THE YEAR OF
LIVING DANGEROUSLY

OTHER BOOKS BY STUART BARNES

Smelling of Roses

THE YEAR OF LIVING DANGEROUSLY

Rugby and the World Cup 1995

Stuart Barnes

RICHARD COHEN BOOKS · London

To Lesley

British Library Cataloguing in Publication Data:
A catalogue record for this book is available from the British Library

Copyright © 1995 by Stuart Barnes

ISBN 1 86066 027 4

First published in Great Britain in 1995 by
Richard Cohen Books
7 Manchester Square
London W1M 5RE

1 3 5 7 9 8 6 4 2

Designed by Behram Kapadia
Typeset in 10/12 Linotron Palatino by
Rowland Phototypesetting Ltd
Bury St Edmunds, Suffolk

Printed in Great Britain by
Butler & Tanner Ltd, London and Frome

Contents

Preface

The 1994–5 season was one in which much of the world was a rugby stage. From the epic Bledisloe Cup battle in Australia at the end of the southern hemisphere season in 1994 to the culmination of the World Cup on a memorable June afternoon in Johannesburg, the game dominated sports headlines in an unprecedented manner.

The doomed traditionalists will remember the year with nostalgia and regret. We were witnesses to the long-awaited demise of amateurism, and the battle between player and administrator was as gripping as any action on the pitch. In England, the climax of this struggle was the dramatic dismissal and re-appointment of Will Carling as England captain. In the *dramatis personae* of this book, Carling is listed as the Prince of England – a description which was the unwitting harbinger of tabloid headlines to come. The post-season prince-and-princess story has no place in this record; besides, burdened with the status of ex-player, I will face enough hostility for my opinions from those who believe that the game's participants become life members of a club in which any criticism must be kept between four walls. This view leaves no room for retired players to enter the ranks of the media, so I shall declare myself an ex-player no more and be damned. Of course, I hope that any appraisals will be taken in the constructive and often lighthearted manner in which they have been offered, but if not, that's too bad.

There were occasions during the season when my exile from this club strained relations with its active members. That is a sad but unavoidable feature of a sport that is only now learning to cope with the dazzle of the stagelights, still a novelty when it has for 100 years been a game for 'gentlemen'. Where image-consciousness in players was once perceived as a vanity which could easily be drowned in a vat of beer on a Saturday night, it is now part and parcel of the marketing game. Modern rugby is also a business, and the loss of innocence is inevitable. Off the field, the ethos that captivated me for twenty years has disappeared forever, but from its ashes standards will grow, and with them, drama.

Even so, we shall not see a season like 1994–5 for another four years. The World Cup provided a fairytale finish for a unified South Africa. That nation's invigorating spirit subdued the emergence of the most spectacular physical talent that my generation (and probably any other) has seen: that of All Black Jonah Lomu. For England, meanwhile, it was all too little, too late. The 1995 Grand Slam became a distant memory as Carling's dream and Rowell's vision died.

Throughout the season, other hopes rose and fell, fell and rose. Laurie Mains, the New Zealand coach, and Scotland captain Gavin Hastings were both at one stage in career-threatening free-fall before they spectacularly re-asserted themselves and their reputations; Kitch Christie described his role as Springbok coach as an 'intensive-care' task before guiding South Africa to the World Cup. So many heroes – and a few villains, too. This is the story of those men, who left their mark on rugby's year of living dangerously.

Acknowledgements

Lesley, for her invariably sensible advice.

Adrian Hill, without whose diligent research the book could not have been written.

Sally, my dog and companion throughout the long hours spent pounding slowly on the computer, and Master Oats, whose Gold Cup triumph at Cheltenham kept me smiling through the nights.

Illustration Credits

Allsport:	3b,c; 4a,b,c; 6b,c; 7a,b,c; 8a,b,c; 9a; 10b,d; 13b; 14a; 15b; 16b.
Russell Cheyne:	1a,b; 2a,b; 3a; 12a; 13a,c; 15a; 16c.
Colorsport:	5a,b; 9b,c,d; 10a,c,e; 12b; 14b,c; 16a.
Andy Hooper: (Daily Mail)	6a.

ACT I

AUGUST TO DECEMBER 1994

I n which New Zealand lose to Australia in the Bledisloe Cup and Wales is ridden with angst over the departure of its young princes to seek new horizons in the professional code.

Dawn breaks on the Heineken and Courage Leagues as South Africa arrive on the shores of Britain to do battle with Wales, Scotland and the entire national media.

England begin their World Cup crusade as the Rugby World Cup administrators tamper with martial preparations from on high. In the lesser domains, England sleeps during the Divisional Championship and Oxford meet Cambridge in the hallowed shrine of Twickenham for the Varsity match.

These months also witness the birth of a new breed of alchemist – the professional coach. From Scotland comes the legendary Ian McGeechan to restore the elixir of life to Northampton; Dick Best, once of England, returns to Harlequins, the side the rest of the country loves to hate. Neither will find the atmosphere of the club arenas as comfortable as the clean air of international rugby.

DRAMATIS PERSONAE

Laurie Mains	Beleaguered New Zealand Alchemist
Scott Gibbs ⎫ Scott Quinnell ⎭	The Welsh Princes
Ieuan Evans	The Last Welsh Prince
Will Carling	The English Prince
Dean Richards ⎫ Jeremy Guscott ⎭	English Soldiers
Kitch Christie	South Africa's Coach
Jannie Engelbrecht	Deceived South Africa Manager
Gareth Rees	Oxford University Captain
Jack Rowell	England Alchemist
Dick Best ⎫ Ian McGeechan ⎭	Professional Alchemists

Assorted other soldiers involved in light skirmishing

1

1

Hard Times in New Zealand and Wales

T his year, August, once the month designated for club tours and heroic attempts to shed those Sybaritic summer stomachs, was the month that the Welsh Heineken League began.

Before 26 August, the only action to be seen on the pitch was in the middle of the night via the satellite channel of Sky, my new employers. Pubs in the Antipodean region of Earls Court toasted Rupert Murdoch and Rugby Union as Australia and New Zealand produced one of the greatest-ever internationals. If Colin Welland and his Union-knocking friends did not revise their opinion of the sport after this match, I would recommend another spell on Z Cars.

Australia triumphed 20–16 in a game that will be remembered for a ferocious New Zealand comeback in the second half and the last-ditch tackle by Australia's scrum-half prodigy, George Gregan, on Jeff Wilson in the dying minutes. As Wilson dived over the line, Gregan punched the ball from his grasp. As a Test cricketer, Wilson must have been eager to pack his bags and find another tour, avoiding New Zealand at all costs.

One man who cannot have enjoyed the spectacle was New Zealand coach Laurie Mains. Under his charge New Zealand had suffered eight defeats in fourteen matches. No wonder he rarely smiled. Mains essayed a brave face. 'The players can look forward confidently to the World Cup, knowing that they can put together football like that [the second half].' He might have been able to state that the players could look forward with confidence, but he failed to mention his own position. His captain, Sean Fitzpatrick, offered Mains the compulsory support of his team the day after the Test, adding that he saw the World Cup winners coming from New Zealand, Australia, France, South Africa or England.

How brave. To prove that Englishmen are not scared of a prediction, I bet that either the Labour or the Conservative party will win the next General Election.

Not all the leading lights of New Zealand rugby were so adept at sitting on fences. Their 1987 World Cup-winning captain, David Kirk, said he found it hard to see the All Blacks taking the World Cup if no changes were made at the top. John Kirwan, one of New Zealand's great wingers, was even more forthright. I thought my outbursts with selectors were regarded as temperamental, but Kirwan made my dia- tribes seem positively United Nations. After accusing Mains of 'losing the plot', he added, 'If we get the right coach, I think we'll see a dramatic difference. It's up to the NZRFU to show some leadership and maybe make some hard decisions.'

Perhaps Laurie Mains telephoned Dick Best for sympathy. Best re- turned from England's summer tour of South Africa as national coach, but his tenure was to last barely two weeks. The sacking came in the shape of an RFU statement, 'It has been decided that Jack Rowell, the England manager, will assume a more direct "hands-on" involvement.' Best gave the impression that he was slightly disappointed that Rowell did not give him this news directly. Now he knows how players have felt throughout the ages. The moment the decision was announced Rowell stood alone. Rowell's description of the England side as an 'inherited squad' gave a clear indication of his future plans to those who knew this intricate man, and indeed his attempts to re-style England before the World Cup were to be one of the most significant campaigns of this rugby war.

Away from the field, the forces of old and new were already meeting head-on in the battle for the soul of the sport between amateurism and professionalism. As so often, the catalyst was Rugby League and the venue, Wales, where die-hard amateurs could be forgiven for quoting a line from Bob Dylan's 'It's Alright Ma': 'Money doesn't talk, it swears.'

Scott Gibbs fired a shot across Rugby Union's bows as he headed north to St Helens. 'Players and officials keep on covering up what is going on in the Union game,' he declared. 'Every player in Wales knows that when you play on a Saturday you get a few quid if you win. Players get the cash after the game. The hypocrisy of it all sucks.' Mr Welland might wince at such transatlantic jargon, but he would doubtless raise a northern pint to the content of Gibbs' statement. Russell Jenkins, the chairman of the Welsh Rugby Union amateurism committee, retorted: 'If Scott Gibbs would like to give me names of players and amounts involved, I would be pleased to receive them.' The fact that Gibbs was not prepared to betray his own friends or risk his own neck meant that nothing could be proved and the matter was closed. The word hypocrisy is apt.

Cardiff RFC chief executive and former Welsh fly-half Gareth Davies joined the debate. He too muttered on the subject of hypocrisy, 'They say you can't be a little bit pregnant, so we have to decide whether we're going to be amateur or professional.' Davies firmly believed that the game was moving towards full-time professionalism, although the staunch protectors of the old ethos might well have made the defenders of Rorke's Drift seem pliant in comparison.

All this talk of dismissals and money seemed rather corporate to a simple ex-player. By 27 August I was itching to see some real action where it should be – on the pitch. I returned to Wales, the land of my education but other people's fathers – I am pure Essex stock. I had joined rugby's band of voyeurs: the sporting media. Two weeks from my first appearance as Sky Sports presenter of live Rugby Union, I was prepared for the nerves that rarely afflicted me during my playing days. My only nerves that day, however, concerned the late appearance of my new comrades, Tony Bodley of the *Express*, Peter Jackson of the *Mail* and beaming Barry Newcombe of the *Sunday Express*, for lunch at Champers, near Cardiff Arms Park.

Wales was still awash with talk of money. Watching Cardiff play Bridgend, I pondered the benefits of performance-related play. It was a terrible match, an impression heightened by my memory of the Bledisloe Cup. Despite their fifty points, the only Cardiffians to receive a handsome financial reward would have been Derwyn Jones, the 6ft 10in Celtic version of Martin Bayfield, and Mike Rayer, whom I have long considered the finest full-back in the British Isles. In contrast, Adrian Davies, who was supposedly challenging Neil Jenkins for the poisoned chalice of the Welsh fly-half berth, probably owed Cardiff a hypothetical week's wages. His display conjured a surreal vision of Wales' inelegant incumbent at No. 10 sipping champagne and smiling as he watched a video of Davies' performance.

As my train returned me to Bristol through the Severn Tunnel, my parting thought in Wales was that 'Jack Brown, the leading rugby bookmaker in these parts', according to the match programme, would be the only gambling Cardiffian to make a profit on the season's League. As I write, Cardiff are joint top with Pontypridd, leaving me feeling decidedly stupid and perplexed at the state of Welsh club rugby.

As the season in England had not yet started, it came as little surprise to find Rugby Union hidden between fascinating articles on trampolining and darts for the disabled in the next day's press. Welsh people are justified in feeling neglected. A perusal of a few Sunday papers of proof-reading intensity barely enlightened my fading knowledge of the Welsh club scene. In England the League lifted clubs, but in Wales, where club competition was already strong, it somehow achieved the opposite. Yet if the clubs now appear more anonymous to those of us who live east of the River Severn, one man still illuminates the sport in Wales: Ieuan Evans.

On the first Saturday of the season Evans scored a hat-trick for Llanelli in the derby against local rivals and defending champions Swansea. Stephen Jones of *The Sunday Times* described the Scarlets' flying wing as 'Merlin reincarnated'. Jones, as a proud Welshman, would understand the role of mythology in the Celtic world. Evans may not be Owain Glyndwr, the scourge of the English in times past, but none the less it was he who buried the sword in the Triple Crown ambitions of Carling's England in 1993. That feat alone consigns him to history, but in isolation it does not provide a full picture of Evans. Despite appalling injury setbacks throughout his career, his lightning change of pace and direction have inspired listless Welsh sides. His display for the British Lions against the Maoris of Wellington in 1993 was one of those performances that left players grateful to have played with him. He is articulate, but not challenging, his calm intelligence a blessed contrast to the threatening skinhead culture behind which Wales sought to hide in the late 1980s. If ever a man has been a talisman for his side, it is Evans.

Those talismanic qualities were to serve Wales steadfastly in the season's first important international of the season, a World Cup qualifier against Romania in Bucharest on 17 September. Defeat would leave them needing to beat Italy in order to avoid the so-called 'group of death', featuring Australia and the Springboks, in South Africa. Even in their 'glam-rugby' pomp of the mid-seventies, Wales would not have fancied such a group; in the success-starved 1990s it would provoke mass scenes of national despair. Welsh rugby would be keen to avoid the humiliation of having to qualify for another World Cup by facing such powers as Spain and Portugal, although, to look on the bright side, Neil Jenkins could become the world's leading international points-scorer playing such opponents. As it turned out, of course, Wales were to ensure their place in the 1999 tournament via a much safer route: hosting the thing themselves.

Romania led 3–0 and were dominating the game before the Welsh captain and wizard scorched over for a try to settle Celtic nerves. Dehydrated in temperatures of around 100 degrees, Evans inspired his country to a narrow 16–9 victory. If Evans had become the symbol of Welsh rugby, Wales could claim a second world-class threequarter thoroughbred in Mike Rayer. One week after Cardiff's victory against Bridgend, I was delighted to read that Rayer had been Cardiff's mainstay in a hard-fought victory over Pontypridd. With Evans and Rayer shining and a victory in Romania to supplement their status as Five Nations champions, Wales could be forgiven for breathing a collective sigh of relief. But barely had they exhaled before the news came on the wires: 'QUINNELL MOVE STUNS WELSH RUGBY'.

6

The previous season No. 8 Scott Quinnell, described by national team manager Robert Norster as 'a catalyst for the side', had typified the pride and the power of a new generation. His try in Wales' first victory against France for twelve years had set the game alight. My neighbours in Bristol could almost feel the shudder from across the Severn when he headed north to Wigan. Rugby legend Barry John labelled his departure 'another massive blow to the Union code'. John's assertion that Wales could not compete financially with Wigan raised few eyebrows, but his claims that 'Union does not compete with League today when it comes to action and mobility' and 'Union has to take a long hard look at itself' certainly did.

Britain was not the only country to suffer the depradations of League in September. It was to prove a good month for the scouts in Australia as well. Anthony Herbert, the twenty-eight-year-old centre, switched codes but the major signing was that of Garrick Morgan, a man good enough to keep a 6ft 7½in salmon like John Eales out of the Australian team. Ewen McKenzie voiced the thoughts of top international Union players throughout the world when he complained: 'The lowest-paid Rugby League player would be doing better than a senior Wallaby,' although the Australians were trying to rectify that one. In New Zealand no players defected to Rugby League in September, but Canterbury did lose the regular services of All Black scrum-half Graeme Bachop. Bachop, a twenty-seven-year-old unemployed carpenter, signed a one-year contract to work in Japan with the Sanix Chemical Company. His provincial coach, Vance Stewart, commented: 'Japanese companies have become a bigger threat to New Zealand than Rugby League.' Perhaps one of the giant Japanese car plants in Wales should recruit some Welsh internationals – Honda RFC, top of Heineken Division 1, an intriguing thought.

If South Africa's Louis Luyt had the autonomous control of world rugby that he seems to possess in South Africa, such a thought would delight him. He is a man driven by power and a need to dominate, and the contrast with Dudley Wood, in his last season as RFU secretary, was quite delightful. Wood gives the impression that he left ICI to administer a game he loves without the hassle of corporate back-biting and wrangling over money. He may sound antiquated; he is, in fact, the traditional English gentleman and the players, almost uniformly, dislike him. Yet he is far from the bogeyman so many people think he is. In a newspaper article on 28 August Wood was questioned about his similarities to King Canute. He retorted: 'I like being modelled on King Canute. He is one of my favourite characters.' In the trample to join the commercial world, it would be sad to see the players becoming incapable of sharing such humour. Wood presided at the RFU and Courage Press Conference which opened the season on 31 August at Twickenham. I left with the impression that he was more interested in Courage's beer brands than the ensuing debates on the game.

If Wood seemed in relaxed mood, the RFU president, Dennis Easby, was clearly prepared for combat at an earlier stage in the season. On the relationship between committee and players, he said: 'A lot of the deterioration in our relationship comes from their [the players'] ignorance. They have refused to talk to me since I became president . . . and that is very sad.' Easby added: 'Contrary to popular belief, the players will tell you that they prefer the freedom to follow their professions, vocations and family interests.' A report commissioned by BBC Wales and published in October would question such an assumption.

On the players' side, England hooker Brian Moore slated the RFU for 'their grudging, niggardly, piecemeal approach. We tried to make progress and they refused to do anything. The way it worked in the past, you can't have confidence in the RFU.' Examination of the commitment that the England players gave in September makes observers sympathetic to their pleas. On the first two days of the month the squad requested their first two days' leave of absence from work for fitness tests at Bath University. What a way to spend valuable holiday time! I was driving back from London on 1 September, and my sadistic side toyed with the idea of a visit to Bath University. Sickened by my baser tendencies, I drove on, vowing never to criticise players for a lack of fitness.

Jack Rowell also announced that there were to be fortnightly training sessions in midweek. At Marlow, the venue for those sessions, Martin Bayfield explained the rationale. 'Our aim is to be working together every couple of weeks, even when there is no Test match imminent, so that we become like a club squad when we meet the best of the world in the World Cup.' It seemed that no England player could be interviewed without mentioning that tournament. Traditionalists still blow the trumpet of the Five Nations but the priority of the players was self-evident.

England's captain, Will Carling, admitted that 'the World Cup has got to be our chief goal'. Carling himself was a man under the spotlight in September. The eyes and ears of the media awaited the ear-splitting wrench as he lost the support of his mentor, Geoff Cooke, Rowell's predecessor. Many expected Rowell to appoint his own man to the captaincy. The reason he kept faith with Carling can be explained by his decision to alter England's style, rather than the personnel. Two radical changes would have been too drastic with the World Cup less than a year away. Rowell also admired Carling's potential and proven ability, and to strip him of the captaincy would probably have hurt his sensitive nature to such an extent that he would have been irretrievably lost to the side. Carling certainly reacted positively to his re-appointment. 'It's very flattering that Jack wants me to continue, but at the same time it's meaningless if I'm not performing at the required level,' he said. 'Continuous performance from me is necessary, otherwise the appointment counts for nothing.'

Under Geoff Cooke Carling had never said such things. I was encouraged, and wrote as much in the *Daily Telegraph* of 12 September. Little did I realise that it was not so acceptable for an ex-player and journalist rookie to remind him of this when his form deserted him later in the season. Doubtless England's captain did not find it amusing, but it was impossible not to smile when he was quoted as saying that 'form and fitness are the most important criteria for playing for England and the captain is not excluded from that rule', only to suffer a series of slight hamstring twinges in the next month or so.

Carling was adamant – as were many of the England squad – that the injuries were not imaginary. Numerous team-mates at Harlequins were less certain. As the relationship between Rowell and Carling struck a fairly positive note the pressures of being a Harlequin began to show. Club rugby would not prove to be Carling's favourite way of spending a Saturday afternoon in the months ahead.

If any area of Rugby Union was viewing World Cup year with trepidation, it was the Courage First Division clubs. Rowell and Carling were urging their players to rest and prepare for the Armageddon of South Africa. Carling argued that an adverse national performance in the summer would have long-term detrimental effects on the future development of the English game. He was right. Nor could players be criticised for setting personal goals – the highest of which would be a place in the World Cup squad – yet everybody knew that a fundamental conflict did exist. Only twenty-six players would be chosen to represent England. Those twenty-six would rely heavily on the 124 other players who strain away on Courage League Saturdays to keep their clubs in the hunt. If nothing else, rugby is a team game, and nothing is more likely to cause dissent than a prominent member of a club deserting his team. Tim Rodber, Dewi Morris and Brian Moore were club captains. To attain glory for self and country, these players could be risking the valuable respect of their peers.

Despite Courage magnanimously stating that they would prefer a tame end to the season to a poor England showing in South Africa (they had cleverly invested in sponsorship of England as well as the League), the matter was not that simple. The inability of the RFU to act decisively on this question represented one of the strongest arguments offered by advocates of professionalism so far. An amateur body like the RFU committee could only advise. This guaranteed that by April, players whose clubs were still in the Cup, or battling at the top or bottom of the League, would be left with a personal choice that would be patently unfair: risk your England place, or risk sacrificing your friends. Some choice. If a firm decision was made from on high the whole issue would be out of the hands of individuals and the blame could be gratefully aimed elsewhere.

Another thorny issue created by the ambiguous state of the game is the relationship between the clubs and the RFU. The RFU clearly perceive that the interests of the national team surpass any other consideration. I had my doubts about such a concept as an amateur player. Imagine what the burgeoning number of professional coaches, whose livelihood could depend on club success, make of it. In September, Bristol, Gloucester, Leicester, West Hartlepool and Sale all employed professionals to run their clubs. Rugby's petty hypocrisy dictates that they are known as 'directors of rugby', but their influence on the playing side is pervasive. In addition, Ian McGeechan had been appointed in a professional capacity at Northampton. How would a Scot feel about an English amateur body weighing the odds for or against him?

The very presence of professional coaches was the first wave of a movement that would leave a bitter taste in the purist amateurs at headquarters, although John Jeavons-Fellows, the chairman of the RFU competition sub-committee, emphasised that amateurism was far from dead when his committee announced that, in the interests of England players, only one side would be relegated from Division 1 of the League in 1995. At the start of the season most onlookers reached the conclusion that only Orrell's Dewi Morris might be involved in such a struggle. Quiet whispers drifted on the air from Bath and Leicester. 'What about the race for the League Championship? That might affect a few more potential World Cup stars.' Who was to predict the trials and tribulations of Northampton and Harlequins at this stage? I certainly did not.

2

Old Acquaintances

On the Monday before the commencement of club hostilities I wrote a preview of the Courage League season. Displaying rather more Courage than sense, I not only analysed each team but predicted their final League standing. Experienced as a player I might have been, but as a pundit I remained a novice. Unsurprisingly, I tipped Bath for an unbelievable fifth consecutive title, but the rest of my predictions in the *Daily Telegraph* on 5 September are rather more embarrassing for a self-declared expert. My prediction was as follows:

1	Bath
2	Wasps
3	Bristol
4	Leicester
5	Harlequins
6	Gloucester
7	Northampton
8	West Hartlepool
9	Orrell
10	Sale

I saw little to change my perception of that pecking order on my first day as Sky Sports' sweating, greying rugby presenter. It was both fitting and ironic that my new career started for real at my spiritual sporting home – the Recreation Ground, Bath. And what more appropriate opponents could there have been than Bath's local rivals, Bristol? It was the game I used to dread losing more than any other, just as it is the one Bristol players can barely dream of winning. Television hype built up the fixture, but the dreariness of the match itself hardly surprised me. Bristol boasted about their formidable pack, Bath struggled to win ball, but eventually the favourites won the match with relative ease. The skills of back play seem to have bypassed Bristol's threequarters. Wins for Harlequins, Leicester, Wasps and Orrell suggested that the season would be as predictable as ever.

In fact the most impressive aspect of the day was the presence of Bath's new corporate stand – the Teacher's Stand. It is the only physical testimony to an unparalleled period of success in English club rugby. The reason for the club's failure to move with the team is inextricably interwoven with the recent resignations of John Carter and John Gaynor, the secretary and president, who had the courage to actually initiate action rather than spend three hours in a committee meeting discussing the contentious issue of hand towels or blow-driers in the toilets.

In the second week of the season the Sky bandwagon rolled north to Orrell, traditional home of mushy peas and monstrous forwards. The mushy peas were still available but the pack had departed. Few fancied their chances against a Leicester team which had allied itself to the gospel of running rugby – in word rather than deed at this stage. The match itself was historic. In a week when more points than ever before were scored in the First Division, Sky chose the lowest-scoring League game. Dark words were muttered in the studio.

Leicester maintained their winning ways by 6–0 and as 6–0 matches go, it was appalling. In the *Telegraph* I called it 'a banker for the worst match of the year'; perhaps I should have written 'millennium'. I described Leicester's running style as 'mythical'. Normally Orrell is an enjoyable venue, but I left that Saturday wishing that I was a fishing presenter. Elsewhere, Bath ensured that Northampton remained point-less; Gloucester trounced West Hartlepool and Bristol likewise Sale. Things were looking grim for the north. The one match that shocked the club world was Wasps' fifty-point demolition of Harlequins. Wasps had never been so popular.

As the season got into its stride, October started with a Sky visit to the club match on everybody's lips – Blackrock College against Young Munster. It was roughly the equivalent of providing live coverage of Lingfield versus Glentoran while Manchester United played Arsenal. Despite a vague sense of embarrassment when English friends asked which match Sky were covering, I was secretly delighted to be back in Ireland.

It was my first experience of club rugby in the Emerald Isle, but I received a familiar reception from the people. Within Ireland, the men of Munster, in the fiery realms of Limerick and Cork, are not impressed by the Dubliners. The city of Joycean drinking sessions in my super-ficial dreams is the city of middle-class bourgeois values, according to Munstermen. Certainly rugby has a far more 'professional' background

there – doctors from Dublin, dockers from Munster. Munster have dominated the All-Ireland League since its inception, but the Dublin folk
argue that a game based on passion can only inspire poverty at higher
levels.

It is hard to refute such an argument, but in Ireland my logic is a
regular victim of defenestration. Watching Young Munster receive a
rare spanking, it was obvious that rugby is not the sport of poetry in
Munster. Ireland's legendary flanker Fergus Slattery, a staunch son of
Blackrock, was delighted with the performance of his side, while Tony
Ward, one of Sky's most valuable and charming guests, took defeat in
the manner appropriate to the sport. Ward, a swarthy Munsterman
who now lives in Dublin, epitomised the Dublin–Munster split in his
distinguished playing days. Strutting and classy on the pitch, his rebellious and superstar image off it did not endear him to legions of
Irishmen. It appears that Ward still inspires more affection and venera-
tion in England than in Ireland, but as Tony would probably admit,
Irish rugby is not the land of logic.

Even as I sampled the dark stuff deep into the dark of Dublin, logic
was applying itself forcefully at the head of the Courage First Division
in England. Bath won the traditionally tight away fixture at Gloucester,
while Leicester stole away from Sudbury with a win that cast the Wasps
in the role of the revolutionaries who lack the pragmatism to achieve
power. In contrast Leicester had it, with a capital P. At the bottom of
the table there was a more Irish feel to events, with Northampton losing
at home to Bristol. Four straight defeats left them bewildered in the
basement of Division 1.

On the following Saturday I would see Northampton in the flesh for
the first time in the season, against Harlequins. I was to be startled by
the performance of Northampton. While in Sale a player, Paul Turner,
performed the role of guru, in Northampton the squad awaited miracles
from former Scotland and British Lions coach Ian McGeechan. The
Northampton players clearly held McGeechan in awe. Anybody who
can coach Scotland to a Grand Slam, given the limitations of their playing resources, deserves respect. Yet Northampton reminded me of helpless children cast into the big, bad world once they were alone on the
pitch. McGeechan was clearly surprised that this Northampton baby
needed so much weaning.

The side's problem stemmed from the arrival in the early 1990s of one
of modern rugby's great players, New Zealander Wayne Shelford. Most
Kiwis believe themselves to be gifted with unique insights into the sport;
Shelford actually is. The club captain might have been John Olver but
'Buck' Shelford was the boss. Youngsters at the club, like Tim Rodber,
proceeded on fast-track learning curves under the tutelage of a master,
but even as they learned to play they forgot to think. In Shelford's

day, the England squad loved to mock the Northampton players in the national team with constant taunts of 'Buck says . . .' Lighthearted it was, but as with most humour, there was an undeniable and debilitating truth behind it. As an army officer, Rodber should know that it is not always conducive to a healthy future to blindly follow the leader. Northampton appeared to be a rudderless ship, unable to comprehend that a coach can provide only a framework within which players themselves must make decisions.

The recent phenomenon of autonomous tactical control being held by a coach is responsible for many of the failings that have afflicted the decision-making of captains from Will Carling through to skippers in Division 3. When he was assistant manager of England, Dick Best once asked Rob Andrew about a decision made during an international. He could not understand why England's second phase of attack had been aimed at the heart of the opposition defence when the other side of the pitch had been unmarked. Andrew's retort, that it was what had been agreed on a chalk board before the match, was a chilling indictment of such structured coaching. Northampton appeared to be deep in this tactical mire as Harlequins won a match of low quality. I wrote on Monday 10 October: 'Northampton have far too many good players to face relegation, but the club will never return to the lofty heights of the Shelford era unless the coach points the finger at each individual and says, "The Buck stops here – think for yourself."' At least part of my thinking seemed fairly flawed back in October.

That away victory for Harlequins lifted the team to a results tally of three wins and two losses. It appeared that the motivational qualities of the new captain, Brian Moore, were chiselling a more determined Quins team. In retrospect, the club's problems were clearly not far below the surface. Moore's commitment might have inspired seasoned veterans, but with the exception of Carling and the perpetually unfortunate David Pears, Harlequins possessed one of the least experienced three-quarter lines in the First Division. The result was spectacularly average rugby behind the scrum. The more nervous they became, the more mistakes were made, the more the England hooker forced caution upon them. In the midst of such mediocrity stood England's captain, Will Carling. Carling's club rugby has appeared to promote amateurism to a height that matches his highly professional approach to the international game. Throughout his Harlequins career niggling injuries have co-incided with non-international weekends. Although he has lifted his game to majestic heights in all of Harlequins' Cup finals, notably the epic against Bath in 1992, he was the epitome of the club's apparent indifference to their League aspirations. At Franklins Gardens I described Carling as 'slouched, uninterested in the entire proceedings', and commented that it looked as if he considered the result and his lack of contribution an irrelevance. It was a view espoused that day by Les Cusworth, the England backs coach.

As Carling's early-season enthusiasm for the club scene vanished, so did Moore's hopes and expectations. Hamstrung, he watched Leicester accumulate in excess of forty points at the Stoop Memorial Ground. Orrell came, saw and conquered; the journey to Bath yielded nothing, and suddenly Harlequins were a side in decline. It was a state of affairs that brought joy to most English club players. Poor Harlequins have consistently failed to inspire affection from any quarter. Their aristocratic image, perpetuated by the club's officials, has left the Quins friendless in the democratic world of League rugby.

Undoubtedly Carling was scratching his head, wondering why he had joined the club. He confessed that he was asking himself this question with increasing frequency. As he pondered, his form started to drift. His performances throughout October were far from international standard. His relationship with Moore became strained, as did his previously improved relationship with me. Since Carling had stated, as we have seen, at the season's opening that a poor run of performances would be punished by England's selectors, it was inevitable that someone would revive his comments when his form dipped. To criticise Carling is a decidedly risky business for journalists. On England's 1994 tour to South Africa, Peter Jackson of the *Daily Mail* mused on the likelihood of the captain being dropped from the Test team. It was a speculative and, as it proved, incorrect punt, but Jackson was clearly within his rights. The reaction of the squad was to ostracise him. Players would be fined if they spoke to him, although a few disregarded this dictat. I do not remember any journalist being cold-shouldered for discussing selecting or dropping any other player.

It was touching that Will Carling's colleagues were supportive, but their reaction seemed exceptionally immature. When I questioned Carling's form on 31 October, I discovered why his close friends in the team had responded in such a manner. Carling is a very sensitive man. He is neither arrogant nor aloof, as many critics have maintained, but painfully shy and vulnerable to criticism. My column was certainly not a personal attack, but within hours of reading it Carling called me. He was reasonable and honest on the telephone, but I could almost hear the hurt. As one of rugby's highest-profile players he should be used to the barbs of newspapers, yet, at the age of twenty-nine, he still seemed unable to shrug off the comments of outsiders. Perhaps the silver spoon Cooke gave Carling when he appointed him the national captain at twenty-two had become a burden. Whatever the truth, October was not a good month for Carling or the Quins.

England's captain may not have enjoyed his Saturday afternoons in October, but Dean Richards, the player many consider to be the finest tactician in the English game, most certainly did. Despite all the debate about the number of games in which a player should appear in World Cup year, Richards trudged on week after week. A true team man, he enjoys his club rugby and the company of his weekly comrades as much as the glamour of an England international. Psychologists, dieticians and fitness gurus may be dragging Union into the modern sporting world, but the solid figure of Richards remains a reassuring symbol for the traditionalists. 'Deano' espouses similar opinions to those of the players of yore. The best way to stay fit is to play; none of this fancy peaking and troughing for him. The Australians and New Zealanders have taken players to new levels of athletic excellence since the first World Cup, but Richards remains unchanged, almost timeless.

Shirt hanging down outside his unflattering shorts, socks collapsed round his ankles rather than rolled down, a toothless grin and genial but genuine resolve; Richards is the rugby player of legend. He is not interested in image, and to him the media attention is not an opportunity to promote himself but a burden which makes him uncomfortable. If Richards was inclined to promote himself, he would not need to manufacture an image – he has the perfect one already.

The heart and soul in whichever team he represents, Richards is a player of awesome proportions. His physical asset is his bearlike strength, which can kill an attack or turn an attacker in the tackle, thereby creating turnover ball. He is not a natural athlete, but he is a natural ball-player. Watch him under a high ball and his skills are evident. Some spectators may wonder how it is that a man who lumbers rather than strides is always beneath the ball. The answer is that Dean Richards possesses such a rugby brain that he invariably knows where the ball will land. This season he added a new determination in his training. Never one to do two sit-ups if he could escape with one, he applied himself with a dedication that astonished some. The result is a new streamlined No. 8, according to the big man himself. To me he will always be the reluctant hero, happier playing cards with Jerry Guscott than working on the weights with his fellow forwards. His rivalry with Ben Clarke for England's No. 8 shirt was shaping into one of the most exciting of personal battles this year.

Superficially the antithesis of Richards – athletic, good-looking, marketed and modelled – Clarke has more in common with his rival than most people would suspect. Despite the glamour that surrounds Clarke, he, like Richards, enjoys life's simpler pleasures – real ale rather than fine wine, National Hunt rather than fancy Arab Flat horses. Clarke is 'one of the lads'. Like Richards, he has absolutely no superstar aura. He remains close friends with colleagues from his Saracens and Cirencester College days. Clarke still delights in quiet escapes to his parents' home in Hertfordshire, where Bath players swear his mother pampers him.

A Ben Clarke Christmas party has its share of Guscotts and Catts, but you'll also meet seventy-year-old supporters and drinking friends.

On the pitch, however, Clarke is the opposite to Dean Richards. Where Richards orchestrates his forwards, Clarke is himself the battering ram. He has an extra pace that makes him a formidable proposition to defenders trying to stop his rampaging. He also has an ability to drift wide, taking ball outside centres, to the understandable horror of the opposing backs. Clarke is the incisive weapon, Richards the shaper and organiser; Clarke the athlete who does not look natural on the ball, Richards the footballer who looks anything but an athlete. Merge the two, and opposition teams would find themselves facing a monster of Frankensteinian proportions.

Sadly for England, only one of them could play at No. 8. It would be a question of Clarke's mobility against Richards' nous. On 22 October Jack Rowell arrived at Bath for the first collision of these two Titans. It was also a match of massive significance in the race for the First Division title. Both Bath and Leicester swaggered to the Recreation Ground with 100 per cent records. Despite a stutter in Bath's form, home advantage was expected to prove decisive. A crowd of 8,500 packed into what is surely the most scenic venue, but, I acknowledge, the most inadequate stadium in Britain. People were hanging from trees, perched on precarious Georgian window ledges. Rugby Union at club level had arrived. Leicester's Tony Underwood, on the other hand, had not arrived. Muttering regretfully about the M4 and heavy traffic, he eventually took the place of a youngster called Jamie Hamilton on the bench. The fact that Leicester did not censure or even drop him reveals the long reach of amateurism within the sport, as well as one reason why Leicester have struggled so long to emulate the more ruthless West Country side.

Despite the absence of Underwood Junior, Leicester left the ground with a merited point. Bath had thrown away a 20–9 lead created by their more imaginative back play. Jamie Hamilton, the coltish-looking emergency wing, scored the try which tied the match and Dean Richards emerged a points victor over Ben Clarke. Leicester's growing confidence was revealed the next week when Sky covered their League match against Sale. A comfortable victory saw the Tigers sitting content, top on points difference, as the Courage Leagues waved goodbye to October.

3

The 'Boks are Back

W ales could be forgiven for thinking that it is October, and not April, that is the cruellest month. What did T.S. Eliot know about rugby, anyway? On the day that Romania were dispatched to the World Cup 'group of death' containing Australia and South Africa after their humiliation by Italy, Wales lost the man who meant so much to the national cause – Ieuan Evans. All of Wales despaired when the news of Evans' broken leg, sustained in a Llanelli versus Cardiff Heineken League match, leaked. Emyr Lewis, a former Llanelli team-mate who had moved to Cardiff in acrimonious circumstances, was one of the first to visit his bedside – that is what Evans means to Wales. Quinnell at the end of September, now Evans; national coach Alan Davies must have been wondering whether life would have been easier at Nottingham, his former club.

Defeat against Italy later that month would probably have given Davies no option but to return to club rugby. It was a game that Wales would eventually win, but it was one of the saddest experiences I can recall in the rugby cathedral of the National Stadium.

As I crossed the Severn Bridge, just hours before the kick-off, the old Welsh arrogance was absent from the radio news and views. The Celtic bard of rugby was no more. The importance of victory was stressed as the prime concern – but they were playing Italy, for God's sake. Rather than build up their own team, the pundits hyped Italy on the strength of a two-Test series against a clearly complacent Australian side. A 23–20 loss marked them as formidable opponents. Even Aussie captain Michael Lynagh had warning words for the Welsh: 'They've been building towards this one for a long time.' Alan Davies confirmed that a win for Wales was vital. 'We want to play at altitude right from the start [of the World Cup]. We must be aiming to reach the final, and that is being staged at 6,000ft above sea-level. We don't fear New Zealand – in fact, the players want to play them.'

A 29–19 victory granted Davies his group of New Zealand and Ireland together with Japan, who were to qualify later in the month. But the manner in which the win was achieved suggested that Davies' buoyant World Cup aspirations were nothing more than bluster. On a night created for rugby, Wales dominated the forward exchanges but could translate their superiority into only one score, for Wayne Proctor. Fittingly, it was full-back Mike Rayer, Wales' one incisive international, who set up the try. A crowd of around 35,000 became increasingly frustrated as Wales stumbled like novices in midfield. All the press headlines the next day were dedicated to the Welsh version of Grant Fox, Neil Jenkins. He scored twenty-four points, which took him to a new Welsh record of 308 at the tender age of twenty-three. Jenkins was ebullient. 'I think I have grown into the No. 10 shirt. We have a lot of talented players and we would have liked a few more tries, but the tries will come.'

The booing of the Welsh crowd suggested otherwise. The Jenkins vision of rugby was not the one that made a generation dream of playing at No. 10 for Wales. He was right to say that Wales would have liked a few more tries – we all would have done – but while they continued to pick Jenkins it looked increasingly unlikely to happen. The manager underlined his real concerns. 'We improved on our performance against Romania, but there is still plenty of room for more.' Robert Jones, the so often neglected scrum-half, was rather more blunt: 'I think Italy showed us how to play football tonight.' He was not referring to Roberto Baggio.

To compound the demise of the beautiful dream that was once Welsh back play, the last fit Welsh thoroughbred, Mike Rayer, broke a leg in two places playing at Treorchy for Cardiff on 15 October. Rayer, desperately unfortunate not to have been selected for the 1993 Lions, now looked unlikely to make the trip to the third and biggest yet World Cup. A week later, he would have found himself playing against the host nation, South Africa, for his beloved Cardiff in front of only 15,000 spectators at the National Stadium. The attendance was a more lucid comment on the state of Welsh rugby than the blind optimism of Alan Davies or Neil Jenkins.

While Welsh crowds pronounced a verdict on Welsh rugby with their feet, South Africa were preparing for their tour of Wales, Scotland and Ireland in yet another of the endless series of Tests they have played since returning from their sporting wilderness. The visitors were Argentina, a country with whom South Africans have a great affinity. Hugo Porta, surely Argentina's only rugby superstar, by this time Argentinian ambassador to South Africa, cannot have been too disappointed with the Test series. On 8 October South Africa beat Argentina 44–22; a week later the margin was 46–26. Porta must have approved of José Cilley's sensational twenty-one-point debut at fly-half. The England management dutifully requested a video of the match and watched it until Les Cusworth could almost speak Spanish. This was World Cup year, after all.

Perhaps England would underestimate Argentina, whom they were due to meet in Pool B of the World Cup, but, after their ruthless trouncing of Rowell's men in Cape Town, the Springboks would never suffer such a fate. The Welsh are a nation of rugby historians, and the pre-eminence of South Africa in the story of the game is as undisputed as the validity of the international ban they suffered for their deeply rooted apartheid views, symbolised by the once-shamed Springbok badge. Such an abhorrent system infiltrated the very bloodstream of so many South Africans, but my experiences from England's summer tour earlier in the year convinced me that the new hyper-exposed travelling players were dedicated to changing this perception. They were a far warmer and more relaxed outfit than the Neanderthal types who toured England in 1992 and maintained a detached wariness of the outside world throughout. Their captain, François Pienaar, might look like the incarnation of Hitler's dream, but looks can be deceptive. Gallant in defeat in Pretoria, humble in victory in Cape Town, his leadership qualities were as impressive as any I can remember from my playing days.

The other misconception concerned the level of violence on the field. Nobody who witnessed the extremity of Eastern Province would ever forget that some teams do take the war metaphor too far, but such teams exist in every country. Overall, the England tour was more noteworthy for the breadth of South Africa's rugby ambitions. Jack Rowell returned as a convert to a style of rugby that gave rise to rather more smiles than the turgid efforts that had previously epitomised the English scene.

If nothing else, however, apartheid had taught South Africans the value of propaganda. Innately sensitive to others, the Springbok management decided on a charm offensive – and when the touring party was announced they were to need the charms of Casanova. There in the list was the name of Elandre van der Bergh, the man who had unzipped Jonathan Callard's head in Eastern Province. The English press love nothing more than a story laced with violence, especially if the villain is not an Englishman. Jon Callard's thoughts on the selection were quite understandable. 'His choice for this tour shows what South Africa think of their image.' Not according to South Africa. Coach Kitch Christie understated the point when the *Daily Express* quoted him on 20 October as claiming: 'Our image has been overplayed a bit.' Van der Bergh even said that he would like to speak to Callard. I could not imagine the Bath full-back dropping his teaching duties at Downside for a matey reunion, a beer and a curry. Elandre van der Bergh was apparently roaming the rugby fields of the world singing the Animals' hit, 'Don't Let Me Be Misunderstood'.

Christie added: 'I've spoken to Elandre about the Callard incident, and he told me he didn't mean to rake the guy's face.' The standard rugby inquest again: 'I've asked him and he told me – what more can I do?' As if to emphasise good intentions, James Small, the fiery Natal winger, was axed from the squad for disciplinary reasons. Apparently he broke curfew along with André Joubert one night. Banning a man for having a few beers summons rather ambiguous thoughts in this author. 'We're coming to Britain to play hard, fast, exciting rugby as a very disciplined side,' insisted Christie. 'No one's coming to fight.' Music to the ears of rugby fans, but not to those of the media.

Having played in South Africa, I believed Christie, but few were interested in the playing side of the game. The other topic of controversy was the drug situation. South Africa selected three players who had previously tested positive. The tour manager, Jannie Engelbrecht, offered South Africa's view before he was even asked: 'Since re-admission [to the International Rugby Board] in August 1992, no Springbok has tested positive. This side is demonstrably clean.' It was hard not to sympathise with Rudi Straeuli, an outstanding No. 8 who felt 'at times it seems they're putting the blame on us for everything that is wrong with rugby'. Just how the mountain peasants burned for witchcraft in seventeenth-century Europe felt in the face of the Counter-Reformation. It was no surprise that the most vehement attack came from a liberal South African journalist, still fighting the very real ghosts of Springbok allegiance to apartheid. Gavin Evans wrote in the *Guardian*: 'The overall package is one of foul play and drug-abuse offenders.' And I thought they were in Britain to prepare for the World Cup.

The South Africans' first match, played, as I said, in front of a pitiful 15,000, hardly excited the critics or the fans. Against Cardiff South Africa gave a lacklustre performance in conditions unusual to them – driving rain. They won 11–6 but it did not impress Cardiff captain and Wales centre Mike Hall in the process. 'I think a couple of the Welsh clubs will have a chance of knocking them over.' Hall will not be cast as a prophet in a Greek drama. Only Ruben Kruger on the flank and André Joubert at full-back impressed. It was to be the start of a sensational tour for Joubert, who managed to look the world's most accomplished and most brittle player at the same time.

South Africa had been on the road for seven months even before the tour began and Kitch Christie's view that they were overplayed looked close to the mark. François Pienaar appeared grateful for an injury that prevented him from playing in the first two matches. 'Our season started at the end of February, so when we get home from this tour we will have played for over nine months, made two full tours and had nine Tests. It has been tough . . .' When unthinking advocates of amateurism complain about South African players they would do well to have a quiet discussion with Pienaar. It is not only the love of the sport that drives the Springboks on, but the weight of public expectation. To be a defeated Springbok is not far removed in their macho mentality from being a eunuch. Even before the tour, Christie was revealing the burden of expectation. He described the job of creating a team for the World Cup as 'an ambulance, intensive-care task'.

After the midweek match against Wales A at Newport, talk of ambulances was rife in the press. The Springboks emerged comfortable 25–13 victors, but rugby was not the issue. The *Daily Express* opined on 27 October that 'South Africa scored three second-half tries to overcome Wales A at Newport, but soon went back on their pre-tour pledge of no foul play'. Any defence of the team met with even meatier headlines. 'BOKS COACH GIVES STAMP OF APPROVAL TO ROUGH TACTICS'. That report continued: 'Pienaar and Christie are the most successful partnership on the South African domestic scene and their Transvaal team does not take prisoners.' After Transvaal beat England, Jack Rowell cited them as one of the best teams he had ever seen. The word 'violence' was never mentioned.

The problem for the South African management was that faced by legions of British forwards. The press generally like simple answers; an explanation of rucking sails over their heads. For South Africa the problem was exacerbated because they were talking to people with preconceived ideas. Christie defended his team. 'If you are lying on the wrong side of the ruck, any place in the world, you are going to be rucked yourself . . . it's logical because getting the ball is what it's all about.' It's a pity today's British referees do not have such a clear understanding of the game's objectives. Rudi Straeuli, captain for a second match, added, 'Players were warned for rucking, but we were not going for the man or kicking him in the face. We were simply rucking for the ball.'

From the gloom of a wet Newport to the sizzling passion of Stradey Park, home of Llanelli. In 1972, before the Scarlets faced New Zealand, it was rumoured that fifteen coffins were delivered to the ground. The players would rather die than leave the pitch defeated – the war metaphor again. The one touring side who had not lost to Llanelli were the Springboks. Today they rose to the occasion. Christie described it as 'the first time on tour that we have played in a stadium packed with passionate supporters'. Four tries and thirty points later, the Scarlet fire had been utterly doused by a record defeat. Boots flew again – the *Express* claimed that 'Silly Schmidt [Uli, the hooker] should have been sent off . . . it seems that the Springboks cannot stop themselves'. As they moved on to Neath, South Africa's rugby players were convinced it was the English press who could not stop themselves. Few newspapers carried the honest words of Rupert Moon, the Llanelli scrum-half: 'I was not aware of any cheap shots. People are making too big a deal.' It was a pity that hardly anyone noticed that the South Africans were starting to play the quality of rugby they had promised before the tour.

In Wales the press corps hunted for spurious tales of controversy on the pitch, but it was in England that the controversy exploded – and it was away from the field. The battleground was once again the festering debate about the sport's soul versus money. On 1 October, BBC Wales announced the result of a poll conducted on their behalf by Beaufort Research. It revealed that nine out of ten Welsh players wanted to be paid for playing. It was easy for the RFU to claim that players such as Rob Andrew, a London chartered surveyor, did not want payment, but in Wales financial circumstances are very different.

The attitudes to loose change are even more diverse in South Africa, and a story that started in Eastern Province and saw the light of day in the Bath clubhouse was to have the rugby press salivating and the rugby world beyond Twickenham screaming, 'Hypocrite!' Blame it on the strength of the beer in the Bath bar, but Mike Catt, showing a total absence of sense, opened his heart to a *Mail* journalist called Mark Ryan and revealed that he had received payments in his playing days at Eastern Province. South African-born England international Catt was quoted as saying: 'I was paid £200 per match, cash in hand, by Eastern Province before each game.' Eastern Province promptly denied Catt's allegation, but to the rest of the rugby world, tired of England's arrogant air of moral superiority, it was the moment to strike. Vernon Pugh QC, the International Board chairman, ordered the RFU to look into the matter – 'It does not matter where it happened . . . it is in breach of the amateur regulations.' As Catt was a member of the England squad, it was time to see whether England were committed to the defence of amateurism, or whether the charge of jingoistic hypocrisy was to be levelled at them. It will surprise few from outside England that it was the latter.

Dudley Wood, the RFU secretary, said: 'Even if we had factual information from Catt we would not persecute a player for what happened under the jurisdiction of a different union.' Yet Catt was now under the RFU jurisdiction, and he had admitted that he had breached the rules of amateurism. Wood, right to defend Catt, but wrong to speak against backhanders thereafter, added: 'The International Board are well aware that payment for playing has been alleged to be widespread and it is now a question of what they're going to do about South Africa.' It was a matter of rumour that he wanted the IB to act on breaches of regulations in South Africa, while in England a player's statement should be ignored. Once again, Twickenham was cast in a less than flattering light.

'My view is that he was playing under the jurisdiction of another union at the time and so the problem is not confined to Catt, but fourteen other players as well, who are South African,' elaborated Wood. 'We will have to talk to Catt and, depending on what he tells us, we will have to contact South Africa for them to inform us exactly what was going on in their unions a couple of years ago.' After such statements it is doubtful whether the southern hemisphere will ever take English accusations of professionalism seriously. What Dudley Wood failed to accept was the fact that Catt had admitted his offence, whereas his former team-mates had not. In a sport that seems capable of taking action only on someone's word, it was strange that England refused to act on the word of one of their players. Rugby players throughout the world would be delighted. Catt's only crime was to be naïve enough to confess; the RFU cast themselves as a union of double standards.

Those standards came to light elsewhere in October. This time the issue was club versus country – a perennial sporting problem. Two international coaches, one former and one current, eloquently proved that the sport is at a painful watershed in the debate over amateurism. Ian McGeechan, once of Scotland and British Lions and an amateur coach, now of Northampton and contractually obliged, remarked: 'It's unfair. The Rugby Union is putting unfair pressure on clubs and players to say they can't play. If they want to play, they should be allowed to. The Rugby Union says it's an amateur game, but then they tell players when they can and can't play. It wouldn't happen in soccer, and that is a professional game.'

Jack Rowell responded by reminding us that 'the players voted to rest the weekend before Romania and Canada and something has got to give in a hectic season'. A weaker man would have had to have forced the players to sacrifice the respect of clubs and their colleagues to appear strong. Rowell did no such thing, knowing that at this stage of the season, rest was not critical. 'I have not received any appeals from players, but it seemed clear that a few were going to be reluctant to desert their clubs, even in England's cause. I want a squad which is happy in their rugby at all levels. However, the ban will apply for the League weekend preceding the Five Nations Championship matches.' This ban would take effect before England's visit to Wales. Neither Northampton nor Harlequins, the surprise props at the bottom of the table by that time, were to be impressed at this utterance, yet I wonder whether the players who voted for the embargo back in August have ever castigated themselves for not considering the possibility that their clubs would be near the foot of Division 1. I do not blame them – I would have felt the same about Bath.

As October ended, Harlequins and Northampton ought to have been watching the Asian World Cup qualifier between Hong Kong and Singapore. Here a real crisis revealed itself. Hong Kong broke the international points record, beating Singapore 164–13. Despite the severity of the setback for Singaporean rugby, Terence Khoo, the man responsible for all thirteen of his side's points, commented: 'Hopefully, we can learn something from this.' That was an official brave face.

It was Japan who clinched the last spot in the World Cup, beating South Korea 26–11. The Korean manager, Yoon Jae-Seon, explained: 'The true difference between the two sides was their bigger foreign forwards.' Two Tongans and a Fijian had swayed the match, but at least South Korea had not faced a crash-course Oriental in the shape of Graeme Bachop. If he fails to make New Zealand's World Cup squad, who knows? He could be lining up against his former colleagues in Bloemfontein, my favourite South African city, on 4 June 1995. How ironic it would be if New Zealand, poacher of Pacific Island talent supreme, found their own talent being poached by Japan.

4

A World Cup Warning

As the season moved into its third full month, international tension began to grip the rugby world. It might not quite have been Munich 1938, but November was laden with significance for the World Cup.

The eyes of analysts and bookmakers were turned to the international arenas of Britain as six World Cup teams graced the United Kingdom. Wales, Scotland, England and Ireland would represent the Home Unions, while South Africa and Romania, and in December Canada, would provide foreign opposition. The USA also travelled to Ireland as a last-minute replacement for the Namibians, who cancelled their trip, although two narrow defeats against Argentina had forced them into the murky depths of rugby's non-qualifiers. The United States epitomise the old world of rugby amateurism. The sport's popularity lies in its almost bohemian advocacy of individualism. Rugby has become a haven for dope-smoking liberals, tired of the militaristic regimes of gridiron, with a less than gung-ho mentality. They may never be rugby's world champions, but they are great fun to spend some time with. Their amateurism was emphasised by their manager, Jack Clark, who admitted that although they do not pay International Board tour allowances, they do now pay for travel to home matches. Doubtless their 26–15 defeat in Dublin, in which they played with spirit, was not viewed with too much consternation; nor was victory greeted with abundant elation by the Irish, the most relaxed of the 'serious' rugby nations. Coach Gerry Murphy complained that 'our line-out will have to improve by 300 per cent if we are to compete effectively against England at the start of the Five Nations'. He could have added 'in near-hurricane conditions'.

The bonhomie and relaxed atmosphere of Irish and American rugby would be as puzzling to South Africans as socialism was to Ronald Reagan. New Zealand excepted, no country is under more pressure to succeed in the sport. In New Zealand there is little else to do and the cricket team is useless, while in South Africa rugby holds all the solemnity that some Boers offer their distorted macho God. Male pride and superiority create a situation where failure is intolerable. In the darkness of apartheid, South African sportsmen generally accepted such an interpretation, but the boycott, the return to the light and the dismantling of apartheid has opened their eyes. In 1992 South African rugby players did not find the free world an easy place to understand; by 1994, they might well have been exhausted with touring, but the beneficial effects of their prolonged education were evident. Most of the arrogance of yesteryear was stripped away. The national media, while hostile to the image of South African rugby, admitted that individually the players were good company. Some claimed that the South Africans who toured Britain in 1994 were far more approachable than the England team that visited South Africa earlier in the year.

Seven months of touring might have opened Springbok eyes, but nothing could have prepared them for their opponents on 2 November. The previous Saturday's fixture in Llanelli marked the furthest west they would journey into Wales, while the following Wednesday they travelled into the almost Conradian 'heart of darkness' that is Neath. To write of Neath and a Joseph Conrad novella in the same sentence smacks of poetic licence and pretentiousness, but there are similarities. The inherent fear of the jungle and tribalism that pervades the atmosphere in Conrad's masterpiece is faithfully reproduced by the tribal crowd at Neath. The Gnoll is a small, dark and unattractive ground befitting a town in the shadow of Port Talbot Steelworks. The local rugby club is the social diversion and support is every bit as fanatical as at any football club. In the days of the late 1980s, when Neath reigned supreme in Wales and Bath in England, the club battles were blood-curdling affairs. A staccato chant of 'Neath, Neath,' would build in intensity, supporters banging the advertising boards in a rhythmic, ominous drumbeat. It was almost a relief to lose.

If the atmosphere was intimidating, so was the look of the team. The Welsh All Blacks, as they are known, adopt a confrontational style of which even the grizzliest South Island rucking coach in New Zealand would be proud. Their very appearance seemed a statement of intent. The poetic Welsh teams of the seventies had long flowing hair, summoning up visions of Celtic bards and Van Morrison records. Neath was all skinheads and menace.

Even before the Springboks arrived in Neath, the omens for the match were not good. In the 1960s, when the apartheid-happy Springboks toured and the disgracefully fraternal committees of the Home Unions welcomed them in Britain, the biggest enemy to South Africa was a man of Neath. South African-born Peter Hain, who would be an official guest at the post-match function in 1994, was then an anti-apartheid activist, now Labour MP for Neath. Even off the pitch, the Welsh club had troubled South Africans in the past, and, to their credit, refused to play them. More ominous still was Neath's recent match against the touring Australians, a game dominated by violence. Bob Dwyer, the articulate Australian coach, was famously to describe Neath as 'the bag-snatching capital of the world', a reference to the testicle-twisting habits of the rugby team.

The match resulted in another victory for South Africa, by a narrow margin of 16–13, but rugby was not the winner. Neath attacked their illustrious opponents with a frightening intensity that soon boiled over into scenes of outright violence. Tian Strauss of Western Province, captain for the day, compared them with Tucumán, an Argentinian side of unique infamy who were banned from playing a touring team for two years. At the end of the game the Springboks ignored rugby protocol, at least half of them running from the pitch without shaking hands. Strauss even gestured at the partisan crowd. He explained: 'I don't think you can be friendly after a game like that.'

Jannie Engelbrecht, South Africa's diplomatic manager, confirmed: 'This was not rugby. If this is the rugby of the future, then I want no part of it.' He should have realised that Louis Luyt, South Africa's Mr Big, had no plans in the future for him anyway. Luyt was to sack him when they got home. It is hard to believe that Neath, widely perceived as the villains of the piece, could be so abrasive in their post-match comments. Gareth Llewellyn, a captain whose media skills do not match his line-out capabilities, predictably struck the 'hard man' chord – 'It is a hard game, you get on with it.' Nobody could doubt Kitch Christie's final observation that it was 'a black day for rugby', and in the broadest sense.

Engelbrecht, the master of tact, did not need long to brush aside the South African objections that seethed long after the match. 'We are seeing the match as an isolated incident and we look forward to our next game at Swansea on Saturday,' he said brightly. That comment will probably win the award as Rugby Union's understatement of the season. Thankfully, even the sensation-hungry British media could do little but eulogise a performance as brilliant as St Helens, home of Swansea, had ever seen. Swansea, the Welsh champions, strode on to their pitch confident that they could repeat the historic victory achieved against Australia in 1992. They left it in a ragged state of bewilderment. I could not believe my eyes when the score flashed up in London, where I was presenting the match between Harlequins and Gloucester. Swansea 7, South Africa 78. André Joubert helped himself to four tries, thirty-eight points and a guaranteed berth in the Test team.

Pundits acclaimed Joubert as the world's greatest full-back, yet only months before he had been axed from the Springbok squad, albeit for only twenty-four hours, for having an unofficial beer too many. It was good to see an individual like him triumph. I first met Joubert in 1991, when I captained a Barbarians side against Scotland. He initiated a counter-attack from beneath his posts which levelled the match at full-time. He was obviously a great attacking player four years ago, but more importantly here was a man who was proof that sport could overcome social obstacles. There was little or no arrogance in Joubert, no rage about the sporting boycott, just a desire to play the game around the world, meeting people en route. After the events at St Helens, Joubert probably sent President Nelson Mandela a gracious postcard. 'Love it in Swansea. Wales is not too bad, a bit wet, but don't ever go to Neath. Love, A.J.'

Bags packed, the Springboks travelled north with all of Scotland trembling after their Swansea triumph. The tour was advancing according to plan. The first team Christie wanted assembled by the end was clearly taking shape. It looked as if he could soon leave the 'ambulance' about which he had muttered in October. Instead it was the Welsh who looked hospital-bound. Mike Ruddock, Swansea's coach, could provide scant hope for his country. 'We were savaged by a very good side. At this moment I don't think I can offer Wales any advice on how to approach the international at the end of the month.' There was little to console in the words of Alan Davies, either. 'I was pretty depressed before I even got here,' he said. His misery was to be compounded by news from the club scene. Cardiff, still proving me stupid, continued to pound away at the top of the Heineken League, beating Abertillery 50–12. Sadly, Nigel Walker, the Olympic hurdler turned international winger, dislocated a shoulder, while Nigel Davies fractured a cheekbone, leaving two more backs unavailable to the national side. If Jason and the Argonauts bemoaned the enmity of the gods, one can but imagine what poor Alan Davies was thinking.

Such was the mood in the Principality that it was likely the whole of Wales was rather hoping South Africa would not return from Scotland. Certainly, the South Africans seemed happier north of the border. Perhaps the pessimism that matched the gloomy autumnal weather was too much for the instigators of the Welsh depression. Buoyant after their Swansea win, the South Africans raised British eyebrows when they pinpointed Scotland as the more difficult of the two forthcoming Test matches. Kitch Christie thought the extra passion of Scottish rugby would test the mettle of his men. How the Welsh demi-gods of times past must have groaned to hear such a damning indictment of their national treasure. Yet those of us who had witnessed the carnage left in Scotland by New Zealand the previous season put the South African comments down to naïvety, or false flattery.

It seemed hard to take Scottish pride seriously when Bath's David

Hilton, a selection for Scotland A to face the Springboks, explained his Pauline conversion from Bristolian to Scotsman. 'I mentioned to my Bath colleague, Andy Reed, at training about that side of my ancestry [his grandparents were Scottish]. It was a casual remark.' Such is the nature of patriotism and Scottish selectorial policy. Hilton added: 'I've got to learn the words to "Flower of Scotland", but then again, I don't know too much of "God Save the Queen", either.' At least sporting mercenaries wage their wars with a smile.

On 9 November, Hilton and friends walked on to the mud of Melrose and into the Scottish history books with a 17–15 win against South Africa. Amid the euphoria of the visitors' flowing form against Swansea, we had forgotten two facts: first, that the corollary of a settled Test team is often a demoralised midweek team, and second, that South Africa were still uncertain of themselves in the mud. To see such an accomplished player as Gavin Johnson play like an unpromising novice proved both of them. The three points that mattered came in the dying seconds from the boot of Duncan Hodge, a promising twenty-year-old fly-half. It was a boost to the morale of Scottish rugby, but even the winning captain, Kevin McKenzie, kept his feet on the ground. 'We are all realists. That was their second team. I'm sure it will be different a week on Saturday.' Kitch Christie's comments hardly smacked of despair. 'We are naturally disheartened, but we can't expect to win all the time.' I wonder how South Africans would accept such a comment made after a quarter-final defeat against England in the World Cup? 'Scotland A gave us a lesson in rucking but I have to say that the weather was not conducive to good rugby.'

Next out was the Test team, who overcame a Combined Scottish Districts team 33–6 on 12 November. It was a less than impressive performance, doubly concerning because Joubert limped off with a hamstring strain. The earlier comments of Pienaar and Christie regarding tiredness were beginning to sound prophetic. The Districts captain, Sean Lineen, felt Scotland had a chance. 'But they will need to put in some strong tackles,' he warned. The midweek side gave the Test team the perfect build-up when they defeated another combination side, the Scottish Select XV, 35–10. Eric Peters, another Bath man, performed magnificently as people started to wonder why Bath were competing in the Courage Leagues and not the McEwan's League in Scotland. Greg Oliver, the Hawick scrum-half, also professed himself confident of a win for his country in the Test.

Although François Pienaar fuelled further hope when, twenty-four hours before the kick-off, he announced: 'We still have a long way to go before reaching our full potential,' the bookmakers were rather less sceptical about the South Africans' chances. The Springboks trod the turf of the majestic new Murrayfield, 67,500 seats of pristine blue,

5–1-on favourites to beat their hosts. As I sat in Sky's studio in Bristol attempting to impress upon viewers the long-term significance of the South-West versus London (minus all internationals), the rugby world, excluding the 127 spectators and three Alsatians who paid to watch a riveting divisional match, awaited the Springboks' return to Murrayfield. Having lost eight consecutive internationals, Scotland were under as much pressure as their opponents. Even the bagpipes sounded unconvinced.

By full-time the tartan hordes were wishing that South Africa had never returned from the international boycott. The 34–10 result was a hammer blow to a nation in disarray. How fitting that one of the best performers was a man who symbolised the new South Africa – the Cape coloured wing Chester Williams. Joubert and Rudi Straeuli were again outstanding, but it was Williams who caught the eye of so many purists. He played so well that even the pro-apartheid die-hards who remain isolated in various Transvaal *doorps* must have been glad to have him in the jersey of their beloved Springboks. How often have you heard the racist rubbish about only white South Africans enjoying the physical contact of rugby? Gavin Hastings found out that the truth can hurt. Hastings is renowned for his strength, but as Scotland trailed 34–3 he launched a counter-attack in the direction of Chester Williams. Williams stood square and awaited the impact. The result of the collision was as conclusive as that of the match. Hastings was stopped in his tracks and dumped to the ground, helpless, as Williams remained on his feet and regained the ball. I wrote in the following Monday's *Telegraph*: 'Hastings had more chance of blasting a hole through Table Mountain.'

The game itself was proof of South Africa's good intentions. Joost van der Westhuizen, a scrum-half with the athletic capabilities of Gareth Edwards, unlocked a Scottish blindside defence as tight as an open barnyard door in the first half. It was merely the preliminary to twenty-four minutes of powerful, sublime rugby that resulted in four sizzling tries. In that brief spell, South Africa issued a statement to the world: the Springbok learning process was nearly over. Their one area of vulnerability looked to be the line-out, where Andy Reed (yet another Bath man) and Doddie Weir performed with some credit for Scotland. The day, however, belonged to South Africa.

It meant nine straight defeats for Scotland under the now beleaguered captaincy of Gavin Hastings. All he could offer was: 'I'm gutted. My advice to Wales next week is simply to tackle.' When I heard that I thought, that should be no problem for Wales, it's about all they do. Pienaar was still not completely satisfied. 'You have to be a team, not a bunch of individuals,' he complained. 'There were too many individuals out there today.' The South African captain might not have been too impressed, but the bookmakers were. Odds on South Africa for the World Cup were slashed from 7–2 to 11–4, making them second favourites to Australia, at 5–2. Scotland were a best-priced 66–1. I have seen racehorses win at 66–1, but I refused to believe that Scotland's price represented anything other than a complete waste of money.

According to the leading spread-betting operation, Sporting Index, there was very little money being laid on Wales for the following Saturday's international in Cardiff. Their opening market suggested that the Springboks were expected to win by a margin of between fifteen and eighteen points. Such was the confidence in South Africa after their taming of the Scots that by the kick-off this had increased to a seventeen-to twenty-point margin.

The odds on the midweek team beating Pontypridd at Sardis Road would have been considerably shorter. Even without Neil Jenkins, Pontypridd has become a difficult place from which to escape with a victory. It was a rare culture shock for the South Africans to travel up the Rhondda. At least two of their journalists grumbled that they could not understand why Tom Jones sang about 'the green, green grass of home'. A little more time spent in the community would have convinced them that the people are not as bleak as the scenery. That is a sadness of modern touring: it is taken so seriously that sides need the right sort of hotel, training facilities – even leisure facilities – which insulate them from the outside world. The time when rugby players used tours as opportunities to discover an unfamiliar country is fast disappearing into antiquity.

But Pontypridd were not to cause an upset. The Springboks did fail to score a try for the first time on tour, but they left the ghost valley of the coal-mining industry with a 9–3 victory. Dennis John, Pontypridd's coach, thought them beatable and urged Wales to attack them wide out in the international. As his team had played a Springbok midweek side that bore no resemblance to the Test XV, his comments are worth noting only as an illustration of how highly coaches value their own opinions. Alan Davies was more realistic on the eve of the match. 'They came on this tour looking for a team and that's what they've got now.' Even the normally ebullient Ieuan Evans, sidelined by injury, sounded a pessimistic note. 'What's most important is that we expand on the particular pattern of play we have developed over the last few years. I want to see us being able to vary our tactics, in the middle of a game if necessary.' Once upon a time, Welshmen might have thought the priority was to win. Just as South Africa had been humbled after their boycott, so Wales learned humility in the dark years of the early 1990s when New Zealand and Australia regularly ran up cricket scores against them.

Wales were not to prove us all wrong – they did lose, but the raw courage of their performance was immense. South Africa's perception that Welsh rugby lacked passion was shown to be erroneous. After sixty-five minutes Wales led 12–10 through the accuracy of Neil Jenkins, the man growing into the blessed No. 10 jersey. But class prevailed eventually, and a Hennie le Roux penalty and Chester Williams try gave South Africa a surprisingly difficult, but well-earned victory by 20–12. Even the most patriotic Welshman would be hard pressed to deny that three tries to nil merited success. It was fitting that the scorers were Straeuli, Williams and Joubert. Together with Ruben Kruger, they had been the players of the tour, while Pienaar's leadership qualities had silenced the many critics who saw him as a one-dimensional figurehead.

The primary reasons for the respectable margin for the Welsh were the towering performances of Gareth Llewellyn and Derwyn Jones in the line-out. The Springboks were annihilated in this facet of play, and it was to become their greatest area of concern before the World Cup. Christie admitted: 'They shocked us in the line-out, but they never really troubled our defensive line in the backs.' Welsh manager Robert Norster was also fulsome in his praise: 'Our line-out was magnificent and Derwyn Jones had a magnificent debut.' Jones had also learned his lesson from the kicking he had received in the earlier tour fixture at Newport: not once did he lie on the wrong side of the ball.

As François Pienaar's side waved farewell to the Principality, bound for Ireland and the two final matches of their tour, the relief at a mission successfully accomplished was almost tangible. 'We are definitely going somewhere now,' declared Engelbrecht. Little did he know that he would not be part of the ride for much longer. Christie conceded that, as far as the World Cup was concerned, 'this tour has proved that we now have the central core of our Test side'. It would be the nearest he came to admitting that he was happy until South Africa won the World Cup.

If South Africa allowed themselves a collective sigh of relief, so too did Wales. They might have lost, but they had not been psychologically savaged. Gareth Llewellyn, who had added to his burgeoning repu-tation, summarised this feeling when he admitted that he was 'pleased with the all-round performance'. How can a nation with the glorious rugby tradition of Wales be delighted in defeat? How could he be content when he had supplied an abundance of quality ball for Wales and they had not even troubled South Africa's backs?

The answers can be found back in October, when Wales rejoiced in victory over Italy and Neil Jenkins assumed the role of Welsh hero. Llewellyn was certainly convinced of the talents of his fly-half. 'I rate Neil Jenkins the best goal-kicker in the world at present, and possibly the best fly-half as well,' he declared. The best fly-half in the world must have a habit of ensuring a certain flow of tries. Jenkins' record was less than impressive against any bar the Iberian countries. Perhaps Jenkins does have all-round footballing skills, but in the Welsh shirt he was hiding them rather well. It was an awful conundrum for the selectors. Should they drop a man who scores all their points, or keep a man who limits their game? If Alan Davies seriously believed in his side's ability to reach the World Cup final on 25 June, he needed the courage to alter his style. I suspected he would be secretly honest and select the tackling, kicking Jenkins to apply his own efficient brand of damage limitation. That had been the story for Wales against South Africa, and the pattern looked likely to be identical for the next international against the equally formidable French in Paris.

5

Down the Road to Dynamism

It was time for English minds to turn to the international season. Their first opponents would be Romania at Twickenham on 12 November – not as glamorous as the neighbouring fixtures for Scotland and Wales, but equally important in testing their mettle after the South African mauling they had received in Cape Town in the summer. Before that, however, there was the small matter of the only round of Courage League matches to be played in November. England's players were granted a rest while the RFU and others, notably me in a lonely studio, tried to convince everyone that the restructured second-rate Divisional Championship was truly important to the development of the game.

The future of the English game depends on the health of the club system. That is why players such as Rodber, Bayfield, Leonard and Moore were so committed to playing for their clubs in the week before an international. Their determination forced Jack Rowell to retreat, or at least to show flexibility.

After the 5 November matches the Leagues would be exactly halfway through. The major fireworks occurred at the Memorial Ground, Bristol, where the anachronistic men of letters from the West Country beat the anachronistic men of letters from the Midlands. It was Leicester's first defeat of the season. Inspired by twenty-six points from Mark Tainton (a West Country Neil Jenkins who causes Bristol's selectors identical headaches), Bristol stormed away from Leicester in the second half to win 31–22. The result was marred for Bristol only by the news that Bath had again been victorious and had gained a two-point lead in the League. Bath top, Leicester second, Wasps third and Bristol fourth – there was little heart-attack material at the top of the First Division.

At the other end of the table, conformity was not the norm. West Hartlepool were near the bottom, but Sale and Orrell refused to become the northern whipping-boys. This left three of England's most famous clubs scrapping in the dustbin of Division 1. Northampton, so recently the great pretenders under the control of Wayne Shelford, had a mere two points. They faced West Hartlepool at home in one of the dogfight bankers. Despite the excellence of their home wins against Wasps and Bristol, Hartlepool are about as useful as a vegetarian in an abattoir when they play away. The other game, attended by yours truly with Sky, was at the Stoop Memorial Ground, home of Harlequins. The visitors, Gloucester, had six points, as did Harlequins. A win would push either side to a mid-table position of relative comfort; defeat would leave the losers only two points clear of the bottom if Northampton won. A vast majority of neutrals were supporting Gloucester. The West Country club represented the common face of rugby. The Shed may be vociferous and rude, but Kingsholm generates atmosphere. The club has an intense family feeling that endears it even to the bow-tie-wearing Bath rivals.

Harlequins are a very different club. The English may be unable to shrug off their obsession with the class system in society, but a sporting institution that actually styles itself as an aristocracy is something else. The whole ethos of the Harlequins club is that of amateurs versus professionals. There is always a vague sense that the committee feel embarrassed to play League rugby.

On the playing side, such an attitude has long been consigned to history, but perhaps some of that pervasive spirit has rubbed off on the team. Their League record is outstandingly average when one considers the quality of players they have had at the Stoop in the last seven years – Winterbottom, Coker, Carling, Moore, Skinner, Halliday, Leonard and countless others. Brian Moore had loudly proclaimed his determination to change this record of mediocrity, but before kick-off on 5 November he was still struggling in vain. A few more defeats and the Quins' committee could start to consider the prospects of hosting the likes of Fylde, Wakefield and London Scottish. At this stage of the season I made them around 9–1 for relegation. If I had offered odds I suspect there would have been a legion of optimistic takers.

Problems notwithstanding, the Londoners were the favourites. Gloucester had been winning friends with their style of flowing rugby – yes, flowing rugby. Under Barrie Corless, their rugby-mad citizens applauded the heresy of back play in front of their very eyes. They were not finding it easy to win matches, however. Although Gloucester were level on points with Harlequins, they had failed to earn a single point away from home. Visitors to Gloucester find it impossible to understand, but the West Country club do not like to travel far from their home.

The atmosphere at the Stoop was better than usual. Harlequins rely on the supporters of the away team as they have very few of their own, despite the popularity of their jersey as leisurewear. The Gloucester crowd knocked some of the crust from the old Stoop pie, jeering at any

Harlequins internationals who were spotted in the gloom and rain of an English sporting winter. Of the two clubs, Quins might be the ones associated with champagne rugby, but the conditions suited them more than Gloucester with their new fluidity.

In front by 9–5 with minutes left, Harlequins appeared to be on the verge of two points, although their performance did little to convert any Sky Sports viewers tuning in by mistake to Rugby Union. Then came a moment that would be cherished by all men of Gloucester and most rugby neutrals. It epitomised the new image of the West Country club. Mark Mapletoft, a 5ft 7in full-back who looks to have an international career as a fly-half, marked another ball that Harlequins had kicked away. Twenty metres in front of his posts, he spurned the sterile safety of touch, turned his back on the Quins and tapped the ball. After running 5 metres he changed pace so dramatically, coming to an abrupt halt, that the Harlequins defence froze, a ragged terracotta army. Prop forward Andy Deacon timed his run so well that he looked like a portly, pale Jerry Guscott and several pairs of hands and 70 metres later, Gloucester wing Paul Holford was under the posts. They had won the match and retained their friends.

Things were not so cheerful in the Harlequins bar. There would be no more League rugby before Christmas; Harlequins would have a long wait before attempting to haul themselves clear of relegation. Just as I carried my ante-post betting slips for Cheltenham around, for comfort, during the winter, so did a legion of rugby fans and players harbour the wild dream of Harlequins in Division 2.

As the Courage Leagues retreated into the most ridiculous two-month isolation, the white rose of England emerged to prepare to face Romania. During Geoff Cooke's tenure English supporters had had a good idea what they would get for their money. Under the new management of Rowell and Cusworth, the direction of the national team was shrouded in mystery. Rowell espoused the word 'dynamic' throughout his glorious seventeen-year reign at Bath. In the West Country it was widely believed that he would expect England to mirror the style which Bath had evolved. Yet under Rowell, Bath had suffered from a multitude of misconceptions and forgotten facts. At times they were emotionless automatons, on other occasions free spirits. Few could pin down the essence of the club's style. It was hardly surprising, because nobody could categorise Rowell, either.

His early Bath success revolved around the bounteous talents of backs like John Palmer and John Horton, but by the time Bath started to win trophies, the most influential characters were the rugged West Country forwards Gareth Chilcott and especially Roger Spurrell. By 1988, they had reverted to being a running side; by Rowell's double-winning departure in 1994 the team was a fifteen-man unit. Under Rowell's guidance,

Bath had remained at the pinnacle of the club game through constant evolution. What a contrast with England, who found a static forward power that conquered the northern hemisphere and then lost the ability to develop. It was all or nothing: kick every ball, as in the 1991 World Cup semi-final against Scotland; or run every ball, as witnessed by the tactically bereft final against Australia. Personnel changed but the style did not. When Geoff Cooke belatedly recognised this in 1994, England's players were no longer able to react to their manager's challenge. It was for this reason, I believe, that Geoff Cooke resigned so suddenly. He knew that his era had passed. Cooke's role in England's emergence from the underbelly of international rugby should not be under-estimated. When he arrived, the team lacked any organisation or disci-pline and was crying out for somebody of Cooke's detailed planning. Rowell, on the other hand, is not such a person, and it is unlikely that he would have achieved what Cooke did if he had been appointed in 1988.

By 1994, though, the problem was very different. Now England's fault was an excess of organisation and discipline. Like a benevolent dictator, Cooke had schooled the players so well that they seemed incapable of thinking for themselves; to progress they needed to change, and Rowell was the right man to help them do so. England had become a settled unit with a core of players, including Carling, Moore, Andrew and Rory Underwood, who appeared to be almost a club within a club. Rowell's presence shattered this debilitating cosiness. Nobody knew what this enigmatic man was thinking.

On the England tour to South Africa, his awkward 6ft 7in frame could be seen wandering quietly around the training pitch, absorbing the methods of the players and coaches at work. Rowell was biding his time to good effect. At Bath he had been an institution for long enough to know everyone and everything within the club, but he was new to England, and used the tour to form his impressions. At Bath Golf Club Rowell is renowned as a man who keeps his own company on a Sunday-morning round. In previous years that was his time to weigh up and evaluate Bath's performance of the day before. I suspect (it is impossible to know in Jack's case) that it was the time when he judged characters as well.

The Rowell philosophy veers steeply away from that of his England predecessors. Man-management has been a Rowell forte for as long as I have known him. Just as he was strong enough to back down in the England versus Romania/club versus country debate, so he is big enough to stress that a game can only be won by the players. His greatest compliment to his Bath teams was never technical appreciation but the free use of the description 'special human beings'. That is the biggest 'secret' behind Bath's success.

His social habits reflected his penchant for strong characters. Rowell was rarely an early-to-bed-Friday man for the sake of it. Never a school-master, more a manager, he relied heavily on trust. If somebody lets him down his reaction can be spectacular. It was the Spurrells, Tricks, Chilcotts and Halls who were Rowell's drinking friends – the wild boys. I have sat up with Jack Rowell drinking until 6 a.m. only to discover that he was due at a board meeting in Amsterdam that afternoon. The social habits of a beatnik and the work ethic of a demonic Margaret Thatcher make him a unique character. His generosity in the wake of the Bath Cup final victories was legendary in the city. Champagne flowed throughout the day chez Rowell, yet at the same time his parsimonious side was equally famous. He may be a former managing director of Golden Wonder, but the chances were evens that a packet of crisps offered by Jack Rowell would be past its sell-by date.

Like a fine wine, the man is an acquired taste. He is certainly far from perfect. At Bath he was rarely the one to tell a player he was dropped – that was the role of the captain. Some players did not appreciate him; they saw him as a scheming Machiavellian character, and to a certain extent they could be right. Rowell is a man driven by success and sacrifices have been made. Even men like Roger Spurrell, his most loyal of lieutenants, were left out without warning. Yet all the disappointment expressed by the host of players dropped by Rowell should not mask the fact that loyalty is one of his intrinsic instincts. Like Cooke, he would defend a character who served him well, but when a firm decision was needed, emotion was driven deep into the recesses of his formidable mind.

This toughness made Rowell the perfect man to inherit Cooke's team. The other element he would need to succeed would be humour. Having resigned from the adrenaline rush of his career on the board of Dalgety, Rowell is not one to sit idly around between internationals. His wife Sue mocks his inability to relax; Les Cusworth, England's backs coach, receives videos from side-on, front-on, every angle. Rowell had one mission only, to win the World Cup. The Grand Slam would be a bonus, but other Englishmen had coached the team to such success. No one had ever organised the winning of a World Cup for England. The danger for Rowell was the fact that he had no other vocation to provide a safety valve for the pressure. At Bath he adamantly refused a penny's-worth of expenses, although he travelled there twice a week from Market Harborough, on the other side of the country. By never accepting any-thing from the club, he felt himself free to turn his back on it when he wished. It was an escape route that Rowell would have found difficult to take because, for all his mental toughness, his heart will always be at Bath. Even as England manager he continued to overtly support their efforts.

At international level disentanglement is more difficult. Rowell can leave whenever he wishes, of course, but the media spotlight casts a cruel glare, and it might not be so easy to do so with his reputation intact. He was well aware of the added pressure when he accepted the challenge, and if he did not have one of the most sardonic senses of humour with which to confuse and strike fear into much of the media, one questions whether he would have been as keen to take up the post.

So to those who could claim the most minimal knowledge of this intricate man, World Cup year would be a fascinating experience. Rowell's first anticipatory comments before the Romanian international were typical. He does not believe in hidden agenda – in fact, it came as a surprise to most of the press how openly he spoke on selectorial matters. 'We have got to find out who is going to play full-back and we have got to find the best back row, specifically our first-choice openside flanker,' he said. Such comments placed enormous pressure on the incumbents in those particular positions, Paul Hull and Steve Ojomoh. They had been arguably England's two players of the tour in South Africa, but both were relative newcomers at international level. Rowell also held memories of poor Paul Hull performances for Bristol against Bath, while Ojomoh was yet to convince the manager that his commitment equalled his ability. This was Rowell's trusted test of newcomers.

His comments on Will Carling were also pure Jack Rowell. An established player would be placed under more subtle, but none the less obvious pressure. 'The captain is looking forward to making more of an impact. Will has got to play well to keep his place in the team. I have seen him play several times this season and he has not always had the opportunity to show what he is made of.' That was his magnanimous way of telling a rather shy, sensitive soul to sharpen up his act. Rowell was more covert in his statement because he recognised that outright criticism of Carling would help neither Carling, England nor Rowell in the quest for the World Cup.

The other customary touch was the salutary warning about the opponents. Romania's last international might have ended in ignominious defeat in Italy, but Rowell was not the man to build extra pressure on his side by underestimating them. 'The Romanians have some big men, and even Wales will admit that they were lucky to beat them earlier this season,' he cautioned. If Jack Rowell thought the world might believe Romania were on a par with New Zealand, he would have said so. This extravagant evaluation of the opposition caught on with Will Carling immediately. Romania's near Test-strength team had been beaten 26–16 by Oxford University, but Will advised us all not to read too much into the result. Even a Sloane with one 'O' Level in domestic science could work out that something was adrift in such an appraisal of Romania. Carling almost gave the game away later when he admitted:

'It would be nice to crush Romania as a lot of people expect.' And so it was, but Carling remained defiantly deceptive even in his post-match comments. 'It was nice to score today, but it was a very hard game to play in. If you'd offered this scoreline beforehand I would have taken it.'

Rowell added a string of his beloved superlatives in his analysis. 'We showed the dynamic rugby that we have been seeking. Bayfield was outstanding, Rodber immense [we would become thoroughly bored with that description of England's favourite army recruiting officer] and Andrew absolutely majestic.' He also offered the typically critical appraisal of the performance. 'We played with great ambition, sometimes too great an ambition, and that led to a number of errors.'

Rowell's summary, though downbeat, was accurate, despite the 54–3 margin of victory. While blind patriots prepared Homeric eulogies to England, more astute observers were less impressed with the overall quality of their game. The result was a substantial win for an international in terms of points, but this was the worst Romanian side most people had ever seen. It was almost impossible not to wince at the cruel television close-ups of defeated and dejected Romanian faces. The glib 'they never gave up' was summoned in countless post-match interviews, but the pictures gave the lie to such banalities. Given that the players have lived through the appalling recent history of Romania, it would be morally reprehensible to criticise them for not taking the match too seriously. Their perspective on life is based on rather different models from those of most other rugby-playing nations.

England scored six tries, of which four were attributable more to demoralised opponents than to incisive attacking play. Some of the players recognised the creative shortfall. Tony Underwood, who looked back to his best form, appeared bemused when a BBC reporter expected a mood of total elation. The man almost choked on his patriot's microphone when Underwood Junior elucidated on the work England needed to do. Too many unforced errors were made, not enough chances taken. Steve Ojomoh played well and, superficially at least, Dean Richards was not missed. In fact he would probably have been a liability: he would have ambled around the park, bored with the metaphorical massacre. Richards is a sporting warrior and needs a real battle. No such battle occurred against Romania. Other notable performances came from Martin Bayfield and Tim Rodber. Their director of rugby at Northampton, Ian McGeechan, was at Twickenham to support them and inadvertently assisting his 'auld enemy' in the process. In contrast the back line did not function smoothly. Carling looked uncomfortable playing a more fluid game, and passing errors abounded. It was a performance that relied too exclusively on physical power and porous defending, but at least the team were attempting to play with dynamism.

Carling confirmed the point when he revealed, 'We've realised the dynamic style is something we have to have to be successful in South Africa.' The ominous question of whether England had enough time before the World Cup to master such an approach hung, like a guillotine, over Rowell's head.

My Monday column in the *Telegraph* reflected my doubts and ended with the sentence: 'Perhaps the sterner test of . . . Norman Hadley and his Canadian mounties will reveal more on 10 December.' Already Cardiff's position at the top of the Heineken League had made me look a fool in Wales and Orrell's mid-table comfort belittled my thoughts on the English club scene. Rowell's charges were to join that list of torturers in December.

Meanwhile, poor Theodor Radulescu was, unsurprisingly, considerably more impressed with the men in white. 'England are certainly stronger, faster and bigger than Wales, to whom we lost earlier in the season. The hardness of England came as a bit of a shock to our younger players.' In the lead-up to the game Romania may have been lured into a false sense of security. If they relied on the press for information they might well have been unaware that they were even due to take the pitch at Twickenham. The British media had forgotten about the existence of the Balkans state since the demise of Ceaucescu. One man monopolised the stage – Carling's centre partner and media rival Jeremy Guscott, the golden boy of English rugby, who had been sidelined by a groin injury for a year.

It was one of rugby's most publicised comebacks. Guscott claimed he was 'as nervous and excited as when I first played for England five years ago'. That was not how Guscott described how he felt before his first cap to me. Sitting down in the Moon and Sixpence, one of Bath's most popular restaurants, the relaxed, composed Guscott casually admitted that he was not looking forward to the experience. 'I've heard they [the England team] are a bunch of Oxbridge tossers.' If Bath Football Club was a parochial place in the mid-1980s, Jeremy Guscott was the epitome of unworldliness.

Guscott was born with a precocious sporting talent. Some would say he was born to play for Bath. He joined the club as a mini-rugby player and, despite the lure of six-figure transfer fees, it looks increasingly unlikely that he will ever play for any other rugby club, Union or League. Strangers who meet Guscott are surprised by his approachability. Nicknamed 'Precious' by his England team-mates, Jerry has a reputation for arrogance that has frequently outstripped Carling's. This perception is based upon his play – he is and has a duty to be arrogant on the rugby field – and a misinterpretation of the paradoxical insecurity and aggression he radiated in his early years. Born into a close-knit family – his father, Henry, is Jamaican and his mother, Sue, a serviceman's daughter

– Guscott sneered his way through youth, never louder than on the rugby pitch, where he was sure of his gifts.

He was a local boy to the core: 'I had no ambition to play for England. Even as a Colt I wanted to play No. 10 for Bath.' Yet when Guscott did win his spurs, away to Waterloo, Simon Halliday remembers: 'He kicked a few penalties with his right foot, then a few with his left, just for a laugh. Everyone said, "Who is that?" but we knew how good he could be. So did he, and he told us all on the journey back.' Halliday and David Trick both had a quiet word, but it did not quell the rebel. In 1989, one day he was a noisy club player, the next a rugby superstar and British Lion. The chip on his shoulder was replaced by an aloofness that was more studied than his Bath team-mates realised. He was trying to prove a point, but in the process he started to lose his friends, as well as a place in the Bath team for a Cup semi-final.

Guscott, now nearing thirty and maturing in the mellowest of manners, happily admits that it was rugby, together with parental responsibilities, that made him grow up. The man who strode out at Twickenham to face Romania was no longer the posing, immature Guscott of the early days, but the real Guscott: a man with a vicious tongue, an engaging sense of humour and a capacity to endure marathon drinking sessions. Needless to say, he and I get along well nowadays.

Guscott's relief at being able to return to the international fold was heightened by the arrival of the man he had known all his adult life as a coach. 'Many aspects of my life have changed, but what is familiar is the sound of Jack Rowell organising a team. What England need is Bath's habit of winning games.' What England also needed, which the relaxed, wine-sipping Jeremy Guscott would never say, is a reborn, fully charged Guscott. He has an extra injection of pace that promises drama whenever he touches the ball; additionally, he has a consummate feel for the game in both hand and foot. Guscott is England's complete threequarter, and his form would be imperative in the preparation for South Africa 1995.

On 27 November, England announced the team to face Canada in 'the sterner Test'. Two changes heralded the return of one familiar face and the exit of another. Although Steve Ojomoh had played well against Romania, he misread Rowell's wishes by excusing himself from the motley assortment of matches known as the Divisional Championship. England specifically requested that Ojomoh played openside for the South-West to give him the match practice he couldn't get at Bath while Andy Robinson occupied that berth. He had forgotten about Rowell's judgement of character. After the Romania match, Rowell had made a pun about 'England's embarrassment of Richards' in the back row. For Canada the Leicester Titan returned to No. 8 alongside Rodber and

Clarke, who moved to No. 7. The public clamoured for Neil Back, forgetting that this trio had played as a unit in victories over New Zealand, Wales and South Africa and had yet to taste defeat. Rowell's gamble was that England's loss of athleticism in Ojomoh would be compensated for by the tactical skills of Richards. The other alteration was the removal of the forwards' favourite scrum-half, Dewi Morris, for Bristol's sharper Kyran Bracken, another sign of England's honourable running intentions. Rowell, as elusive with his words as ever, announced: 'These changes are to try different combinations and should not be looked at in the context of dropping players who are left out.' Bath players had heard it all before.

So November ended miserably for Ojomoh, Morris and Scotland. Wales deluded themselves that matters were relatively satisfactory; for England they were, but the real heroes of the month had been the Springboks. Their style of play and Test match triumphs had struck a chord in the hearts of all true rugby supporters.

Perhaps the biggest losers of the month were New Zealand. They did not even play a game but they lost John Timu, veteran star of twenty-six Tests, to Australian Rugby League club Canterbury Bankstown. In this context the words of Louis Luyt sounded an ominous note for those who claim to protect and support the game: 'Rugby has been run on a very old-boys'-club basis and people don't change easily.' If the International Board could not stop the drain of the Quinnells, Garrick Morgans and Timus, somebody else within the game would have to do so. Season 1994–5 was shaping up, not only as a World Cup year, but also as a revolutionary one as we tiptoed into December.

6

Dark December Days

For me December started with a literary jolt when I was asked to contribute a piece to the England versus Canada match programme. Such contributors are normally members of the twenty-caps-plus club. While I had blazed my way through headlines in the manner of Andy Warhol's fifteen minutes of fame, most of England hardly knew me, or, if they did, it was as 'that twat who put club before country'. When I ran on to the pitch to play Scotland in 1993, one supporter asked, 'Who's that bloke who looks like a darts player?' Now I was earning a living writing for the benefit of these people, not to mention my bank manager.

Having very limited experience of Canada – I visited Newfoundland once in a drunken stupor, with Fergus Slattery – I was not finding the article the most straightforward task. It was a relief when the normally dreaded telephone distracted me from my tribulations. 'Best's back,' a voice on the line said. It sounded like some Batman plot; I didn't know what he meant until my source clarified his terse comment. 'Dick Best is back in rugby,' he explained patiently. 'He's been appointed director of coaching at Harlequins.' Judging by the rumours that flew around south-west London faster than the overhead jets, Best had signed the best deal in club history. He owed Jack Rowell an unexpected vote of thanks for sacking him from the England assistant manager's post.

Best's appointment strengthened the number of contracted professionals on the club scene. It was becoming clear that the professional priorities of coaches would eventually tangle with the amateur demands being made on the England players. How can the likes of Dick Best accept that Harlequins internationals could be coerced into missing games that might cost his club a place in the First Division 'elite'? I wasn't sure whether I could smell a barbecue outside my house or the whiff of gunpowder. In another life, Guy Fawkes' profession would be a director of coaching and his target the Rugby Football Union offices in the Twickenham complex.

Best was not the only man joining Harlequins. West Hartlepool lost two of their better forwards, the volatile No. 8 Mick Watson and Simon Mitchell, a well-regarded hooker. Unlike Best, they could not take up residence at the Stoop immediately because of the 120-day qualifying period. This is how the sport attempts to prevent 'poaching', a move which in football circles is known as 'a transfer'. This rule appears to be another of the RFU's ostrich decisions, the powers that be seeming too frightened to lift their heads from the sand to face reality.

Despite a youthful reputation equalling that of soccer's Tommy Docherty as the man with more clubs than Jack Nicklaus, I remained rooted in Bath for the last decade of my career. A sense of loyalty enveloped the club and helped to make the place both enjoyable and successful. I believe in the benefits of loyalty, but in League rugby, where achievement is paramount, players will move if the need arises. It is a reality of the Courage Leagues and it is unlikely ever to disappear. Far from being a deterrent, then, the qualifying period is merely an inconvenience. Even worse, it hinders the game's career-minded amateurs. If a player is a member of Newcastle but is offered a plum job in London, why should he wait 120 days before joining Richmond or Wasps? The situation is farcical.

In theory the players keep themselves fit by continuing to play for their old club until the registration period is complete. I for one would not have wanted to play with someone who would soon be joining a rival club. West Hartlepool's statement reflected the view of any sensible club. 'Both players wish to continue playing for West during the 120-day qualifying period before they can appear for Harlequins. It must be highly questionable whether the players who transfer to a rival club by choice during the season will have the level of competitiveness so essential to success and so vital in the First Division. In the interests of equity and club morale, there can be no compromise on this stance.' The London-bound pair were never again to wear the shirts of West Hartlepool. Their ambition looked rather like a game of snakes and ladders.

Harlequins themselves were suffering an unpleasant phase of landing on snakes at every throw. They were not quite back to square one, but that appeared to be the general direction in which they were heading. The other board players were less than concerned. I was rather dismayed, however, with Sky's decision to send the cameras back to the Stoop on 17 December for the fourth-round Pilkington Cup match against Saracens, table-toppers in the Second Division. When the draw was made, the Sky rugby team's opinions on which game to cover were neatly split. The recent recruits, myself and Jamie Salmon, wanted to travel to Yorkshire for Wakefield versus Gloucester. This was the game we considered most likely to throw up a rare Cup shock. The experienced television men, however, were adamant that the 'story' was the struggling Harlequins and their big names, Carling, Moore and Jason Leonard, himself once a Saracen. After a heated debate, both Jamie and I accepted that the peculiar demands of live televised sport made Harlequins the match to be at. An element of hope and prayer also hung in the air.

That Saturday dawned a typically wet, grey December day. Even in a tropical climate, the Stoop holds little joy for me, but on such a dank, dismal afternoon it was a positively wretched experience to cover the match. All the climatic depression would have been forgotten, though, if Saracens could have avenged the 'theft' of Leonard. It would have been rendered acceptable even if the two combatants had offered a stirring Cup tie. Sadly but predictably, neither the dream nor the hope would be realised. Our first live Pilkington Cup tie finished a respectable second behind Orrell versus Leicester as the worst match of the season for television viewers.

Festooned with Christmas decorations, the Harlequins clubhouse had an unaccustomed seasonal air, but the match was a total turkey. In the best English traditions, players ran at tacklers, rather than space, and the spectators left feeling about as satisfied as England cricketers must have been with their performances in Australia. Harlequins 'triumphed' 9–5, but the meaningful statistic was the one that told us there had been a line-out every two minutes. Not a game for the uninitiated – not a game for anyone, for that matter – but Harlequins were through.

As luck would have it, Wakefield did cause a Cup upset by beating Gloucester and the Sky crew all blamed one another for the choice of the Stoop. The only other First Division team to lose was West Hartlepool, who fell in the land of pies and peas to Orrell.

Two days later I huddled around a radio, awaiting the draw for the fifth round, praying, 'Please do not give Harlequins an attractive home tie!' This time my wish was granted. Harlequins would not be overly perturbed by the prospect of a visit to Second Division neighbours London Irish and there was no danger that the fixture would be deemed a fascinating experience for Sky viewers. The two big matches were Orrell versus Bath and Bristol against Leicester. The Sky selection was unanimous this time: Bristol and Leicester, and a two-minute drive from my house. A fine choice.

It was a pity that my last memory of English club rugby in 1994 was such a disappointing one as the Quins Cup tie. It did little justice to one of the most entertaining three months on the club circuit I can remember. Jack Rowell had preached the rugby revolution according to the gospel of the Bledisloe Cup and Transvaal. To their credit, the First Division clubs rose to the challenge of producing an infinitely more attractive sport. Not only were Wasps following the gospel with the fervour of the fanatic, but such remorseless, grinding sides as Leicester, Orrell and West Hartlepool were busy tearing down the walls of set-piece rugby. Even the militant Shed smiled at the exploits of new Gloucester. Old advocates of 'trudge' rugby, like Mickey Skinner, were beginning to appear rather politically incorrect. It was a Scotsman, Ian McGeechan, who pointed out just how much the change in style would benefit the national side: 'The significant change in First Division rugby has seen many clubs open out their attacking approach, and that must help England.'

While the new attitude might have been assisting England, the gains were hardly mutual. The RFU's failure to structure the season left the clubs in tentative mood as they faced 1995. Bath coach Brian Ashton sounded a note of concern: 'With internationals and divisionals, it's been very difficult to maintain any continuity at club level. In fact, when we resume the League programme in the New Year, it will be like starting a new season. Who knows what's going to happen then? What happens on the Saturdays before internationals? England have already said they want their players to rest the week before Five Nations matches. What if Scotland and Ireland request the same?' I could think of nine other clubs who would envy Ashton's problems, but the point was clear. The clubs were being given a raw deal and potential battle lines were being drawn up in the club-or-country debate.

Meanwhile, oblivious to England's administrative vagaries, South Africa prepared themselves for the final match of an enjoyable tour that had gone a long way to silencing so much of the hyperbole surrounding their arrival. Their victories against Wales, and especially Scotland, focused attention back to the quality of their rugby.

The Springboks had arrived in Ireland at the end of November to meet the Combined Provinces, whom they beat 54–19. Their finale would be the traditional end-of-tour match against the Barbarians. There are a multitude of modern rugby minds who argue that the Barbarians are an anachronism; that in the pressurised world of modern rugby there is no longer space for them. Many players argue that the opposite is true, that precisely because of the pressure that chokes the sport, they love the concept of the Barbarians. The Barbarians are probably the embodiment of all the amateur virtues in which the Dudley Woods of this world believe. Their expansive game is made possible by the players' awareness that only that day's result is at stake, and to play for them against a major touring side is an opportunity to compete against the best without the patriotic pressure of impending national disgrace. Additionally, in a game where time for socialising has almost disappeared, it remains a rare joy to mingle with players from other countries.

The Barbarians team to face South Africa had a diversity of talent, from Welsh captain Robert Jones to Philippe Saint-André of France, Ian Jones of New Zealand, Simon Geoghegan of Ireland, Scott Hastings of Scotland, Jonathan Callard of England and even a Canadian, Al Charron. There was little doubt that the Barbarians were motivated for the match. Some saw it as an unofficial international, and Jeff Herdman, their coach, developed that theme on the Thursday before the game. 'The South Africans will be determined to end their tour with what would amount to a Third Test victory.' However, close analysis revealed that South Africa clearly did not view the match as such, even before the game. The Springbok side showed five changes from Cardiff: the management had magnanimously decided to use those players who had been close to Test rugby but had not yet quite sniffed the intoxicating air of a full international. It was a gesture that emphasised the good nature of a successful and contented touring side; it did not suggest the mental edge needed for an important game.

Robert Jones voiced the Barbarians' determination. 'We owe it to the Barbarians tradition and also to the Lansdowne Road crowds, who have their first chance of seeing the Barbarians play the tourists. It is a great honour to play for the Barbarians.' Like many others, Jones also had a personal point to prove to his own national selectors: 'With the Five Nations Championship coming up and the World Cup on the horizon, this game is a great chance for players to stake claims for places in their national squads.' The likes of Neil Back and Callard were undoubtedly thinking along similar lines. Jones, one of the shrewd-est brains in British rugby, pinpointed the Barbarians' game plan. 'The South Africans struggle without first-phase possession, as was the case when they struggled to beat Wales, and we aim to play on their weaknesses.'

The Barbarians may have trained like an international squad, but a visit to the Guinness Brewery on the day before the match underlined that, win or lose, it was only a game. It was not even a skirmish in the rugby war that was being waged.

The match itself was a triumph for the Barbarians. They won 23–15 and probably saved the club for the immediate future in the process. Tries for Saint-André and Geoghegan, backed up by Callard's boot, proved too much for a South African side that appeared rather less than desolate in defeat. Pienaar's appraisal of the game and the overall tour would be a fair summary. 'The Barbarians were more motivated than us. We tried to play Barbarians-type rugby and it backfired. They scored two tries off our mistakes. But we have conceded only eleven tries against fifty on tour, and we are 40 per cent better than when we started back in October. And we won the two Tests.'

He could have added that South African rugby also won many friends, which may well have been the most triumphant aspect of the tour in a general sense. But Springbok minds, anticipating the World Cup, remained uneasy. Losing to the Barbarians was not in any way damaging to their morale, but the factors behind the defeat were of grave concern. Simon Shaw, an England back-up, and Ian Jones, the great All Black, dominated the South Africans in the line-out, while André Joubert signed off the tour for them with an inept display of goal-kicking. Joubert had been the player of the tour, but his imprecision with the boot was symptomatic of South Africa's slightly casual approach, compared to that of the battle-hardened England and Australian sides. Journalist John Robbie, once of Ireland, now the voice of South African rugby, had little doubt about South Africa's problems. 'There are still glaring deficiencies in the line-out and you have to question whether the half-backs will be able to dictate play against strong opposition. And they have a weakness in the lack of a goal-kicker.' Robbie's opinion scarcely made their odds for the World Cup, 11–4, seem attractive.

When the South Africans flew home for a well-earned break, it was hard not to wonder just how much they would improve before they met Australia on 25 May. They had proved enough on tour to suggest that only a magnificent side would overcome them once they were home and inspired, but they had looked at least susceptible.

It was not until February that I remembered to ask Jon Callard if Elandre van der Bergh had offered him a beer on the night after the Barbarians match. Callard confirmed that they had bumped into each other in the foyer of the Berkeley Court Hotel. An invitation was extended, but Callard declined it. A pity, they could have compared notes on the rejuvenation of South Africa's rugby reputation.

As the South Africans departed they remained very much on English minds. England were confidently expected to win their group in Durban, while the bookies narrowly fancied Australia to overcome South Africa in the first game of the tournament. That would leave South Africa needing to beat Romania and Canada to qualify as runners-up and face England in Cape Town. The Rowell video library of South Africa was fairly extensive by the time they flew home.

Not only were the England management thinking about South Africa, some of them were actually visiting the country. Jack Rowell and John Elliot attended a Rugby World Cup managers' meeting to thrash out the logistical details of hotels. During the summer, they had pinpointed a luxurious and isolated beach hotel north of Durban. It was exactly what England wanted, but unfortunately it did not suit the Rugby World

Cup administrators, who had decided to allocate hotels to all the teams without consulting them. Mr Rowell was not a happy manager. 'We want the appropriate accommodation for this event. The players have got to feel comfortable about their surroundings and where they will be spending a comparatively long time. After all, this is one of the biggest events of their lives. A handful of other countries feel the same, especially those who are committed to making the rugby life as attractive as possible to the players in order to retain them in the sport. We have an assurance that the position will be reviewed.'

In theory, the rationale behind Rugby World Cup's decision was quite acceptable. They claimed that their aim was to create a 'level playing field' for all the sides. Perhaps the fairly lopsided history of apartheid in the country engendered this ennobling spirit of community. Socialism seemed a fading force in the world at large, but in rugby, brotherhood appeared to be all the rage. England's concern stemmed from the fact that they would be one of the best-supported nations in the tournament. The players are always delighted to see the flag of St George abroad, but twenty well-intentioned travelling fans staring at a few of them playing bridge in a hotel bar is not really conducive to relaxed preparation. In the furtherance of their level playing field, perhaps the Rugby World Cup authorities guaranteed that each country would be supported in equal numbers, but somehow I doubted that there would be an abundance of Romanians or Tongans to distract the preparation of their heroes. England also indicated that, as they were to be based in Durban, where humidity is a serious problem, it would be even more difficult to create a level playing field on the pitch, since Argentina and Western Samoa were far more comfortable in these conditions. If they wanted to create a really level playing field, they should have organised the tournament in a non-playing country, because South Africa would have an unfair home advantage.

Rowell left Elliot in South Africa and returned home to await the outcome of England's bid to break free of the restrictions of Rugby World Cup and its socialist organisers. He was doubtless interested in whether RWC would note the heavy-handed hint in his reference to those countries 'committed to making the rugby life as attractive as possible to the players in order to retain them in the sport'. Consider the 1994 roll call of defections, notably those of Scott Quinnell, Garrick Morgan and John Timu, and it was easy to understand Rowell's implicit warning. On 3 December Sir Ewart Bell, the RWC chairman, issued a statement that suggested that his administrators were disciples of the RFU's ostrich philosophy: 'So far as I am aware, no manager is going home saying that the thing is not being organised in a satisfactory manner.' I imagine Jack Rowell was forced to retreat to the jealously guarded wine cellar at his home in Bath when he heard this offering.

If that statement startled him, the announcement of the decision to send all eight quarter-finalists to the Johannesburg–Pretoria area after the group matches must have made him apoplectic. RWC's reasoning was that all sides should have an equal opportunity for altitude training. Doubtless this had nothing to do with commercial decisions. As England would play only one match at altitude – the final, if they progressed all the way – they were understandably upset. It was more important to establish a base in Cape Town. It is an irrelevance that nearly everybody who has ever visited South Africa rates Cape Town as a better city in which to spend any time than Johannesburg. England had been nothing if not thorough, and John Elliot, the silent partner in the English management team, tersely announced: 'We have taken advice from a sports scientist and we would prefer to stay at sea-level for as long as we can. We don't see any benefits in gaining altitude experience and then returning to the coast.' For a sport determined to progress, it is sad that the detailed planning of individual countries can be nullified by the decidedly dictatorial whims of a RWC committee that seems intent on arresting the development of the game through the creation of this wonderful level playing surface.

Yet England had not given up hope of reversing this policy decision. It was one of those rare occasions when the entire weight of the national press corps was behind them. I hold up my hand and admit that my reasons were utterly selfish. The thought of wandering through Cape Town up to Table Mountain, along the coast to bars like Blue Peter with their stunning vistas, was rather more appetising than spending three weeks in Johannesburg, the world's most violent city, by reputation at least. RWC needed to be prepared for a media backlash if our social plans were to be shattered.

Even as England battled for independent World Cup arrangements, the future stars of the 1999 tournament were battling for the Divisional Championship at Wasps. Well, that was what I told my Sky viewers – at any rate, those who thought London versus the Midlands a more interesting proposition than the Barbarians versus South Africa on BBC1. It was also what the sponsors, CIS, propounded and, of course, it was the official line of the RFU. The reality is that the CIS Divisional Championship is an antiquated concept now that the Courage Leagues are so strong. The other reality is that the CIS sponsorship deal is a fairly attractive proposition to the RFU committee.

A second consecutive week in the echoing Wasps ground was rather less than exciting. My mood was hardly improved by the match that unfolded before my eyes. London, who had been the only divisional side to play any positive rugby, led the Midlands 15–10 five minutes into injury time. The Midlands had spent more time killing, as opposed to using, the ball when suddenly they awoke from their slumber to score a late try through wing Harvey Thorneycroft. Richard Angell kicked the conversion and the Midlands, a fifteen-man cure for insomnia, were England's divisional champions. I would willingly bet that whichever team is finally relegated from the Courage First Division, they would beat the Midlands comfortably. I would also lay odds that the Midlands will win the 'Least Popular Rugby Champions' award for the 1994–5 season.

After the Midlands' grinding victory against the North, during which Martin Bayfield sat in a Sky studio in Bristol, predicting that they would be easily the worst divisional side, Dave Scully, the North captain, called them cheats – a reference to their kamikaze style of killing the ball. It was little surprise that the Midlands adopted this approach: they had selected as their captain the thirty-four-year-old former England flanker Gary Rees, the king of slow-ball rugby. As the Midlands celebrated their Championship win, Tony Jordan, the generally genteel London coach, described them as 'exceptionally cynical'. Even Steve Bates of Wasps, one of rugby's most relaxed personalities, fumed: 'My view is that we are doing our domestic game a disservice by protecting the player on the ground. In the World Cup in South Africa next summer, for certain, those who get on the wrong side will be seriously raked out – and referees will allow that.' In layman's terms, Bates was advocating a serious kicking. It sounds barbaric, but within the game it is universally accepted that if you try to prevent the ball being played by falling offside you will be kicked. Rugby Union players have little time for those who complain about backs or legs being raked. The head is different, and Steve Bates would never support kicking anyone there. Nor would François Pienaar, but imagine the reaction of our national media if he had spoken in terms as plain as Bates'. It is no coincidence that of all the English clubs, it is Wasps who have the biggest reputation for using the boot. I would argue that 99 per cent of the time it is within the spirit of the game; it is also a fundamental reason for the excellence of their ball-recycling. London rightly felt that the triumph of the Midlands was a regressive step for domestic rugby, but it was interesting to note that they did not possess enough variety in their own game to nullify the Midlands' destructive tendency. Captained by Bates and dominated by Wasps, London revealed a naïvety similar to that of which Wasps have been so often accused. They would probably win the League now and join the Make Stuart Barnes Look an Idiot Club – as the season marched on, membership continued to grow.

A prime member of that club is Robert Jones of Wales, the victorious Barbarians captain. In 1993 it was Jones who sliced through my head with his studs, leaving me to play a week later against Taranaki wearing a huge turbanesque bandage. Jones has spent his career making opponents look foolish, but was now out of favour with Alan Davies and his fellow Welsh selectors, who preferred Rupert Moon. Moon's heart and soul are as big as those of any Welshman, but his talent is not quite their equal. Jones suffered playing behind packs that looked as if they hailed from Knotty Ash compared with Ackford and Dooley in their prime. Skill was sacrificed for size, and when Jonathan Davies headed north and Robert Jones was dropped, the ambition of Welsh rugby died.

But Jones' desire to play for Wales has never faltered throughout the traumas of recent years. In the summer he left his career with the Swansea Building Society to join Western Province in South Africa and prepare himself for a tilt at Rugby Union, rather than windmills, come summer 1995. He admitted how important the Barbarians match against the touring Springboks had been for him. It was just as well that he acquitted himself well, because he paid a price for their win, a price only too well known to Ben Clarke and myself. In November 1992, we represented the Barbarians against Australia, both keen to push for England and British Lions berths. Bath were playing Waterloo – 'A load of shit from the middle of the Second Division' was, I think, my description – in the Pilkington Cup. The rest is a matter of record: the biggest shock in Cup history, and the most abuse ever from the tongue of Jack Rowell for Ben Clarke and Stuart Barnes.

I don't know what reception Jones was given in Swansea after leading the Barbarians to success, but I doubt that Mike Ruddock, Swansea's coach, congratulated him. In a League match, the All Whites, the defending champions – minus Jones – achieved the distinction of losing 12–10 to First Division strugglers Abertillery, a club I considered about as successful as the defunct mines in the grimy Gwent Valley. The defeat left Swansea in a hopeless position, out of reach of this season's League title. The very mention of the words 'South Africa' was apparently still leading to psychological collapses in West Wales' premier town.

While Swansea stuttered, Cardiff maintained their mocking ways, remaining top courtesy of a 19–6 victory over my first club, Newport. My only hope of being proved right about their incapacity to win the League lay in the Rhondda Valley with Pontypridd and the deadly boot of Neil Jenkins. He scored twenty-four points in a 29–13 local derby against Treorchy, silencing their male voice choir. It was a cruel irony – a man I so often decry as a No. 10 was my prime hope of retaining a vestige of self-esteem in matters relating to the Principality.

There were more serious concerns for Welsh hopes the following week. Emyr Lewis, Wales' bullish No. 8, damaged a leg, ruling him out of the formidable challenge of a January trip to Paris. Alan Davies' luck did not appear to be turning at all. He might not have enjoyed the end of 1994, but my own horizons brightened when Neath – never let a bad word be said about them – beat Cardiff 21–3, leaving Neil Jenkins and Pontypridd in with a chance of winning the League.

7

Bangs and Whimpers

For Neath, conquerors of top-of-the-table Cardiff, December was a good month outside Wales as well – and in probably the least likely setting to find a pair of Neath players: the Varsity match. The presence of Matthew McCarthy at fly-half and James Reynolds on the wing for Cambridge was a reminder that rarely is anything as it seems in sport. Try telling the Springboks that Neath have two members studying in one of the world's most 'civilised' universities – they would never believe it. Nor would they believe that Brian Thomas, Neath's rugby architect, has a formidable Cambridge-educated brain. In fact the university has long had extensive links with Wales. In contrast, Oxford have a tradition of Commonwealth students, the brightest of whom are the Rhodes Scholars. Bill Clinton, in his non-inhaling days, was a Rhodes Scholar, as was Phil Crowe, an Australian international in my distant university days.

The second Tuesday of every December is the day on which the majority of these graduates have their sporting moment in the sun. Very few progress to long-term recognition. It could also be described as the day when much of England casts all sense out of the window. Twickenham is always packed for the occasion, and not just with drunken undergraduates (my favourite class of supporter in my three Varsity matches) but the entire City of London. Louis Luyt would tear out his hair to see such unrefined 'old-boy' behaviour. Sixty-year-olds who can barely remember where Oxford is, and certainly never played rugby, scream at the young men with a raw tribalism that would unquestionably lead to ejection from a football ground. The pin-striped suit seems to be something of a behavioural *carte blanche*.

More senseless still, the entire national press corps arrives en bloc for a game that is a glorified school match. Never does England reveal its rampant snobbery and pomp more obviously than at a Varsity rugby match. At least the rowers are actually good-quality teams; Oxford and Cambridge rugby sides would not hold their own in Division 2 of the Courage Leagues. Most perplexing are the hordes who watch the game without even a hint of old allegiance. There can be only two reasons for the crowd: the opportunity for businesses which fail to obtain tickets for England internationals to entertain guests in front of a host of retired sportsmen speaking for a living; or, more simply, an excuse not to work on a Tuesday. Any decent rugby would not be recognised by the majority of spectators, but it is a real bonus for the knowledgeable few. The 1994 Varsity match was to be such a game.

My interest was rather more avid than usual because I had played for forty minutes against Oxford University for an invitation side called Major Stanley's. I think we lost 80–58 – defence was surplus to requirements. The exciting style of Oxford's play impressed me; so did the healthy tradition of drinking, which had survived undeterred by the lectures of the long-faced health fanatics who preach against excess. I endured a long night's session with Oxford's Canadian No. 10, Gareth Rees. Any fly-half who tips the scales at 14st has earned my support.

The eve of the match was another heavy night. That was the occasion of the Vincent's Dinner for members of the Oxford University sportsmen's club of the same name. Held at the Café Royale, it was a far from abstemious affair. The evening passed in a blur. One of my few recollections was of Jack Rowell, another Oxford graduate, being tackled down the stairs by *bon vivant* chef and celebrity Keith Floyd. Rowell never did enquire about Floyd's availability for South Africa.

Leaden-headed, I arrived at 'Twickers', as it must be known on Varsity match day, in time to speak at a lunch for fairly disinterested customers from supermarkets, leasing companies and the like. A competition was held, with a prize for the person who could predict the correct score, or came nearest to it. Conspiratorially, I let my table know that Oxford were certain to beat Cambridge well. The Make Stuart Barnes Look an Idiot Club was expanding still further. My opinion was based on first-hand experience. Perhaps I should have remembered that journalism, broadcasting and wine are not conducive to playing against fifteen fit athletes. But even Tony Rodgers, the Cambridge University coach, claimed that his team were 'rank outsiders'. Lyn Evans, the Welsh coach of Oxford, would make no other predictions than: 'If we don't freeze in front of the big crowd, we will put on a show.'

The Oxford show was scripted to star fly-half Gareth Rees as the ringmaster. I had interviewed him the previous week. Only four days after the Varsity match, he was due to play for Canada against England. He was in pursuit of a unique double that, in his own words, would make him 'happy, but not completely shocked'. He would regret such optimism by 4 p.m. on Saturday 10 December. The week started wonderfully for Rees, however. After fifty-five seconds he dropped a goal to send the favourites flying out of the blocks. Thereafter things degenerated. Oxford's handling became too ambitious for the occasion and Cambridge, inspired by Reynolds and guided by McCarthy, edged home 26–21, despite a late Rees try and a rally that left even the most cynical journalist holding his breath. Five tries, forty-seven points and a game of rugby that emphasised an apparent re-birth of ambition in the sport. Oxford had lost, but their heads were held high.

None took defeat with more grace than the burly twenty-seven-year-old Rees. Oxford's inspiration had performed below his standard; fitfully brilliant, he nevertheless failed to provide the tactical direction so imperative to a side high on adrenaline, low on experience. The Varsity match had been Rees' victory banker. Now he would have to lift himself for the challenge of England. Few doubted that he would not be capable of re-asserting his presence at Twickenham.

Rees had played at Twickenham as an eighteen-year-old Harrovian for Wasps against Bath in the 1986 Cup final, when his precocious maturity helped Wasps push us to the brink of despair before our inevitable recovery. Since then his career has marched on mercurially. He is perhaps North America's greatest-ever rugby player. He has an assassin's boot. He kicked last-minute penalties to beat England A, then, more famously, the land of his father, Wales, in Cardiff. In the summer of 1994, he kicked a late penalty to secure victory against a France team en route to a series victory in New Zealand.

Rees is too heavy to have great pace, but he is razor-quick in speed of thought. He considers himself the rugby equivalent of a quarterback and he throws the ball quarterback style, with almost as much accuracy as Steve Young of the 49ers. When you drink and talk sport with Rees, he constantly uses the word 'vision'. He has it on the pitch. His role is to keep the team moving forward by the most suitable method, boot or hand. He is a thinking fly-half; he is also a drinking one. After the Major Stanley's match, Rees was at the centre of the Oxford roisterers, an attitude that bucks the new athletic rugby trend. He has been criticised for being too rounded a fly-half; I would prefer to praise him for being a fully rounded individual.

If Rees was an army officer, his troops would follow him; he is a team man, moulded on the Canadian experience. 'Canada have been breaking new ground since 1986 and we perform for each other; we like and respect one another,' he says. Canadian rugby developed a pioneering spirit which engendered the attractive club mentality Rees epitomises. A Harrovian yes, but first a Canadian. 'For me, the highlight of rugby is playing for my country. That has always been my main motivation.'

Nevertheless Rees must have suffered after the Varsity match. It would be a tough four days for him, leaving the world of student rugby for the crunching reality of the international game, and against an England side committed to improving on the Romanian victory. As he reflected on the pain of defeat, his countrymen were facing an Emerging England XV, 110 miles away in Bath. They had selected a largely second-string side but even so, I shuffled off to Bath, gingerly respecting a hangover that had worsened throughout the Varsity match. While a second team cannot indicate the strength of the Test team, they are a barometer for the morale of the tour. By watching the midweek team, I could gauge whether Canada would live up to their growing reputation at Twickenham.

I left the Recreation Ground depressed, and by more than my hangover. Emerging England crushed Canada 34–6. The visiting side had not even looked like an international squad; they looked as bad as I felt. Youngsters like Tony Diprose, Rob Hardwicke, Nick Greenstock and Richard Hill indicated that England's long-term future looked positively rosy compared to Canada's immediate prospects. The other Richard Hill, my former Bath colleague and England Emerging coach, issued a challenge for the understatement of the season: 'I think we've given the Canadians something to think about. I just feel that England can deny Canada possession.' Who knows, there was a chance they might just score a few points, too. My mood stemmed from the obvious slide in Canadian fortunes. The world of rugby needs new forces with long-term potential, and Canada and Italy had appeared the two most likely candidates before the match at Bath.

The build-up to an England versus Canada fixture is never likely to have the same intensity as one to a Five Nations match, but it was evident that this was a little different. It was another central stage in the unveiling of England. The clock was ticking, and England were merely five matches from the World War proper. Canada would be for real.

On Wednesday 7 December rumours leaked out about the fitness of Paul Hull, one of the players under Rowell's scrutiny. He was apparently doubtful because of a persistent Achilles' strain. Little did he realise that an archer called Catt was about to shoot an arrow into his international career. Rowell was typically ambiguous in his comments. 'When a player reports an injury and then sees a replacement joining us in London, ready to step in, the injuries rapidly improve. Players want to keep their places.' I recall a bout of flu that miraculously disappeared when Marcus Rose arrived as cover for me in Scotland back in the mid-1980s. Although Hull was to start the match, he would be replaced by Catt midway through the first half. While big Jack kept the pressure on Paul Hull, his tactics towards Dean Richards changed. Here was the old head whom Jack wanted to encourage. 'Richards is outstanding. His attitude is first class, he is slimline compared with a few years ago, and he wants it. If our back row works it will be formidable.' The back row in question was Rodber, Clarke and Richards, a trio which had already destroyed Wales and South Africa earlier in the year. England had not yet lost with this unit in alliance.

Carling followed Rowell's lead: 'Dean has developed a mental hardness and ruthlessness . . . when Dean talks everybody listens . . . he has the respect.' He also maintained two of Rowell's other themes. 'We want to progress from the Romania game . . . reduce the error rate and increase the cohesion.' He was right in this prognosis, but the next took some believing. 'Canada are a strong powerful side who will be hard to break down.' You should have added 'for forty minutes', Will!

If Carling was perpetuating Rowell's favourite trick of convincing the world how powerful his side's opponents would be, the Canadians helped him enormously. Giant second-row forward Norman Hadley, a cult hero, was adamant: 'England look uncomfortable with their new plan. When we put pressure on them they will go back to a kicking style with which they feel more comfortable.' Canada were sponsored by Canadian Club whisky. I can only assume that such optimism was based on a close working relationship with the sponsors. Even Gareth Rees sounded a warning to the home team. 'We are a physical team, and if England are not ready for the physical side of Test rugby after their month's lay-off, then that's fine by us.'

Canada started well enough, and at half-time England had been forced to rely on a faultless display of goal-kicking from Rob Andrew for their lead. Canada were 18–0 down with no chance of winning, but the margin looked wildly distorted. Yet nobody could have envisaged how brilliantly England would attack in the next thirty-five minutes. Six tries followed – more than England scored in the entire previous domestic season. The Underwoods claimed three, two for Rory this time; Bracken scored one of England's finest tries in modern times and replacement full-back Mike Catt ran in a brace as he exploded into the reckoning as England's regular in that position.

Later that night a Yorkshire boxer called Henry Wharton would be outclassed by Chris Eubank. He did not look half as dazed at the fight's conclusion as Canada did at full-time. England's continued development was now seriously threatened. How does a team develop further after such a stunning effort? Andrew's goal-kicking was a perfect twelve out of twelve, but the real bonus was Mike Catt. Incisive and imaginative, he ran beautiful angles. Most impressive of all, when he breached a defence he showed tremendous maturity by having the sense to slow down and wait for support. For too long England players have had a lemming-like capacity for running head-first into the nearest group of defenders. It was tough on Hull, but to be, and to beat, the best, difficult decisions have to be made. Bracken's inclusion at Morris's expense had also been a hard call on Morris, but it was another inspired selection – Rowell himself mused, 'At times quite inspirational.' The manager also allowed himself another favourite word when describing Bracken's try. 'It was breathtaking. I have seen nothing better than the team-work involved in Kyran Bracken's try.'

Carling continued his pre-match theme. 'They were a hard side to play against and I was absolutely delighted with our performance. We didn't make as many errors as we did against Romania.' Carling sounded ridiculous when he called Canada hard, but they did compete, and this was a mighty English performance. Canada's beleaguered coach, Ian Birtwell, groaned, 'I think England have improved substantially.' Surprisingly, the press were not universally impressed. It was as if they could not believe that England could improve so dramatically.

Rowell expressed unease with his back row but there was no doubting their formidable firepower. England were close to a settled team. Under the tutelage of Rowell and Cusworth, they were developing some flexibility in their game. Geoff Cooke had created something sturdy, but he lacked that architect's vision to build the sublime, something like a World Cup-winning team. Now England waved goodbye to 1994 as serious contenders for the main prize.

The rugby situation was rather more gloomy north of the border. Sky arrived in Edinburgh the week before Christmas to cover two of the Scottish Inter-District Championship matches. When a national hero like Gavin Hastings is the target of adverse media attention, the state of the sport in Scotland is all too apparent. The unwelcome attention concerned not only Hastings' suitability to lead a side which had lost its last nine internationals, but even his place in the team. The only point overlooked was that Scotland did not have a suitable alternative at full-back.

Having presented three divisional matches and the horror of that Harlequins Cup tie, the role as Sky's rugby presenter seemed to me more appropriate for one of sado-masochistic tendencies than for a rugby follower. Scotland was to compound what had been a morbid month for our television crew. I joined the rest of Sky's team at Murrayfield, having flown up business class from Bristol. I cannot fathom the difference between business and economy class on these shuttles. It seems that the flimsy curtain is all that divides passengers. It was definitely not the food.

The temperature was arctic in the extreme. Thankfully, I knew that Murrayfield, one of the world's most modern stadia, had undersoil heating. My complacency was shattered within seconds of paying my taxi fare. A downcast executive producer, Piers Croton, informed me that the match between the Scottish Exiles and the North and Midlands was likely to be cancelled or, almost incomprehensibly, played on an adjacent park's pitch which was not blessed with heating. The tale of woe that unfolded convinced me that England does not have a monopoly on inefficiency. The underground heating at Murrayfield might be able to make toast when it is on, but unfortunately the extreme cold of a minus-10-degrees night had caused a fuse to blow. Even more unfortunately, the Scottish Rugby Union had not thought it necessary to install a warning system. The ground staff arrived the next morning to find the pitch frozen in places.

By mid-afternoon the sun had thawed much of the surface, but not the area shaded by the majestic, towering new stand. By 4 p.m. Sky were still awaiting a decision. SRU chief executive Bill Hogg was adamant that the game would be played on Murrayfield, the ground staff equally confident that it would not. By around 5 p.m. the ground staff's opinion had carried the day, and the match was moved to a park's pitch beyond the range of extensive live coverage.

While I sat in a frozen studio – the Scottish Rugby Union, in their wisdom, think bare concrete is as much as television presenters deserve – poor Miles Harrison and Jamie Salmon commentated over pictures of Scotland versus South Africa from a barren commentary box on an empty Murrayfield. The crew were diverted from the conditions momentarily when Harrison used the line: 'There's an eerie silence for an international ground.' This one was not induced by the Springboks. The memory of the two of them sitting alone in a freezing Murrayfield is one to cherish.

Two days later, the pitch had thawed sufficiently for Edinburgh to play the Exiles. The Scottish Exiles, captained by Andy Reed from Bodmin Moor, Cornwall, were decisive winners and finished the tournament unbeaten. Nine of their side played Second Division rugby in England – a stark illustration of the differences in playing strength between England and Scotland. The future, in both the long and short term, looked bleak for Scotland; it looked even worse for the Englishmen from Sky who waited for the fog to lift in the south. Eventually it did, and we flew home to warm our toes at Christmas.

Sitting on the aeroplane bound for Bristol, I cheered myself by thinking how much harder things could be. It may have been hotter in Western Samoa, but life was certainly less comfortable. Their players prepared for Christmas by pushing wheelbarrows through the island's villages and raising $US100,000 to fund their World Cup campaign. As Samoa has a population of a mere 160,000 and a reputation as a poor country, this sum testified to the local love of rugby. It was not enough, however, to prevent the loss of another star, Lolani Koko, to Rugby League in the shape of the Sydney City Roosters. It had been a successful year worldwide for the Rugby League raiding parties. The real pressure point was developing in Australasia. A defensive reaction from the Wallabies and Kiwis looked imminent, but how far would rugby bend the rules of amateurism, and possibly shatter the very ethos of the Union code, to counter the drain?

One experimental law change did received the blessing of the more traditional Five Nations committee: the use of yellow and red cards. On 11 December, Bob Weighill, secretary of this august body, was quoted as saying: 'It is largely to inform the crowd whether a player has been warned officially.' He added: 'We were impressed with the control that the cards achieved during last summer's World Cup.' I wondered, albeit briefly, whether Mr Weighill realised that the purpose of the cards flourished in the summer was rather more than simply to inform the crowd, and whether the Five Nations committee realised that the sport in question was Association Football. But it had been a long year, so I did not think too long, or too hard, about it.

ACT II

I n which the war between states escalates into the most traditional of all rugby battles – the Five Nations Championship. The English army prepare their campaign in Lanzarote as the camp followers, the book-makers, wage their odds. The French and English forces are equally confident before the outbreak of hostilities, while the Scots, under the command of their latterday Robert the Bruce, sit watching spiders.

England's alchemist, Jack Rowell, weaves his familiar psychological spells before each match as his army begin a march which initially looks set to end in Johannesburg on 24 June.

France's wizard, Pierre Berbizier, speaks of confident high-veld dreams, but his legions are less convincing. Meanwhile Wales and Ireland console themselves with the gloom that surrounds the proud Hastings troops north of Hadrian's Wall.

The act follows Rowell's triumphant march to the conclusion of a successful, but ultimately pyrrhic, campaign, while Hastings' army rises to defy all bar England.

While these nations cover themselves in glory, the soldiers of Berbizier, Alan Davies and Gerry Murphy scavenge like the retreating army of Napoleon, and the wars end with one head rolling.

In the world of club rugby, Cardiff defy the predictions of the author to lead the Welsh Leagues, while those great rivals Bath and Leicester fight for supremacy in England. The new alchemists, McGeechan and Best, cannot find the right formula as their teams, Northampton and Harlequins, struggle in the mire.

DRAMATIS PERSONAE

Jack Rowell	
Pierre Berbizier	
Alan Davies	The Five Nations Alchemists
Gerry Murphy	
Doug Morgan	
Brian Moore	Agent Provocateur
Olivier Merle	A French Demon
Will Carling	Prince of England
Gavin Hastings	Prince of Scotland
Martin Bayfield	England's Tall Man

8

Towards the War

At last 1995 arrived. For four long years the rugby world had been crossing off the days, waiting for the third and greatest of the Rugby World Cups. The conservative element in the sport's hierarchy, who had so regularly argued that the World Cup was not a true championship without the South Africans, would now have their year. David Kirk in 1987 and Nick Farr-Jones in 1991 were taunted with the 'you only won because we were not allowed to play' Springbok jibes. This time there would be no excuses.

The beatings that the All Blacks and Australia inflicted on the Springboks on their return to the world stage damaged their egos and their confidence, but South Africa, liberated by freedom and humility, had stopped playing the role of rugby's retarded child. Their 1994 British tour had marked them as a serious threat to the previous winners, plus a resurgent England and a confident France. New Zealand's Sean Fitzpatrick was hardly placing his head on the block when he stated that the World Cup winners would emerge from these nations. Louis Luyt, meanwhile, was on equally safe ground when he said that this would be the best-ever rugby tournament. As the bells chimed in 1995, the Rugby World Cup committee dreamed of commercial success, the spectators of the excitement to come and the players of the glory that could be theirs on the field of battle. The skirmishes were over.

While anticipation filled the air from Cape Town to Cardiff and Dublin to Dunedin, I toasted 1995 without the slightest backward glance or twinge of regret at having retired before rugby's greatest year. The public will see only the television and newspaper pictures of Michael Lynagh, Will Carling and François Pienaar in their moments of triumph, like actors delivering faultless performances and taking their curtain calls. The pain, the sacrifices and the sweat behind the scenes, like the agonies of the actor striving to learn his lines, will be unknown. To the actor, the glory of success and the financial reward; to the rugby player just the glory. This was to change in the wake of Rugby World Cup 1995, but even money cannot compensate for the horrors of all those hours of training and the harrowing press headlines.

Fourteen previous Christmas and New Year celebrations had been marred by the knowledge that the body was slacking, that I should be training. Retired and laden with red wine, it was easy for me to balance the superficial spotlight with the turgid drudgery that leads to elevation. My satisfaction was compounded by the knowledge that as I drained my third bottle of Burgundy, the England squad were holed up in Lanzarote, with each other, fitness advisers and an athletics track as seasonal companions. It was fitting for the England squad to greet 1995 under the cloudless Lanzarote sky. Rugby was to be their life until June; specifically, it was hoped, until the night of 24 June, the World Cup final. That had been the reason for the Lanzarote trip for four long years. Despite the sunshine, a five-day training camp is far removed from the hedonism of Club 18–30 which, one imagines, Victor Ubogu would prefer.

Overweight and overjoyed at my yuletide excesses, my only pain could be placated by my overtaxed bottle of paracetamol. The players did not dare indulge in such luxury before their departure on 29 December.

'Christmas pudding, another glass of Rioja, dear?'

'No thanks, I'd better go for a run.'

The risk of one renegade calorie too many would be too great to carry to Lanzarote. Under the gaze of Rex Hazeldine, England's fitness adviser, there is as much chance of getting away with carrying flab as there is of walking through Heathrow Customs with a kitbag full of cocaine.

A twenty-year jail sentence might even seem lenient compared with the humiliations heaped upon the squad walruses. Hazeldine has sadistic tendencies. Poor Steve Ojomoh must have spent Christmas on a diet of mineral water and low-calorie soups. Only those utterly dedicated or obscenely fit, like Rob Andrew and Mike Catt, do not tremble in the shadow of Hazeldine. Fatness checked, it is time for the fitness tests, a private hell for poor old Victor. A great advocate of dynamic power – and therefore a favourite of Jack Rowell's – Ubogu has a fitness level that generally peaks near the mark of an overweight forty-year-old.

Team spirit takes the form of an intimate meal for forty-plus men. In Lanzarote eating is hardly an Epicurean feast. Neither Bacchus nor Keith Floyd own timeshares on the island. The meal is accompanied by a floor show that is rather like Wimbledon Football Club – high on effort, low on skill. Tiring quickly of that, the boys toast in the New Year, gazing into each other's eyes. The vision of Guscott and Leonard swaying together, eyes locked, is one that pushes the concept of team spirit over the edge.

It was a vision that made me glad to be a rugby voyeur and no longer a participant. It must have appealed a lot less to all the players' wives or girlfriends. Widowed by Rugby Union for six months, they do not even have the consolation of the glory. The RFU was likely to send them to South Africa for a fortnight, a good gesture, but hardly compensation for the pressures that this amateur sport places on relationships and family life. Even as couples were reunited at Heathrow on 2 January, English thoughts were preparing for Ireland and the third step on the road to Johannesburg.

It was England captain Will Carling who provided the eager press with their first soundbite of 1995. 'The game in Ireland is a huge match for us. It sets the pattern for the rest of the Championship. Losing would be a near nightmare, but we still have to prove that our new style can work in the hotbed of the Five Nations. I am very confident that our new style of involving all fifteen players in ball-handling can work.'

This initial statement was unusual in that Carling placed extra pressure on his team by describing it as a 'huge match'. Rowell preferred the low-key approach, so often a smokescreen, but in the current circumstances acceptable. Carling was right to be confident about England's more flexible style and justified in expressing concern, but because the side was in the early stage of a conversion on a massive scale, defeat would not be a fully fledged nightmare.

I believed such a defeat was to be feared less than a pyrrhic victory. England's pack had proved that they possessed the power and presence to challenge for a third Grand Slam. Yet a Grand Slam based on grinding forward play could only promise mediocrity on the unforgiving grounds of South Africa. I wrote in the *Daily Telegraph*: 'It is not inconceivable that the passion of Dublin could be one game too early for a side coming to terms with their liberated style.' Discussing the need for swift decision-making, anathema in much of England's recent history, I predicted: 'Mistakes will occur and defeat could ensue, but that is part of the learning curve that needs to maintain its sharp progression if England are to conquer the world.'

It was easy for me to sound so reasonable; unfortunately, many sports editors prefer heads and headlines to rational analysis. It would be a tremendous achievement for England to maintain their commitment to a long-term target in the face of the guerilla warfare that the Five Nations Championship so often resembles. It would be difficult to seriously criticise England if they were to creep inside their protective set-piece shell. In the eyes of the world, Rowell had yet to achieve real success at international level. Canada and Romania may be International Board opponents, but the traditionalists who overpopulate rugby accept only the Five Nations sides, Australia, South Africa and New Zealand as 'proper' rugby teams. Hence the paranoia when Wales lost to a strong Western Samoan side in 1991. If things faltered, Rowell would surely consider utilising the set-piece experience of Andrew, Carling and Moore.

Although England's performances in the autumn convinced many of the side's potential, others, notably Mickey Skinner, seemed dubious about the likelihood of them winning *and* enjoying rugby at the highest levels. Carling, too, clearly had a few lingering doubts. To convince himself and his team, he contrasted Rowell's England with Cooke's team which he captained to consecutive Grand Slams: 'Compared with the 1991 and 1992 Grand Slam teams, our forwards potentially have a different level of mobility. The last generation was a restricted set-piece side. This lot look to me as if they are operating in a higher league. That is without disrespect to the magnificent winning players of recent years.' It may not have been disrespectful to them, but it certainly cannot have been music to the ears of Carling's great mentor, Geoff Cooke.

The Cooke era was made and eventually undermined by the extreme discipline of the austere Yorkshireman. England's on-field strategy was Cooke's entire creation. With control up front, England accumulated convincing but conservative victories. They failed to expand their full potential in the last World Cup because they held that vision too long. It is unfair to claim that men like Ackford, Dooley, Winterbottom and Teague were lesser players for it – they merely acted on instructions. Carling's assertion that the 1994–5 England had more to offer was, in reality, an indictment of the man who made him and revived English rugby. The change was one of managerial philosophy, not playing ability. There can be no doubt that Cooke was always in charge of his England, just as Rowell now seemed to have the omnipotence of a Turkish potentate with this side.

The future historians of the game were sharpening their pencils for a Rowell-finishes-what-Cooke-started chapter. That would be a fair reflection of the contributions of both men if England were to claim the 1995 World Cup. When Cooke gathered the reins of power few people would have expected England to re-emerge as a world force this century. Their perennial position as favourites for the Five Nations is testament to his qualities.

Indeed, once again England were unanimous favourites, albeit narrowly from France, for the 1995 tournament. What was not unanimous was the evaluation of the significance of the Championship. Some believed it was the least consequential Five Nations for four years, being undermined by the World Cup. Such an opinion was flawed on two counts. First, the tournament has a unique importance of its own. Australians, New Zealanders and South Africans frequently criticise the quality of the rugby, but the sense of occasion is envied throughout the southern hemisphere. Just look at the BBC's viewing figures for *Grandstand* on Championship Saturdays for proof of its popularity.

The International Championship offers a unique opportunity for five sets of patriots to give vent to all their national prejudices in a harmless way in front of the 50,000 to 60,000 spectators who pack stadia to create an atmosphere for which Graham Kelly and the Football Association would probably gladly sell Terry Venables. Englishmen, dressed in tweed and Barbours as if to deliberately infuriate their Celtic neighbours, drink side by side with hostile Scots, beguiling Irishmen and depressed Welshmen. In Paris they just drink themselves stupid from one end of the Pigalle to the other. The Welshmen dream of those savage Soho boozing sessions and the French renew their auld alliance for all bar eighty minutes in Edinburgh. There can be few tournaments in the world with such an ambience. Such is the defence of Rugby Union's traditionalists.

The modernists would argue about the significance of the 1995 tournament even more vociferously, but for an entirely different set of reasons. It was, paradoxically, more important, they contend, precisely because of the World Cup. It represented valuable opportunities for practice and bonding; it could even offer the northern hemisphere an advantage to counter the alien conditions of the southern hemisphere. That was the view of Rowell and Carling as England prepared for Dublin.

9

Moi, Monsieur?

W ales, too, were preparing for a campaign that could lay the ghost of 1991, the year in which the proud rugby nation betrayed its national heritage by failing to qualify for the quarter-finals of the World Cup. Portugal away in a qualifier for the 1995 tournament must have represented the nadir of Welsh fortunes. On 6 January, Alan Davies announced his side to play France. Decimated by injury, it was completely unfancied beyond the realms of Welsh fantasy, but it was, nevertheless, a significant selection. Davies recalled the man whom most Welshmen thought the management regarded as an antiquated throwback to the days when skill prevailed over brawn: Robert Jones was to return for his forty-ninth cap.

Beyond the Principality, few understood Wales' omission of the talented terrier. In Alan Davies' defence, it must be said that people did view Jones with excessive nostalgia. Undoubtedly he has always been their most talented scrum-half, but in the dark days of Welsh rugby his silky skills suffered behind a battered and broken pack, and his form deserted him. The evidence in the match with South Africa of Wales' new-found physical presence in the tight five was probably a more convincing justification for Jones' recall than his outstanding performance in the Barbarians' victory over the tourists in December. Jones has always maintained the requisite Celtic *hwyl* (although his derogatory comments after Wales' lame victory against Italy suggest that his thoughts and utterances were not always one and the same), and on the news of his inclusion he said: 'I am as delighted as I was when given my first cap.' Robert Norster, Wales' manager, endorsed the Barbarians display by saying, 'Robert's performance for the Barbarians showed he is as good as he used to be. We need what Robert can bring to the team, particularly to give Neil Jenkins a bit more space.' In fact Jenkins needed the opposite; he played his autumn internationals far too far from the defence, with the result that the Welsh midfield never committed opponents. Robert Norster was a great forward, but he is certainly not a backs coach; most worrying for Wales was the fact that Alan Davies did not seem to understand the problem either. Having scored just two tries in three internationals, against Romania, Italy and South Africa, Wales desperately needed to unearth some old-fashioned Welsh magic.

Davies sounded confident. 'If we want to succeed in the World Cup we have got to go out and take on this Test very positively,' he said, adding, 'The French are very unpredictable.' The second remark, cliché or not, would be proved by hindsight to be a huge understatement. It was noteworthy to hear Davies talk of Wales being positive. Against Italy and South Africa, their performances had been full of determination, defence and organisation, but hardly positive. South Africans openly mocked Wales' inability to fashion a single try-scoring opportunity despite the sterling efforts of Derwyn Jones and Gareth Llewellyn in the line-outs.

Even as the northern hemisphere awaited another pulsating international season the long shadow of Louis Luyt was cast across the rugby world, reminding each team that the prime objective was not ending or continuing the recent Irish success, or beating France, but achieving success in the World Cup. Just when everybody thought the South African squad was settled the news broke that Jannie Engelbrecht had been sacked. He ruefully reflected: 'It looks as if I have been used as a scapegoat, but it was on the cards all the time.' He was replaced as manager by the former Springbok skipper Morné du Plessis. The glory of the World Cup would not find a place on the top table for the man who led South Africa's charm offensive in Britain.

Three days before the international at Parc des Princes, a venue at which Wales had not won since 1975, Davies struck another positive note, which realistically underlined the real strength of his squad. 'A lot of people might be writing us off because of our injury problems, but they shouldn't underestimate the resolve of the players in the team.' He was correct here, but his coaching, on the other hand, seemed all too reminiscent of England's early stodginess: re-organised and competitive to an admirable degree, but shamefully inflexible.

A casual witness at France's training session on 18 January would have realised just how predictable they considered the once-ebullient Welsh team to be. The entire session was centred on reacting to up-and-unders and other tactical kicks. France's urbane manager, Guy Laporte, neatly summed up Wales: 'They are strong in ball-winning and defence and have a good tactical kicker and goal-kicker.' As if stung by such an offhand evaluation, Gareth Llewellyn, unquestionably a great ball-winner but a dubious soundbite man, warned: 'Dismiss us at your peril.'

It was not to be the last time that this sporting cliché reared its overused head.

While Will Carling dominated the world of quotations in English rugby, the Welsh, perhaps missing the autocracy of their injured leader, Ieuan Evans, were far more democratic in selecting their spokesmen. One man who was beginning to dominate the airwaves and print world, however, was Nigel Walker, the former Olympic hurdler who had entered rugby at a mature twenty-nine and forced his critics to eat their words. Plagued by a shoulder injury, Walker has nevertheless developed into a wing of legitimate international quality. He is also articulate and therefore a friend of the media. 'Everyone wants to win in style, but if I don't score and we win with Neil Jenkins banging over a few penalties, that will be fine by me,' he said. Critics scoffed, retorting that this was the only way Wales could win. On the eve of the Paris match, Walker declared: 'The first twenty minutes will be the most important. We have to hold them then, because I believe our front five is the best in the world.' He had the grace to add the rider 'Though I am speaking as a left wing.' Athletics is obviously good for confidence. I have never heard a left wing make any sort of public judgement of a front-five forward on anything other than his drinking capacity.

Walker must have been dreaming of Parisian celebrations after twenty minutes. Wales had not merely held the French, they had dominated them. Derwyn Jones and Gareth Llewellyn were busy justifying the eulogistic admiration for their line-out play, but cruelly for them, Neil Jenkins and friends were proving the critics of Welsh threequarter play equally correct. Although Wales, with a commanding front-five performance, had taken charge of the game, only a Neil Jenkins penalty separated the sides. The gulf in class behind the scrum was illustrated when France finally won some ball. Inspired by a rejuvenated Philippe Sella – he may hail from the prune-growing capital of France, but his rugby was of the champagne variety – France cut the Welsh defence to shreds for two tries that left the visitors to man a depressingly familiar damage-limitation exercise. Such is the spirit of the Welsh squad that they succeeded in this, and walked from Paris beaten, but not humiliated, 21–9.

Yet, Wales had failed to even threaten the French line, let alone score a try. It was not the worst of their ten consecutive defeats in Paris, but no Welsh performance could have been so lacking in inspiration. Alan Davies had instilled a worthy work ethic, but the poetry of their back play was no longer heard. Again Neil Jenkins bore the brunt of Welsh disappointment. If his withdrawn positional game was a demonstration of how he believed international rugby should be played, it was staggering that nobody in the land of fly-halves suggested otherwise. If he was merely obeying Davies, Wales had an even greater problem: an insufficiently assertive No. 10 and a coach who understood little about back play.

French coach Pierre Berbizier was suitably unimpressed. The day before he had baited Wales, 'We do not expect the British, and the Welsh in particular, to take much initiative in the game. It's time they started being more ambitious.' After the match he proclaimed: 'I saw two styles of play today. For the first twenty minutes I saw the Welsh style and then I saw the French style. Frankly, I prefer ours.' Somehow, Alan Davies' assertion that he was happy enough with his team's performance left me with a feeling of sorrow. Despite Nigel Walker's claim that 'we can still be a force in the Championship', the prospect of Wales defending their Championship looked as bleak as a Lowry painting.

At least Nigel Walker had grounds for rather more realistic optimism at club level. Cardiff, my bugbear club this season, helped by the absence of good Welsh sides, continued to taunt me. On 7 January they had maintained Swansea's miserable mood with a 16–3 League victory over the champions, still scarred from their massacre at the hands of the South Africans. On the same day Pontypridd lost 13–9 to Newbridge, leaving Cardiff two points clear. Pontypridd then joined Cardiff at the top with an 11–3 win against Llanelli at Stradey Park. It seemed no coincidence that the demise of the Principality's two leading attacking sides should occur at the same time as the emergency of Wales' most lifeless international midfield.

If Nigel Walker's visions of a Welsh renaissance seemed as wistful as a Caliban dream, French hopes of glory were based on much firmer foundations. The scars of those constant defeats against England had been magically healed by the pulsating 2–0 series win in New Zealand the previous summer. France had earned the right to remember the romance of rugby. Only a French rugby player, in this instance Guy Accoceberry, the scrum-half, could reflect: 'Now life is beautiful, but I know things can change fast.' That was romance and realism combined, but as for confidence, the French had that in abundance. Philippe Saint-André, the French captain and magnificent winger, mused: 'We are just coming into the final straight which has a place in the World Cup final at the end.' Even South Africa and Australia had not issued such bullish statements. The normally level-headed and sanguine Pierre Berbizier seemed afloat on optimism as well. To him 'The tournament was the ideal launching-pad for a successful World Cup campaign.' On the eve of the Welsh game the French side were reputedly already discussing how they would end England's long and painful hoodoo.

In the event France conjured some typically majestic moments, but they were not able to produce a performance of consistent brilliance, which was all that would satisfy the media after the hyperbole of New Zealand. And 21–9 was hardly an earth-shattering victory against a

Welsh side limited in personnel and ability. The best news was the return to form of Philippe Sella. Saint-André showed why he would be most people's idea of a World XV winger by changing angles and bullocking past bemused defenders. Jean-Luc Sadourny looked as dangerous as ever in counter-attack, while Emile Ntamack revealed a range of footballing skills, but surprisingly little pace. Twice Nigel Walker made him appear ponderous. The key to French flair was Christophe Deylaud, the shuffling Gallic, thirty-year-old fly-half known as the Tramp. He returned from Australasia as the new French messiah and was touted as the star of the Five Nations. Against Wales he offered tantalising glimpses of brilliance, but his overall control was lacking. Coach Berbizier admitted: 'We did not see the real Christophe Deylaud against Wales. But we will see another Christophe Deylaud in the next match. I have every confidence in him.' Much of Berbizier's early-season optimism was to prove misplaced.

Laurent Cabannes provided a display that suggested his form was peaking, but, Abdel Benazzi apart, matters were less than satisfactory in the tight five. The front row were adequate, but Olivier Roumat, so often a disappointment in the Five Nations, and Olivier Merle were comprehensively outplayed in the line-out. As England's line-out boasted Martin Johnson and Martin Bayfield, it was an area of serious concern for the Twickenham match in February.

Merle was also involved in an incident that severely dented Pierre Berbizier's pledges of new-found discipline. Merle allegedly headbutted the unfortunate Welsh prop forward, Ricky Evans. The blow itself did not damage the sturdy Evans, but the fall that resulted from it broke his leg. It was bad news for the Welshman but good fodder for the newspapers. South Africa had let people down by not taking drugs on street corners or feasting on opponents' testicles, but the French had saved the day. Headlines suggested that Merle had broken Evans' leg with his headbutt. It was not the case, but as Robert Frost wrote of parts of the press, 'When was that any bar to any watch they keep?'

Thus the French claims of spiritual re-birth were mocked by the British media. France did not take kindly to it. On 24 January, the Fédération Français de Rugby cleared Olivier Merle of violent action. French distaste for the British media was clarified the next day by the FFR president, Bernard Lapasset, when he said that 'it was important to demonstrate we would not submit to indecent pressure'. It was also important for France to win line-outs at Twickenham, however, and Berbizier duly axed Merle in a moment of sublime diplomatic skill. His refusal to select the forward was proof of French good intentions. It is possible that the FFR and Berbizier orchestrated the whole decision. Olivier Brouzet, a better line-out man, replaced him and Berbizier then pulled France's latest tormentor, Geoff Cooke, down from his lofty position on the moral high ground.

Cooke appeared on BBC TV's *Rugby Special* and called Merle a 'hit man'. Berbizier hit back. It was a personal slight to suggest that he would select such a character; we heard that he was considering legal action and finally he issued a withering statement which reminded all Englishmen of our capacity to criticise others when we do nothing about our own offenders. Outside England it is called arrogance. Berbizier fumed: 'Winterbottom kicked Cecillon, Dooley elbowed an opponent in the face, Clarke kicked an opponent last Saturday [all will be revealed], not to mention Rodber, who was sent off in South Africa and played a Test match three days later, in the face of all the rules of the International Board. I let people make their own judgement. What people do and what they say are not always the same thing.' Berbizier's criticism could not be countered. Just as in the Catt payments-to-players case, the Rugby Football Union were condemned for hypocrisy. Ever appreciative of political quick-wittedness, even Jack Rowell sided with Berbizier. 'Merle seems to have been dropped for what he did. It's an example which sets standards for the future and is a credit to the people who took the action.' Rowell, that modern-day Cardinal Richelieu, thus cooled tensions with France and proved that it was not only Frenchmen who possessed great diplomatic skills.

10

A Hole in the Hull, but the Ship's in Shape

As the countdown to the Ireland–England clash began, Paul Hull's hopes of regaining the full-back position, in which Mike Catt had deputised for him all too ably during the Canada match, diminished. Hull had travelled to Lanzarote with the England party, but had been unable to take any strenuous part in practice. England were due to announce their side for Dublin on 9 January. Hull was playing the usual game of notifying the press that fitness would be no problem come the international. It is a form of psychological conviction that supposedly persuades selectors and players alike that they must be picked. England warned Hull, however, that to be in contention he needed to play a full game immediately. Those who profess any knowledge of Jack Rowell would have grieved for Hull's chances of selection when he withdrew from the Bristol versus Bath League derby on the day before the 7 January game.

It would have been an intriguing contest for the selectors: Hull against Callard, England's two full-backs in South Africa, with Mike Catt at fly-half. If Hull had played one wonders whether Catt would have rained high balls from the heavens all afternoon in an attempt to damage other parts of his body.

It was Bath who benefited most from Hull's absence. The champions shaded the League match 10–9. Derek Eves, Bristol's inspiration, admitted that the away team deserved the victory that maintained their position at the head of the League, but Mark Tainton was left to rue three missed but kickable penalties in the last fifteen minutes. Bristol had a similar problem to Wales: an outside-half with a metronomic boot, but an absence of vision. This continually led to try droughts and the understandable though self-defeating reluctance to drop the man who was both the sole points-scorer and the cause of the problems. It was a vicious circle. Neither Bristol nor Wales played with any fluency behind the scrum, yet neither side seemed likely to axe their fly-half. As far as Bath were concerned, it was another day, another win. The only event that marred the not inconsiderable celebrations of Jerry Guscott, Jon Hall and myself was a supporter mistaking Jon for Nigel Redman. It appeared that the pressure of the local derby had rather accelerated the recession of the Bath captain's hairline.

Elsewhere, too, it proved to be the tightest day in the history of the League. It was a magnificent advertisement for the game for those who enjoy heaped spoonfuls of tension in their sport. The Sky cameras travelled just 40 or so miles up the M5 for Gloucester versus Wasps. It was the afternoon's most conclusive result with the Londoners winning 21–16. Rob Andrew gave a faultless display of goal-kicking before the match, to the cheers of the Shed. The rugby world really had turned on its head. Imagine Fidel Castro receiving a ticker-tape welcome in Miami in 1962, and you'll have some idea of how startling the behaviour of the Kingsholm crowd was on this occasion.

Rob Andrew was rather less faultless during the game, but Wasps gained two hard-earned points which left them with an outsider's chance of the title. As has so often been the case, it was Steve Bates who provided the inspiration for the North Londoners. If Bates' legs were as fast as his brain he would have fifty caps. He offered an unblemished display of decision-making and initiated and scored a marvellous try from a tapped penalty in his own 22. In truth he dropped the ball over the line, but anyone who knows Bates would have awarded him the try just for covering 75 yards. Gloucester responded with a beautifully worked back move – as stunning as Gloucester's reception of Rob Andrew before the game – fittingly scored by Mark Mapletoft, the shortest shining beacon ever to illuminate the gloom of Kingsholm. It was a good start for Sky in 1995.

Around the country the League table was starting to look more and more like the nation under the Conservative party: the gap between the haves and the have-nots was growing. The game's leading haves, Harlequins, dropped a vital home point to Sale which left them unsafe and lifted the Cheshire team further from the relegation I had so confidently forecast in the autumn. West Hartlepool, too, managed an away draw, at Orrell, to leave Quins one from the bottom. Predictably, Northampton remained rooted, but only after throwing away several chances to beat Leicester. An 18–20 home defeat offered some hope, but Northampton needed points. Tim Rodber was not too despondent. 'If we beat any of these teams [Sale, West Hartlepool or Harlequins] it will more than cancel out the points they have earned for this week's draw,' he explained, thereby proving that he knows that 2 is a higher number than 1.

The weekend was also notable for the introduction of the card system, still the subject of much confusion. Dave Cleary, the uncompromising Orrell flanker, achieved the honour of the first yellow card for use of the boot in a ruck after thirty-nine minutes of the match against West Hartlepool. The other booked player reacted to his card in a manner that caused the entire rugby world to smile. Graham Dawe, one of Bath's most vigorous forwards, received a warning and proclaimed his dismay, referring to himself as the Gary Lineker of rugby. Norman Hunter perhaps, but not the squeaky-clean Lineker. If odds of 5–1 had been offered on Dawe becoming Bath's first booked man, Ladbrokes might well have been ruined by the rush of successful punters.

Two days later, Northampton received some better news. It was rumoured that England international Steve Ojomoh had signed registration forms for the Saints 'to keep my options open for next season'. While Ojomoh was clearly disillusioned with Bath's reluctance to play him, it was doubtful whether his brooding bulk would become a part of the East Midlands rugby scene should Northampton be relegated. Typically, Bath selected Ojomoh for their side to face Northampton the following week. He would thus get a first-team match and at the same time help to push Northampton nearer to Division 2, thereby ending his own interest in a transfer.

The match was a difficult one for Northampton, but England's edict that all squad members should rest the week before the Ireland international worsened their already monumental task. Bath lost three players to Northampton's two, but the big difference in the strength of the respective squads made the loss of Bayfield and Rodber far more severe for the Saints. The absent captain hardly offered hopeful signals to his side the day before the game when he stated: 'We must beat Sale, Orrell and Gloucester, minimum.' While intimating that his side would lose to Bath, he was also placing his charges under pressure in the matches he had mentioned. It is doubtful whether Rowell would have approved of such psychology. Ian McGeechan, meanwhile, reminded everyone of the mess created by the RFU's unique foresight, or lack of it, in planning the domestic season in World Cup year. Commenting on League matches the week before internationals he said, 'It's absurd – a contrived situation – but no one is going to put his England place in jeopardy and we couldn't put our players in that position.'

Northampton duly slumped to a 26–6 defeat, leaving McGeechan to wonder whether the only position in which his players could be put was that of the relegated team. His only hope – the entire nation's hope

– was starting to look like the Harlequins. Deprived of their triumvirate of internationals, the London club recorded another loss, against a gleeful Wasps. Worse, West Hartlepool snatched a vital 22–21 win against Gloucester, drawing them level on points with Harlequins with a home match against them and Northampton to follow. Leicester remained on Bath's heels with a comfortable victory over Orrell and Sky viewers watched Sale cement their First Division position by 21–9 against Bristol. Inspired by Paul Turner, the Cheshire team made fools of a painfully bad Bristol side and critics like myself. I did not mind on this occasion as I had backed Sale to win and made a healthy profit. So did the Sale clubhouse, where the television evidence of their triumph was on constant display.

At least Northampton and Harlequins were to find respite from their League problems in the fifth round of the Pilkington Cup at the end of the month. As the England–France fixture was a week later, both clubs offered to rest their players for matches against Third Division Richmond and Second Division London Irish respectively and saw out January with their Cup records intact. As far as the Leagues were concerned, things were not so simple. Jack Rowell, content to be flexible before England played Romania, was now uncompromising on the question of players being rested the week before internationals, despite Tim Rodber's increasingly expressed worries. Northampton were due to play Sale the week before England met Wales in February, and Rodber's players, who would be without him for this game, doubtless thanked him for articulating the pressure at Franklins Gardens after their 27–6 Cup win against Richmond. The day's other big matches saw Leicester visit Bristol, their League conquerors, and Bath travel to Orrell. Jon Hall was aware of how tough Edge Hall Road could be, but his focus on glory was firm. 'We intend to dog this one out and aim for another Twickenham win.' As Bath held a Cup record of forty-three wins from their last forty-six appearances, Hall could hardly be accused of boasting, but none the less they were behind until five minutes from the end. Callard's trustworthy boot and a late try from Jerry Guscott sealed Bath's win.

At Bristol the pitch was a bog and, unsurprisingly, their coach, Brian Hanlon, wanted to play. Unfortunately, Leicester were far more adept and avenged their November League defeat in some comfort. The prime reason for January's reversal of form was the return of Dean Richards. The Leicestershire policeman revelled in the heavy going like a good Irish steeplechaser, and proved himself once again as one of England's most formidable rugby thinkers.

In the clash of the minnows, the plans of Aspatria, from Cumbria and Division 4, to beat Exeter of Division 3 were assisted by Harlequins'

David Pears, who videoed the Devon side. The trick had helped his former club beat Bedford in the fourth round, but this time it failed and Exeter marched into the quarter-finals. Poor David Pears, the perennial potential England player. His dream of playing in the World Cup had become less likely than Exeter winning the Cup.

Indeed, while these Cup dramas remained in the future, the position of England full-back was fast becoming the least secure place in the team. Ian Hunter had given a fine display for England against Wales in 1994, only to miss the tour to South Africa in the summer and another three months through another shoulder injury. Pears had not played since he limped off against Natal in that tour's opener and Paul Hull's Achilles' problem had forced him off against Canada. This remarkable series of personal nightmares opened a door of opportunity for one man – Michael Catt.

Catt had produced a devastating attacking performance against Canada, but it would take a brave man to select him for a full Five Nations debut at Lansdowne Road in an unaccustomed position. Jack Rowell, conservative by nature, was to prove his decisiveness to the nation by taking that gamble. Days before the side to play Ireland was announced, Rowell was dropping clues. 'I would be quite relaxed about having Catt play against Ireland,' he remarked. Two days later he named the side, and there, at No. 15, was M.J. Catt, the controversial recipient of Eastern Province expenses. The headlines predicted: 'PURR-FECT'. Not for Hull. The hero of South Africa suddenly found himself a doubtful for the World Cup party, with Jonathan Callard called to the bench in Dublin to act as back-up kicker to Rob Andrew. The cautionary tale of Paul Hull is a convincing argument for remaining level-headed about this amateur sport. For Catt, however, it was the culmination of a remarkable rise made possible by an almost comic-book combination of talent and luck.

I vividly recall my first meeting with Catt. It was a wet Wednesday at Lambridge, the Bath training ground, and a lonely figure stood in the car park watching Jon Callard and I practising our kicking. Another sad fanatic, I thought. As one kick bisected the posts (it must have been Callard's) and landed in the young man's arms, I walked towards him so that his return kick could reach me. It spiralled a full 30 metres over my head.

Twenty minutes later, the same gaunt figure jogged on to the training pitch and my doubts redoubled. He wore an Eastern Province shirt. Bath had witnessed a spate of newcomers from the southern hemisphere, all of whom wore provincial shirts and claimed to be junior All Black or Springbok trialists. But it was only ten minutes before we realised that this was no imitation. The slight, twenty-one-year-old Mike Catt had arrived in England. Eight years earlier, he had belonged to the barefoot world of boys' rugby in South Africa. Only two years later, he would be a full international. He oozes ability but fortune has been his greatest ally.

Catt had followed his elder brother to England for a five-month holiday. His visa lasted only those five months and he did not intend to overstay it. He went to Stroud to stay with an uncle, who duly called Gloucester RFC. Fortunately for Catt, nobody answered the telephone – there can be little doubt that he would be unknown at international level if anyone had. Instead he travelled down the A46 to Bath. Brian Ashton identified a lack of poise. At Gloucester, in their pre-revolutionary days, such faults would not have been remedied. Inspired by Ashton and Bath's host of international players, Catt refined his game so quickly that he made a League debut that season in the furnace of Kingsholm. He helped Bath to sink Gloucester and his career sprinted into orbit. At the end of that season he toured Australia as half-back partner to Kyran Bracken with England's Under-21 side. It had been Rowell who had whispered his name in higher echelons.

England triumphed and Catt returned to Bath with fortune still by his side. 'Le Guscott groin' was to keep England's brightest midfield light out of action and Catt found himself a centre. He was an immediate sensation in the position. His searing pace and running angles endeared him to Bath's genteel Shed equivalent, the Flowerpot Stand. His season ended at Twickenham with an intense celebration of a try which clinched Bath the Cup against Leicester and a brief appearance against Wales as replacement for Rob Andrew. In the summer Catt was selected to tour South Africa. If anyone expected interesting political overtones they did not know Catt. 'I am not political, I just want to play international rugby,' he said. He was not about to shed false tears on the Queen's behalf. To those who prefer top-level sport as a celebration of itself, rather than as a patriotic excuse, it was a relief.

Catt's selection for Ireland did not rattle him. Jonathan Webb spoke of his 'outstanding mental attitude', while Les Cusworth drooled over his competitive nature. Cusworth also called him 'stroppy', a worrying description for a position where poise rather than passion is the key. The use of this word suggests that Catt's greatest piece of fortune was Hull's injury. His flawless entry as an international full-back marked him out as a true No. 15. At Bath he was not finding the technical and positional areas of playing outside-half easy, but at full-back he walked again on his free, spirited path alongside Lady Luck. His positive style of play combined with Rowell's positive selection was a clear indication of England's commitment to a vibrant type of rugby which would be suited to the hard grounds of Catt's homeland at the season's end.

ACT II

The other headline was made by the recall of Catt's Under-21 half-back partner, Kyran Bracken. After Jack Rowell's enthusiastic reaction to his performance against Canada, Bracken's selection was not a surprise. Interestingly, most voices that were raised in support of the redoubtable Dewi Morris came from forwards. Bracken was another sign of England's faster and more dynamic intent. Will Carling's comments certainly started to sound a little sharper, and there was a new, positive note. 'You cannot have too many pretensions to winning the World Cup unless you can go as Europe's best.' It was obvious that if England were to be Europe's best it would be on World Cup, and not Five Nations, terms.

England were not the only side sounding an expansive note. The Irish selection at half-back sent shockwaves throughout England. Eric Elwood, the tormentor of England in both 1993 and 1994, was omitted from the team. An injury had restricted his playing opportunities but a general feeling prevailed that if Ireland wanted to use their potentially match-winning wingers, Simon Geoghegan and Jonathan Bell, it was imperative in any case to choose a more attacking-minded No. 10. Paul Burke of Cork Constitution fitted the bill. Criticism of Elwood centred around his penchant for endless kicking. Cunning and accurate it may be, but it was limiting the possibilities for the threequarters. The selection of Burke was a bold decision because it left Ireland without a proven goal-kicker. When captain Michael Bradley withdrew because of a personal tragedy and was replaced by Niall Hogan, Ireland were left with an uncapped pair of half-backs. It was a clear chance for England's back row to inflict severe damage on the axis of the Irish hopes. Coach Gerry Murphy dismissed concerns about the inexperience of Burke and Hogan but many observers thought otherwise. An international is never an easy environment for an experienced player; to have two half-backs making their debuts suggested that Ireland would need the luck of a leprechaun.

The bookies expected revenge to be on the minds of Kyran Bracken, Tony Underwood and Martin Bayfield, all axed after England's disastrous demise against Ireland at Twickenham in 1994. Ladbrokes made England 3–1 on for the match, while William Hill made them 5–6 favourites for the tournament. France were 7–4, Wales 13–2, Ireland 16–1 and Scotland 50–1. These odds would look fairly ridiculous for two of the teams by the start of March.

Whatever odds the bookmakers were shouting, Jack Rowell was not about to alter his over-modest diplomacy just at the moment when the rugby world really was about to start scrutinising every one of his 6ft 7½in. Romania had nearly beaten Wales, Canada were a big physical team – what about Ireland? 'I can't think of a bigger test in the world at the moment for us than facing Ireland in Dublin,' he said. 'For now the result is more important than the style. Dean Richards believes that this will be our hardest game in the Five Nations and he does not make such assessments lightly.' Rowell's comments about results and style suggested that a short-term win would suffice in the first stage of real war. Long-term objectives could develop with success. He also warned: 'When the Irish forwards are wound up they can become supermen, as we found out when England lost the last two fixtures.' He was hardly inspiring English punters to rush out and grab Ladbrokes' 3–1 on.

Even though Rowell was undoubtedly starting to feel the tension his sharp sense of humour maintained a typically irreverent perspective. Commenting on the presence of new Bath star Simon Geoghegan in the Irish team he said, 'If those Bath moves succeed then my successor as Bath coach, Brian Ashton, is going for a dip in the River Liffey.' It would be difficult – Ashton was to be a guest of mine in the Sky studio in Isleworth, Middlesex.

There was little humour to be found in Carling's pre-match comments, however. From an English perspective there was even less to be jocular about in the horror video the team had been watching. 'We have analysed the video of our 1993 defeat in Dublin endlessly. It has been a revelation to the players who were not present and an awful reminder to those of us who were implicated in that defeat.' I squirm in recollection of the day and can only sympathise with the likes of Bayfield, Carling and Guscott at having to re-live it. It's not the sort of video children should be allowed to watch.

Analysis had long been a watchword of Geoff Cooke's, and his precise preparation was not being thrown away by Rowell's squad in this of all seasons. 'We are entering the most important six months in the lives of all our players,' Carling continued. 'The World Cup is our ultimate aim. It's been our dream to win it. So straight after every match this winter we will be analysing how well we have done and how much we have progressed towards that dream.' How strange it was to hear echoes of Martin Luther King in Will Carling. While the great civil rights leader's avowed aim was the progression of human rights, the England rugby team's idea of progression was slightly more prosaic. 'The Canada match was a step up compared with Romania, and now we are taking one more big stride,' said Carling. Inconceivably, Andrew's big stride took the form of a newly designed pair of boots to assist his kicking. His record in the autumn internationals was a distinctly mediocre twenty-three out of twenty-four. This was pushing the pursuit of perfection too far.

In terms of public relations England were doing little wrong. Only Brian Moore struck an inflammatory note. Most of the pre-match publicity inevitably surrounded England: the one area where Ireland gained a marked edge in hyperbole was the front row. Nick Popplewell had proved himself world class with the 1993 Lions, Peter Clohessy had a ferocious reputation and Keith Wood was touted everywhere as Ireland's wonder man. The publicity intensified after their efforts as a unit in helping the Barbarians to defeat South Africa. Jack Rowell described them as 'a cult'; Moore was more circumspect. 'I'm not averse to publicising new elements in the game, but I want to see what they do against me, Jason Leonard and Victor Ubogu before I think about joining in the acclaim.' The Five Nations Championship will seem a very different tournament without the thoughts of Mr Moore. On match day his parting shot in the *Telegraph* was: 'Let's just say the scrums will be more genuine than a Eubank fight.'

The morning of the game saw the withdrawal of Jonathan Bell, Ireland's bright new winger. It made the decision to select Paul Burke look even more dubious. A bigger sensation than the thigh strain of Bell was the weather. Not one of the thirty players could ever have experienced such ferocious wind – at least, not elementally. Graham Simmons, Sky's roving reporter, could hardly stand as he watched the heavy canvas covering from a television camera blow off the equipment and on to the terrace 50 metres distant. Goalposts blew at 20-degree angles and the touchline flagpoles were flattened throughout the day. Not surprisingly, it was impossible for England to adopt the fluid movement they had discovered in the second half of the Canada match. It was doubtful whether the game could be anything other than a lottery in such conditions.

As the teams ran on to the surface the Irish roar matched the howling gale. It is not an intimidatory noise to opponents – there is little venom in the Lansdowne Road crowd – but it is often inspirational to the Ireland team. The stadium was transformed from a gloomy wind tunnel into a dazzling arena by the floodlights, on full beam from the start. The lights were on at Lansdowne Road, but they would soon be out for the Irish.

Ireland kicked off and, typically, surged towards the English line. A keen well-placed kick by Paul Burke in such difficult conditions offered hope, but England won the line-out near their line, and drove the ball forward into the nearest thing to a hurricane that Ireland has witnessed. The home side were forced to concede a penalty. In previous years England would have kicked for touch and a line-out throw, but on this occasion they were far more positive. Bracken's tap and run 15 metres from his own line told us a great deal about the confidence and dynamism – that Rowellism again – of this England. The days of group discussions were exiled to the past as Bracken set a tone of decisiveness that would be the hallmark of a marvellous performance. England would sustain a pace that was always one, and often two, gears too high for Ireland.

Power was the other invigorating element of England's performance. Before the game Rowell, the *eminence gris*, had questioned the balance of the back row. The Neil Back fan club to which many of the English media belong were even more doubtful about the balance of three behemoths. But all talk of back-row imbalance was swept aside like an empty crisp packet lying on the turf of the windswept pitch. I congratulated myself on my previous forthrightly expressed convictions about the prowess of this back row – Neil Back would not be Prince Hamlet on this stage. Today it looked as though the Eastern Bloc would have found them rather harder to knock down than the Berlin Wall. Ireland had placed immense faith in the running power of Keith Wood. After five minutes he must have realised that he had met his match in the tackling strength of Tim Rodber. Together with Ben Clarke and the colossus of Leicester, Dean Richards, he dominated the course of the game for the full eighty minutes.

Behind the scrum, England's performance was adequate but completely eclipsed by the brutal, primal power of the pack. If England's dream of opening up the Pandora's Box that is the World Cup was to materialise it would be imperative to improve on the precision of their finishing. The chief villain was the man scripted to elevate England from the moderate to the sublime: twice Guscott frittered away golden opportunities to feed Rory Underwood on an overlap. The fact that it took heroic tackling to pull him down was a credit to Ireland, but nevertheless it suggested that Guscott's pace was a little bit lacking. His decision-making was even worse. Rory Underwood is a teetotaller, otherwise he would almost certainly have drunk himself into oblivion. Luckily, his appetite is for tries and not alcohol. Guscott was the prime offender but Mike Catt, who enjoyed a steady afternoon (and one surprisingly short on high kicks), and Kyran Bracken, otherwise outstanding, also wasted clear chances. The biggest concern was that Guscott had not scored a try since his return from injury. Jerry himself had suggested joining Bath's third XV to break the duck. The England squad were starting to hum the theme to *Mission Impossible* when Guscott entered a meeting.

If Guscott was the main concern, his centre partner, Carling, was the biggest reason for celebration. Recent form for Harlequins suggested that he had shrugged off his October indifference, and indeed Carling himself scored the first try, just over eight minutes into the game, although the creator was Rob Andrew and, behind him, the influence of Cusworth and Rowell. A line-out was deflected into Bracken's hands and Andrew took the pass flat. I had never seen him take a ball in such a dangerous position – he was inside Ireland's drift defence and outside their flanker. He was hauled down only a yard from the line, where Carling surged on to his shoulder and over for the perfect start to the battles of 1995.

Nick Farr-Jones, the captain of the 1991 World Cup-winning Australian side, wondered whether he would have lifted the trophy had England played a more aggressive flat-alignment game in 1991. Luckily for Australia, Rowell and Cusworth were not in command to offer this vision to a team used to being led rather than making their own decisions. His knowledgeable concern indicated just how worried the great Bob Dwyer of Australia should be about the next world tournament.

Ireland did not possess the power to compete with England's pack, nor the guile or experience to trouble Catt and the Underwood brothers. England had won by three tries to one, but most significantly 20–8, and they knew the margin should have been greater. Nevertheless, they were suitably pleased with the performance. Tony Underwood, not quite Nigel Walker in soundbite terms but still a man for a good quote, enthused: 'This was the ultimate test. They were some of the worst conditions I've played in.'

Will Carling also sang the praises of the match, and didn't miss the opportunity to use one of his favourite words: 'I thought the first half was awesome. I was very impressed with the attitude and commitment.' He revealed that a psychological plan had worked to perfection, encapsulated by the next day's *Mail on Sunday* headline, 'VIDEO SHOW PUTS US INTO FAST FORWARD'. Before the game, England had watched the first twenty minutes of the victorious Pretoria Test the previous summer. If anything, the first forty minutes against Ireland had been even more impressive, since in the Springboks match South Africa had been unfocused and conditions perfect. Neither factor could be said to have contributed to England's success in Dublin.

Rowell's face beamed on to millions of television screens in England. His only complaint was the obvious one. 'If we had been a bit more clinical we would have scored another couple of tries in the second half.' He preferred to give credit, and with some relish. 'I was critical of the display by the back row in our Test matches in the first half of the season, but Tim Rodber was immense and Dean Richards came up to me and said, "Was that good enough?" I had to tell him that it was.' Rowell was moved to admit that he enjoyed Ireland and that he was 'pleasantly surprised at how well that team could play'. Rumours suggest that the players' contingent (those from outside Bath, obviously) were surprised at how well Rowell could drink.

The manager might have relaxed, but he was still determined to let everyone know he was in charge. The International Board deemed it permissible for a coach to join the players at half-time. The RFU, traditionalists that they are, disagreed. Rowell stood with the team at half-time, uttering not a word. He had made his point. The RFU had appointed the right man to manage the team, but a potential firebrand too. According to the *Guardian*, the RFU committee had already received a letter of complaint from Craig Jamieson, a director of Rugby World Cup, in which Rowell was accused of being abusive to various members of both RWC and the SARFU (South African Rugby Football Union). When I had lunch with Rowell, he laughed off the complaint with an airy wave of his hand. The other held a glass of champagne – I was buying. Rowell's counterpart ('a lovely man', according to the England manager and most people who know him), Noel Murphy, had no complaints about the match. 'We were well beaten. No complaints, no arguments. Dean Richards had a superb game throughout.' As he would later prove for Leicester at Bristol, Richards has few peers in adverse conditions. The bookmakers reflected the general opinion of the nation: England were cut to an impossibly mean price of 4–6 to win the Championship, while the Irish drifted to 50–1. A whole army of leprechauns would be needed now to bring success for them.

The only blemish, apart from the performance of 'Mission Impossible' Guscott, was the yellow card Ben Clarke received for 'stamping' on Bath team-mate Simon Geoghegan. Clarke, unlike Graham Dawe, has never claimed to be a larger version of Gary Lineker; in fact he is one of rugby's gentler forwards. Watching the match in the television studio, Brian Ashton told viewers that Clarke dishes out rougher treatment to Geoghegan in training. It threw a sizeable question-mark over the standard of refereeing and the lack of guidance surrounding the use of the cards. Luckily for Clarke, the team had played with sufficient aplomb to steal the headlines from him.

The *Observer* lauded Carling: 'WILL POWER SPURS ENGLAND TO VICTORY' and 'ILL WIND GOOD FOR CARLING' (an ambiguous headline after a night's celebrating in Dublin, not to mention a prescient one in the light of events at the end of the season). The *Mail* maintained the alcoholic theme with 'ROWELL'S HEADY BREW LEAVES IRELAND WITH A HANGOVER', while Paul Hayward of the *Daily Telegraph* described England's back row as 'DESPERATE DANS WITH AN ABSENCE OF MALICE'. Ben Clarke would not have enjoyed that headline. If the saturation coverage was not enough, it was possible to read the various thoughts of Andrew, Rodber, Carling, Clarke, the brothers Underwood, Ubogu, Moore and countless others whose papers I did not manage to get round to before pub opening-time – and yes, the front row were triumphal on the subject of their victory over their much-hyped Irish counterparts. If it was not the best possible start imaginable for England it was not far from it. The pressure on Rowell and his charges would increase after this compelling performance.

11

Allez Angleterre!

I n contrast to the atmosphere in England and Ireland in January, the national mood in Scotland was muted. The team were carrying the heavy burden of nine consecutive defeats, and the extent of their woes was illustrated by the previously inconceivable calls for the head of Gavin Hastings, their icon for a decade.

On 21 January, while France and England made successful starts to their Five Nations campaigns, Scotland played Canada, a team retreating faster than the Italian armies of British military jokes. Defeat was unthinkable. If South Africa could sack Jannie Engelbrecht as manager after a successful tour of Scotland and Wales, there must have been a strong temptation to ask coach Doug Morgan, manager Duncan Paterson and captain Gavin Hastings to follow in the footsteps of the beheaded Mary, Queen of Scots.

Paterson had announced the Scotland team to play Canada on 11 January. Depending on your viewpoint, the selection smacked of either panic or bravery. Scotland made nine changes from the side conquered by South Africa. Scrum-half Derrick Patterson was consigned to the hated One-Cap Wonder Club to be replaced by Bryan Redpath, while Stewart Campbell of Dundee was selected to make his international debut alongside the recalled and rejuvenated Damian Cronin in the second row. Cronin had moved to Bourges to play third-division rugby and renounce beer in favour of red wine. It was most definitely the best diet of the year. At No. 8 in came Eric Peters, another man devoid of a Scottish accent and with less than a fingerful of first-team appearances for Bath. When the cider-toned Alan Sharp of Southmead and Bristol withdrew with a persistent back injury, he was replaced by David Hilton of Bedminster and Bath. When England met Scotland on 18 March it was doubtful whether Bath's confused supporters would know which team to support. Hilton, Peters and the injured Cornish Scot Andy Reed, all current first-team squad members, could be playing for Scotland; in addition, it was hoped that Andy Nicol, surely Scotland's long-term answer to Gary Armstrong, would be fit after injury and optimistic about gaining a Bath place in the run-up to the season's finale. Then there was Cronin, a Bath man when first capped, who, along with David Sole, first boosted bookings for the shuttle service from Bristol Airport to Edinburgh.

In Edinburgh there was despair for the garrulous Scott Hastings, dropped after fifty-one caps. It would be wholly proper to assume that brother Gavin did not sit in on this selection meeting. Scott was replaced by Ian Jardine, an uncomplicated centre who would be asked to cross the gain-line. Scotland made an important decision to play the mercurial but so far disappointing Gregor Townsend at outside centre. Duncan Paterson explained the choice. 'We've seen flashes of Townsend's potential in the past . . . by playing him at outside centre we can take away the pressure of decision-making.'

If Scotland were becoming frustrated at the length of time it was taking for Townsend's talent to surface, they might also have been wondering about the inevitability of Gavin Hastings' place in the team. The selectors had originally made him captain through the World Cup and then rescinded that statement. Most comments about the security of his position were based on the fact that there was nobody else suitable. It was hardly comforting for Hastings. Many men, subject to such pressures, would have considered retirement and a place in Scottish rugby legend. By playing on, Hastings could be risking ending up like those heavyweight boxers who fight on well past their peak and whose greatness becomes a distant memory.

Hastings is a big man, however. He has an uncomplicated philosophy based on effort and being honest with himself and his team. It was typical of him to strike a bold note when the vultures started to hover. 'Teams ignore Scotland at their peril. We are never more dangerous than when we are written off. The team is in confident mood and the spirit is good.' Wales, too, had warned critics to 'write us off at your peril', but that had proved an idle boast in Paris.

Hastings' prophecy, on the other hand, was fulfilled at Murrayfield, although Canada's performance in defeat by 22–6 left many wondering whether the hapless Romanians, their co-victims in South Africa's 'group of death', would manage to win a single World Cup match. Scotland achieved their first victory this season in conditions little better than those in Ireland. Gavin Hastings, in his moment of crisis, scored seventeen points and Damian Cronin, jet-propelled by his local red wine, scored the only try. Hastings was content. 'This is a good way to start 1995. I would be quite happy for this team to face Ireland, but that is up to the selectors,' he said. Their first win in ten games lifted the murky Murrayfield atmosphere, although Jim Telfer, former Scotland coach and now employed by the Scottish Rugby Union, remained realistic about Scotland's hopes for their forthcoming Five Nations campaign: 'A good Five Nations Championship for Scotland will be two wins and two losses. The bookmakers thought otherwise: Scotland were still available at 66–1 for the Championship.

Despite those long odds, Scotland found themselves 5-6-on favourites to beat Ireland on the first Saturday in February. They also found themselves dismissed as 100–1 outsiders for the Grand Slam (I recall one punter in my local high-street bookies advising me to back them after one too many pints of bitter). Having already lost, Ireland had no price for the Grand Slam, but respect for their ability was reflected in the odds for the Murrayfield game. Considering the favourable comments on England's display of sustained power and control in Dublin, I thought the bookies had paid too much attention to Scotland's traditional grip on the home fixture and punted a moderate amount on an Ireland win.

My coterie of gambling friends, unaware of my frequent misjudgements on the state of Rugby Union, consulted me on the other match to be held on 4 February: 'Le Crunch' – England versus France – the biggest game before the onslaught of the World Cup and potentially one of the greatest in the history of the Five Nations. Under Will Carling, England had achieved a remarkable seven consecutive successes, but France, buoyed by the pragmatic good sense of Pierre Berbizier and the revered series victory in New Zealand, were convinced that the time was right to reclaim rugby's high ground from the 'nation of shopkeepers'. Whatever the French thought, the English shopkeepers were lavishing their hard-earned pennies on the national side – the home team were 1–2 favourites. It seemed a staggeringly ungenerous price, and punters who bet with their heads, rather than their hearts (like me), avoided the match as a betting proposition.

The patriotic punter could hardly draw confidence from the thoughts of Jack Rowell. Throughout his long reign at Bath, he always respected the sporadic majesty of French rugby. Along with his back-up staff of David Robson and Tom Hudson, he had helped pioneer Anglo-French fixtures as a path of progression for Bath. For the majority of his final decade in club rugby, Rowell thought there was little to be learned from the English clubs. Looking at them would have given Bath no more than a stiff neck from peering round at them toiling in our footsteps. French rugby was different. Two clubs were regularly played and both were central to Bath's continual development. Toulon, vanquished amid an orgy of Heineken in Amsterdam, came to Bath and destroyed us with a display of continuity of which England's champions had never dreamed. Toulouse, coached by Pierre Villepreux, also taught Bath a thing or two in one memorable 18–18 draw at the Recreation Ground. Where English players thundered heroically into tackles, the French backed off after drawing their defender and kept the ball alive while remaining in the game. Rowell devoured these lessons, mixed them with his side's physical talents and produced a hybrid that stimulated Bath and kept them as far in front of their rivals as Wigan remain in Rugby League.

Whatever his respect for France, Rowell must have comforted himself with the knowledge that under his guidance, both Toulon and Toulouse had been beaten when Bath were mentally prepared. It was proof that his pragmatism could repel that most clichéd rugby phrase, 'French flair'. Having chosen development through consistent selection he knew that defeat for England would be a severe psychological blow. Victory for France at Twickenham would probably have elevated them to the status of co-favourites for the World Cup. His record of selection as a club coach veered towards safety. Rowell does not build for tomorrow; he wins for today and then analyses the way forward.

His regard for France was such that he openly tempered the theme of continuous progression towards the overall goal of the World Cup. 'The squad want to stick to what we are trying to play – more dynamic, handling rugby. It's the way forward. We have to find ways of scoring tries. We got ourselves in a bit of a fix by thinking that we could win on penalties. If Plan A does not work because of conditions, we will fall back on another, because the important thing is to win.' It was the gospel he had preached throughout his coaching career: plan and develop on the training field, but on the pitch *win*. Occasionally this overwhelming desire to triumph stifled his dynamic master plan as fear of losing took a grip. When that mentality is in the ascendant, do not expect the wings to see the ball. Public disputes with players like Simon Halliday were regular occurrences when Bath's backs demanded more ball. Rowell did evolve to a fifteen-man game, but he would never become a lover of open rugby for its own sake. The cavalier side of his character is saved for the bar.

As an open devotee of the formidable French back row, Rowell also used the French match as the acid test for his own back row. If Cabannes could monopolise loose possession, the likes of Neil Back or Lawrence Dallaglio could force their way into national contention. He expected France to test his ballistic forwards physically, but it was Rowell who issued the mental challenge before the game. 'Our forwards were outstanding against the Irish, but I said the jury was still out on the back row of Tim Rodber, Dean Richards and Ben Clarke a couple of months ago and one swallow does not make a summer.' After Dublin Rowell had answered Dean Richards' rhetorical 'Was that good enough, Jack?' in the affirmative. Now he was telling them to prove it again. Rowell's esteem for the French was summed up by his comment, 'This looks the game of the Championship, although the other three nations might have something to say about that.'

The views emanating from the English playing camp were not all as reverent. Once again, the most verbal Englishman was Brian Moore. He had questioned the quality of Ireland's much-vaunted front row before the Dublin match. Before France, the psychological warfare intensified. Moore was quoted as saying: 'Playing against France in the Five Nations is like facing fifteen Eric Cantonas – they are brilliant but brutal.' Such comments seemed to justify French accusations of xenophobia, although the French camp did not take Moore's comments with any great degree of offence. They probably find the appalling table wine offered at the after-match function a greater insult. Perhaps Moore's remarks were directly related to Pierre Berbizier's throw-away claim that England's hooker had organised on-field provocation in the past. Given France's frequent lapses of discipline in the recent past, Moore would not have needed to say much. The French manager, Guy Laporte, calmed the situation when he stated: 'The first time Brian Moore said something before a match it surprised everybody, but when you have heard it for the tenth time, it is just amusing. He is spinning the same record.'

If France considered England xenophobic, England could justifiably question whether France were bordering on the paranoid. Recalled second-row forward Olivier Brouzet chimed in: 'There are many things I don't like in English rugby, starting with their aggressive style, based on rucking.' If France smiled at Moore's comments, England probably laughed openly at Brouzet's. The French newspaper L'Equipe further stoked the fires of paranoia. 'Let us be in no doubt that the British press will exploit the affair [Merle's alleged headbutt on Ricky Evans against Wales] to fuel its favourite tactic against the Tricolours – hatred of the French.' The shadows of Napoleon and Wellington apparently loomed large over Twickenham as international fever grabbed the country.

Whatever headlines the newspapers generated, there was no doubt that England expected their toughest game of the tournament. Ben Clarke described his opponent, Laurent Cabannes, as 'an absolutely tremendous player', adding: 'Everyone recognises that the French match is a step up.' Will Carling, too, issued diplomatic statements. 'I simply don't go along with these anti-French feelings. I don't want to be associated with that sort of thing. We see them as the side to beat because we have so much admiration and respect for them.' Yet he also emphasised that England had rather fewer 'mental hang-ups' than France. As England had beaten them on seven consecutive occasions, it was a view which was difficult to refute.

Looking inwards, England analysed their performance in Dublin and targeted their finishing as the area in which most improvement was needed. Not surprisingly, the loudest concern was voiced by Rory Underwood. There is nothing worse than a winger spurned, and both Guscott and Catt had ignored him in Dublin. 'It was all very well hanging on to the ball and not seeing men outside, or tackles coming in, when we were on the way to a sizeable victory in Dublin,' he said. The name Guscott found its way into Rory's ear and he added: 'Jerry's his own man and will put things right because next time we simply must make the breaks count.' Guscott, deadpan, proclaimed: 'I will always look at what's on for me first.' It was classic Guscott, playing the superstar as much as an amateur sportsman can, but not really taking himself seriously. In the bars of Bristol such remarks meet with contempt, but those who know the rogue would merely smile in appreciation.

French smiles have been rare events since Will Carling ascended to England's captaincy. Grimaces, rather than grins, were the order of the day on 1 February, when Emile Ntamack, the lithe French wing, withdrew. His departure was accompanied by the warnings of the latest *petit général*, Pierre Berbizier: 'We cannot rely on French flair to pull us through.' Nor could we rely on anything other than Gallic angst as the day of reckoning drew near. The normally balanced Berbizier busily intimated that France would draw motivation from the 'press campaign' that led to the dropping of Olivier Merle. The rugby world thought Berbizier was secretly pleased with both his diplomacy and his selection of the springier Brouzet, but the manager claimed otherwise. 'Olivier [Merle] was rock-solid in the pack and allowed Laurent Cabannes to stand off.' In fact Jack Rowell concurred with this opinion in the wake of France's Ireland match later in the season. Brouzet is a more striking player, far more athletic, but Merle's sheer bulk does lay the foundations for the fliers around him. He is not comparable, in terms of footballing talent, with Dean Richards, but he does perform a similar role in the national XV.

The quotable French captain Philippe Saint-André joined the conspiracy chorus directed at the Saxon element of the Five Nations. On the Merle outrage, he muttered, 'Let's just say we sometimes feel there are double standards involved in eliminating foul play.' The elusive French winger offered more confident soundings too. 'Our win in New Zealand made us believe in ourselves.' To borrow from the wonderful world of horse racing, the form line of a series success in New Zealand should have made France a 'winter favourite' for one of the Classics. In rugby parlance they had two Classic opportunities: the Grand Slam and the greatest prize of all, the World Cup. Even Berbizier was bullish. 'We can dream of an excellent match which could be a fabulous prelude to the World Cup.' How paradoxical that so many of the hopes of France, the most elegant of all rugby nations, rested on their captain, Philippe Saint-André, and Abdel Benazzi, nicknamed the Ugly Ducklings. The

Welsh match in Paris suggested that, inelegant or not, France would depend greatly on these two exceptional talents.

The other key element for France would be their goal-kicking. The duel between Thierry Lacroix and Rob Andrew, both coached by the kicking guru David Alred, would be fascinating. Alred's reputation within the RFU was already tarnished by his foray to Rugby League and an exotic adventure in American football, but to coach France's kicker was tantamount to being a mercenary. Alred's influence on international rugby is growing. He has worked with Neil Jenkins and has regularly coached the Australian kickers. Many Englishmen reared on the imperial tunes of Gilbert and Sullivan might chew their handlebar moustaches in indignation, but the RFU have no right to criticise Alred. Rob Andrew uses him on a personal basis but England's treatment of him has been deplorable. As recently as 1993 he was asked to leave Twickenham's playing surface until an 'official' training session was completed. The fact that he had once been a professional overrode the fact that Dick Best, then England coach, had asked him to help by kicking off for the forwards. His requests for a ticket to watch England have also fallen on stony ground – presumably the coach Rob Andrew has described as 'one of the most useful coaches I have met' is less deserving of a ticket than an RFU committee man from one of *Private Eye*'s rotten boroughs.

I digress. Alred travelled to France and worked with Lacroix, whose opinion on goal-kicking was altered. Not to the degree achievable through the use of a mind-bending synthetic drug, perhaps, but sufficiently for him to concede that a kicker can be constructed by technique, rather than having to rely on pure natural ability. Watching Rob Andrew's crabbed style leaves the impression that Alred has spent more time on his English disciple. None the less Lacroix was confident that the Twickenham crowd would not overawe him, although he admitted: 'The only thing that unsettles me is when a team-mate wishes me good luck.' Kickers are a strange breed. Gavin Hastings professes to be more nervous playing golf with Sam Torrance against Ronan Rafferty and Peter Allis than kicking at goal for Scotland, 'except for the odd occasion when the rhythm's missing'.

The night before the game England received the boost of a 29–9 victory in the A international between the respective sides. Despite the win, the presence of Jez Harris at fly-half raised questions about the strength in depth of English rugby. Harris has been a great servant to Leicester, but he is a long way short of being an international. The men who impressed England A backs coach Mike Slemen were the highly talked-about duo Paul Hull and Neil Back. 'The pair were magnificent. I am not a national selector, but I would say that Back must come into serious consideration for South Africa,' he said. On the morning of the Five Nations match the England back row probably enjoyed their breakfast rather less than their colleagues as Neil Back continued to impress everyone except the selection panel.

As the England team looked across Richmond from their base, the Petersham Hotel, to Twickenham, the sight of a blue sky and late winter sun might well have sent shivers of apprehension through them. It was a day made for a Turner painting of the Thames, but also one for which Frenchmen dreamed. The clichés rained down upon us. 'Paris in spring-time transported to London'; 'Watch the French play with the sun on their backs'. National opinion on the morning of 4 February seemed to presume that if God possesses a nationality it is French, not English. Recent history might have been against France, but the climate was on their side. It was almost temperate enough to grow vines.

Most observers perceived that the Championship and Grand Slam would depend upon this collision. Before the match Rowell singled out Victor Ubogu for what he described as 'fireworks'. Ubogu's primary role in the side was to provide stability and pressure in the scrums. In the past his fortitude had been questioned, but throughout the previous season and the three internationals in 1994–5 he had been solid in the scrums. His greatest asset is his ability to carry the ball across the gain-line, but in this facet of play Ubogu had been markedly less effective so far this season. Rowell decided to propel him forward by 'sticking a rocket up his arse', as the quaint saying goes. By full-time France must have wondered whether Jack Rowell had purchased the entire stock of the Standard Firework Company. The French were certainly blown apart in a manner of which Guy Fawkes would have approved. It was a performance that led Eddie Butler, a former captain of Wales, to lend his name to the *Observer* headline, 'CARLING'S GOLDEN BOYS ARE READY TO TAKE ON THE WORLD'. It hurts a Welshman to concur with such an opinion, let alone express it, but not as much as it hurt the French on a day of sunshine that turned into a black afternoon for the Tricolours.

Perhaps Pierre Berbizier's sardonic comments about the unadven-turousness of British rugby before France's victory against Wales were one barb too many for England. Gallic romantics treated the style (or lack of it) of the British game with much the same contempt that Honoré de Balzac reserved for the English centuries ago: 'English inventions tend to mechanise other nations. England seems bent on seeing the whole world as dull as itself and dull in the same way.' For all the team's success against France in the Cooke era, many British observers fundamentally agreed with that view. But 4 February proved to be a landmark. Not only did the 31–10 victory represent England's best score against France for eighty-four years, but it was based on ingredients which had been absent from those previous grinding, worthy wins. Pulsating pace and power combined to overrun France – afterwards,

Berbizier described England as a 'task force' – and again, England's pack laid the cornerstone. This time France yielded in the loose rather than the tight. English heroes were in abundance.

England shaded the first quarter, although points were not forthcoming. After the match Will Carling compared this period to a chess match, but I doubt that Nigel Short would have enjoyed twenty minutes packing down alongside Messrs Leonard and Ubogu. It was France and Thierry Lacroix who opened the scoring with a well-struck penalty from 40 metres. Dave Alred's hopes of a Twickenham ticket began to look slimmer than ever. In contrast, Rob Andrew started with nerves that had not existed when England played Canada. The remorseless pressure of the England pack gave him the chance to kick England into a 6–3 lead before their maverick centre struck. Richards, Rodber and Clarke, all outstanding throughout, powered to within yards of the French line. A secondary surge left them 2 yards short. Kyran Bracken, tentative during the first twenty minutes, fired a pass to Jeremy Guscott as Mike Catt flew into the line from full-back. One imperious dummy sent Deylaud and Sella sprinting into the new West Stand as Guscott glided beneath the posts for a try that was the cause of celebration and relief in equal measures. Guscott had lived up to his pre-match pledge to 'see what's in it for me first'. In Ireland it was a waiting tackle; against France it was another international try, and the crowd exploded. The only thing that spoiled the memory of the score was the delirious crowd automatically breaking into the spurious 'Swing Low, Sweet Chariot'. Andrew converted, and at 13–3 France appeared to be beaten.

So things looked bad for France at half-time, and they were not much better for Neil Back. Laurent Cabannes entered the combat as the standard-bearer for legitimate fast opensides. Despite his prodigious standing jump, he could not win line-out ball against Ben Clarke; more importantly, like so many other No. 7s, he found it impossible to halt Clarke before the mythical but all-important gain-line. Task forces can look ponderous in retreat, but on a surge they are unstoppable. Clarke and his back-row colleagues were taking ground rather faster than Germany did in Czechoslovakia. As rounded as Neil Back's repertoire of skills is, he could never offer England such an edge.

The second half began with the promise of a French revival. Andrew missed a simple penalty attempt and the ball rebounded off the post into French arms and was swiftly moved right. Bernat-Salles, the replacement winger, received a favourable deflection from Catt's attempted charge-down. Cabannes, finally free from his bruising, losing battle with Clarke, took the move on and Sebastien Viars, the replacement for full-back Jean-Luc Sadourny, sprinted in at the corner. Lacroix's expert conversion opened the door for French aspirations and closed the gates of Twickenham to David Alred.

France needed to maintain discipline; instead they made an elementary mess of Rob Andrew's re-start and the fly-half punished France with a penalty goal. It was clear that the French bolt of lightning would not strike twice; indeed, they would not visit the English 22 with any serious intent for the rest of the match. Brian Moore claimed a points victory for England's front row against Ireland; in this match it was a knock-out. Jack Rowell's rocket up Ubogu's backside helped him to produce the best international performance of his career. Normally resplendent in red Versace jeans and colourful waistcoats, the sweet-smelling Nigerian has often been mistrusted by his fellow habitués of the front row, but today the substance matched the style. Jason Leonard had also been a victim of Rowell's tongue as long ago as South Africa, when Rowell had asked him if he was happy just accumulating caps. Leonard responded positively, like so many before him, and lifted his game to new heights, especially in the loose, where he tackled like a centre.

The occupying army that was the England pack pressurised France into more mistakes and gunner Andrew pushed the score to 19–10. With ten minutes of a match remaining, England have often guarded such a lead; on this occasion the attacks with ball in hand continued. Rory Underwood, underused again as an attacker, turned into a French catcher à la Dean Richards. From the turnover Rob Andrew fired a kick into the corner. Philippe Saint-André, such a marvellous player in most phases, was leaden-footed on the turn and Tony Underwood, with the help of a little push and shove, dived for the score. The sight of Tony, one of the sport's gentlemen, indulging in such fractious incidents underlined England's new killer instinct. But 26–10 was not to be the final humiliation for France. Another surge led to an England scrum 40 yards out and 15 in from the right-hand touchline. Bracken fed Rodber blind. He moved it through the hands Jeremy Guscott-style; Catt took the pass flat, and at scorching pace. His speed shredded the first line of the French defence, but even more effective was the deceleration that drew the final two defenders before Tony Underwood took it on with a searing sprint to the corner. It was a fitting end to a match to which Catt had contributed splendidly. The 31–10 result made my high opinion of France look stupid, but at least Catt's emergence could be counted as a rare journalistic success. Paul Hull had never let England down, but nor did he have the footballing skill to lift the side in the manner of Mike Catt.

The crowd had paid in excess of £1.5 million to watch a match that confirmed England's potential as serious candidates for the World Cup. Will Carling was certainly satisfied after his eighth and most impressive success against France. 'As usual our pack came out on top. It is the mark of a good side that it can keep its pattern and finish like that. It was a great finish to a great game.' The bookmakers reacted accordingly. England were cut to 4–1 from 5–1 for the World Cup while France drifted from 9–2 to 11–2. By 4 p.m. on Saturday afternoon there was little doubt that England's 4–1 was the more attractive price.

Rowell's reaction was a masterly attempt to play down his delight. 'The line-out was a jungle and we have to be able to cope with that. I still don't know where this team is in world terms. The pack is developing a unique style, but we still need to fulfil our aims of putting the ball into the centres' and wings' hands more regularly to acquire the balance we aspire to.' The bald truths of Rowell's assertions were unquestionable, but in the light of England's lamentable lack of continuity only a year earlier, the criticism seemed hard, almost artificial. His very first comments revealed his true feelings. 'England today beat a world-class team 31–10, and that is good news for all English rugby. Our line-out was erratic, but in the rucks and other loose play we were outstanding.' The rooftop bar of the Park Lane Hilton struggled to find enough champagne for a euphoric Rowell later that evening. As soon as I heard him use the key word 'dynamic' to describe the performance, I knew that the demanding devil was in a state of near-satisfaction. Four months earlier he would have readily accepted the vast improvement in an England team that led to his conclusion that 'we are on the edge of a roll, but it hasn't quite started rolling yet'. Now the side were well placed to roll with the best in the world.

Jerry Guscott would never admit it, but he too must have been delighted with the try that ended one of the most fallow periods of his high-scoring career. Mock arrogant before the match, he confessed afterwards, 'You look silly when those liberties don't come off, but you have to back your judgement and it's bliss when things work.' There was little doubt that Guscott would back his judgement again before the end of this longest season in British rugby.

Guscott's partner and captain Will Carling had a brief scare. The president of the Fédération Français de Rugby, Bernard Lapasset, reputedly threatened to report him for deliberately injuring Jean-Luc Sadourny. It took a sensible and honest admission from one of the Ugly Ducklings, Abdel Benazzi, to clear his name. It was tough on Carling, who had deliberately dissociated himself from the tedious but sensational hyperbole and xenophobia that preceded the match. Undoubtedly France had suffered at the hands of the English media, but Lapasset's alleged threat suggested more than a hint of paranoia.

The French coach, Pierre Berbizier, was more realistic, but also rueful. 'The English team were at a very high level and France were only at a good level. England played like a task force and did not permit us to have the ball the two or three times in succession that is necessary to win international matches,' he mused. 'It looks like they are better placed to win the World Cup than we are.' Jason Little, the outstanding Australian centre, joined in the congratulatory chorus. 'They are playing a different style. Their form is better going into the World Cup than it was last time.'

12

Northern Joy, Southern Strains

In the aftermath, as in the pre-match build-up, 'Le Crunch' was perceived throughout England as the deciding match of the Championship. Supporters forgot the painful lessons of Edinburgh 1990, Cardiff 1993, Dublin 1993 and, most recently, Twickenham 1994, when Ireland produced the greatest of all contemporary shocks. Writers on English newspapers (many of whom are Welsh) once again referred to the 'first' and 'second' divisions of international rugby. Even Geoff Cooke, normally an astute player of psychological games, had once suggested that the Five Nations was in danger of losing its appeal as a truly competitive event. Of course, the Celtic nations had arisen and smitten English arrogance before, but memories are short and on the day of England versus France barely one neutral eye turned northwards towards Edinburgh. Scotland against Ireland was summarily dismissed as the wooden spoon decider, even though Scotland had not played a Championship match and Ireland had not been without credit in losing to one of the more powerful English performances of modern times.

Considering Scotland's atrocious current record and Ireland's performance against England, I had, as I said, shrewdly backed the Irish, despite Jim Staples' withdrawal with influenza three days before the match. The flu bug is never welcome, especially in the week before a recall for your country. Conor O'Shea, a less than impressive full-back on his previous showings, returned. It was this change, and the abominable Irish record in Edinburgh, that made Scotland 5–6 favourites. Of the Ireland XV only Brendan Mullin and returning captain Michael Bradley had tasted victory at Murrayfield. Records like this hang like millstones around the necks of less self-assured teams when the media bring them to the attention of the players.

Bradley's charges cannot have been fuelled with confidence by the pronouncements of their phlegmatic coach, Gerry Murphy. 'There is a strong feeling abroad that Scotland are not a very good team, but we will be taking nothing for granted. We recognise that they have some of the most experienced players in the game, like Gavin Hastings, Craig Chalmers and Damian Cronin. They are three players who will be lining up in key positions, so I think it would be very foolish of us to under-estimate Scotland, for after their success against Canada their confidence will be high.' Murphy might not have proved himself one of the greatest coaches, but he has emphasised that the Irish can be shrewder than most. His words appeared to be a smokescreen: for all the hype before the England match, few people expected Ireland to produce a third consecutive win. But Irishmen did believe their side was of sufficient calibre to beat Scotland, and Murphy's comments were a deliberate attempt to alleviate the pressure on his players.

Paradoxically, Scotland, too, were under increased pressure, but for the opposite reason. After a run of nine defeats they had nowhere to fall before the Canada match. With victory came a new pressure: the hope of a rise towards mediocrity. When I met Scotland's coach, Doug Morgan, before Christmas, his haunted visage had suggested that reaching the dizzy heights of mediocrity was about as likely as discovering El Dorado. The man at the centre of the storm was Gavin Hastings. After the South Africa match he gave the impression of a man being drowned by the rain. Canada were not a great team, but Hastings' performance indicated that if he was not exactly riding the storm, he had at least found some shelter. Having broken the run of defeats, he was not about to allow those twinges in his back to stop him playing against Ireland and establishing a new Scottish record of fifty-three caps. Moreover, his presence would be important to such a young Scottish side: he instils his own brand of simple self-confidence that passes, like a benevolent virus, around the changing-room. It had hardly reached epidemic proportions around the country, however.

Jim Renwick, the great Scotland centre and proud Borderer, provoked the mood of despair with his comments on a Five Nations match in Edinburgh the previous season. 'I left bitterly disappointed,' he said. 'I was looking forward to seeing a bit of back play, a bit of adventure. There was none of that, and I won't go back until the team changes its approach.' Renwick's few fragments of hope revolved around Hastings, who 'seems to be sharper than he was this time last year'. His pessimism failed to divert Hastings' intense focus before the match. Questioned about the Scottish record, the captain said: 'The enjoyment of winning my fifty-third cap will come after the game – as long as we win.' Gener-ally a calming influence, he positively prickled when the media asked him if Scotland against Ireland would be the wooden spoon decider. 'I do not support the idea that there are two divisions in the Five Nations. [The wooden spoon decider] is an interesting perception, but not one I subscribe to. We feel confident of getting a victory.'

David Hilton, who made his Five Nations debut as a loose-head prop in that match, later verified that the Scots did believe in themselves. 'We were very confident. We were playing at home and Hastings inspired us.' If the captain was an inspirational force before the match, his performance during the game lifted the whole of Scotland out of the stormcloud that had poured on their national rugby team for so long. It was the bookmakers who were right, again at my expense. Scotland confirmed their odds-on status and prevailed by 26–13; Hastings confirmed his re-ascendancy to the throne of Scottish rugby. Kicking with rather less concern than he says he feels when playing golf with Sam Torrance, he succeeded with six out of seven attempts. Torrance's 3-iron could hardly have been more accurate. Hastings' sixteen points took him past the 500-point mark in international rugby, a tally topped only by Michael Lynagh and Grant Fox.

Hastings was the hero of a game which deviated madly from the plot. In the first twenty minutes Ireland dominated and poor Paul Burke missed several kickable penalties. Gerry Murphy nobly defended his young No. 10 after the match, claiming, 'We didn't lose because we didn't kick penalties. We lost because we didn't get enough ball in their half.' Yet one wonders what effect nine early points would have had on this young Scottish side. As it was, Ireland's misses seemed to inspire Scotland's pack, which, according to the script, was supposed to be crushed by the Irish front row (still lauded, even in the wake of Brian Moore's and Victor Ubogu's demystifying displays). The first half saw three Gavin Hastings penalties to a Burke penalty and yet another Brendan Mullin try. Before the England–Ireland match Jack Rowell had jested about Simon Geoghegan bringing any Bath moves into the Ireland midfield; against Scotland this joke became a reality as the outside centre cut short to hold one defender, the full-back surged through the middle to hold the second centre, and Mullin stealthily faded wide to receive Burke's pass and drift into space. It was a well-worked try which suggested that Ireland's backs could win the game. After half-time, Ireland created another fine score for Jonathan Bell, a most impressive footballer, and matters looked ominous for Scotland – or so we thought.

But Hastings attacked, his chip landing kindly on the boot of Kenny Logan, whose well-directed volley from 10 yards into the goal area contained echoes of Jim Baxter. Craig Joiner sprinted on to the loose ball. Hastings converted, kicked a penalty and suddenly Scotland were not only ahead by 19–13 but were in total command up front. Their superiority was underlined when Damian Cronin, the red wine kid, surged over from a yard for a score which gave Scotland a 26–13 lead. Ireland, lacking any platform, could not recover.

If Gavin Hastings was the obvious hero, the front row of Peter Wright, Kenny Milne and David Hilton also deserved special praise. New boy Hilton was delighted. The leg-lifting exploits of Popplewell were absent, Hilton thought, because the 'referee was looking for it. We went up a couple of gears up front, and the Irish couldn't live with it.' He did not overplay the difference between a club and an international front row – in fact, he went as far as to suggest that in some respects scrums in the Five Nations are easier than those at club level. 'It was like a Cup final. Everything was thrown at you. You've got to be quite a wise man.' There are those who would question the wisdom of spending some of your fittest adult years in a scrum surrounded by a combined weight of 260st. At international level, he said, scrums are 'always compact and you're squeezing like mad. There is instant pressure, but the scrum only lasts ten seconds.' The thought of 26st of pressure lasting 'only' ten seconds is frightening. In contrast, he felt, club scrums are not as tight but the element of pulling, which leads to the horrors of collapsed scrums, is far less evident.

David Hilton is the mildest of men, and to hear him speak with such confidence indicated that Scotland were as comfortable as Hastings had claimed. They were most definitely as motivated. The smiling butcher from Bedminster, mission accomplished against Peter Clohessy, had this message for the press: 'We aim to stuff the critics' words down their throats. This is a fine Scotland side and it can only get better.' As Scotland's players celebrated, the collective sigh of relief from the management was almost audible over the traditional piping-in of the haggis at the post-match dinner. A buoyant Duncan Paterson assured us that there would not be nineteen changes in the team to face France. At last a feeling of relative stability surrounded the Scotland team, not-withstanding the *Sunday Times* headline: 'SLOW START IN RACE FOR WOODEN SPOON'.

As the Five Nations Championship neared the halfway stage, the two unbeaten teams, England and Scotland, had cause to celebrate. In England's case, however, the euphoria had evaporated within days of the Twickenham triumph against France. Despite Sir Ewart Bell's assertion that the managers of the countries participating in the World Cup had left the 1994 RWC meeting happy, Jack Rowell had not. England were desperate to stay in Cape Town in the week leading up to their likely quarter-final, hopeful semi-final and perhaps even the final. Their medical team, whose approach was quickly catching up with the progressive thinking of the Australians, had informed England that they should leave training at altitude until as late as possible. RWC's argument that, by forcing teams to stay in Johannesburg from the quarter-finals onwards, they were being fair to everyone hardly seemed a coherent defence when England had just one match above sea-level – and then only if they reached the final. In a country whose provincial factionalism makes England and Scotland look like great friends, there was more than a rumour that the whole plan was little more than another overt display of power from the good doctor, Louis Luyt, and his Transvaal friends.

England had therefore made an official request to stay in Cape Town. France had been beaten, but not the officials of the Rugby World Cup. 'To meet the request from England would have placed them in a different position from all others. It would have been unfair to adopt their proposals and not to offer a similar choice to the rest.' If England were to reach the World Cup final they would have to travel an extra 3,000 miles. Mr Rowell was not impressed.

The Welsh had a right to be even less impressed. Their problem, unlike England's, was not a medical or logistical matter – it was a matter of plain boredom. Whether a misguided Afrikaner thought that a team from Wales would find the homely splendour of Bloemfontein relaxing is debatable, but the Welsh were adamant that they wanted to spend more time in Johannesburg. Relaxation plays a vital role in preparing for matches in rugby's most important tournament. Bloemfontein has little more to offer than a Hard Rock Café, comfortable beds and an intense dislike of this author. There would be little chance of me travelling to watch Japan in any of their three group matches in dear old Bloem. Disgruntled as Wales were, it did not stop the sponsors of their national Leagues, Heineken, from sponsoring ITV's coverage of the World Cup to the tune of £2 million. Jeremy Wilton, the head of sponsorship at Whitbread, said: 'The 1995 Rugby World Cup will deliver a massive advantage to the brand throughout the crucial summer period.' I was looking forward rather more to sampling South Africa's excellent range of red wine, although the prospect of using Australia humbling Romania as an excuse to travel to Stellenbosch, the epicentre of the wine industry, hardly filled me with joy.

The Australian team, meanwhile, seemed to be in a position to buy a few vineyards as well as a year or two's supply of wine that would not necessarily appeal to their Oak-trained palates. As England players mulled over the possibility of a profit of £10,000 each for a Grand Slam, news leaked that the Australian squad had signed one-year contracts worth between £15,000 and £60,000. In return, the players would undertake promotional work for the national side's sponsors. Dick McGruther of the Australian Rugby Union correctly stated that this did not infringe the laws of amateurism as it did not involve payment for playing. Nevertheless, the deals went beyond the furthest reaches of the spirit of the game. It was clearly a move to check the spread of recruitment to Rugby League – coach Bob Dwyer did not want to lose too many more Garrick Morgans. At the end of the month, Brian Lima of Western Samoa was to prove that at least one southern hemisphere player could resist the lure of the dollar. He turned down the equivalent of £185,000 from North Sydney Rugby League Club to remain a proud bulwark of Western Samoa's World Cup side.

Jack Rowell's view was that the World Cup should be organised with the aim of allowing players to perform at their peak. Comfort and financial security have a part to play in ensuring that their preparations enable them to do so. Providing that peace of mind must ultimately be the best way to rebuff Rugby League. It appeared that only the RFU were denying the evidence of their eyes. Malcolm Phillips, a committee man, said that players did not want to be contracted professionals or to be told what to do. 'As for this season, the squad seem happy with something in excess of £10,000.' Not when the Australians earned six times as much, they weren't. The RFU were later to raise their estimate for those who stayed in the English game after the World Cup to a massive £15,000. Yet despite the figures being bandied around in the southern hemisphere, the England players knew that Grand Slam glory followed by coronation as world champions could offer a career and lifestyle to dwarf the Australian sums.

Vernon Pugh, the articulate Welsh chairman of the International Board, was closer to earth than the RFU on the amateurism question. 'We may have to recognise that amateurism has been abandoned and then do our best to ensure we supervise the consequent changes,' he said. Even Bill Hogg, the chief executive of the Scottish Rugby Union and a long-time amateur ally of the RFU, accepted that change was inevitable. 'We will be recommending that top players should benefit from off-the-field rugby-related activities,' he confirmed. The tide was turning rapidly against the days of the amateur gentleman. It was just as well that RFU secretary Dudley Wood claimed to like being compared with King Canute.

The Welsh, the most fanatical of British rugby peoples, were metaphorically building sea walls in the hope of stopping the tidal wave called England from overwhelming the Five Nations Championship. Thereafter they retreated to the chapels to pray for miracles. To a small child, the fulfilment of a dream may be a bicycle at Christmas; to me it is an ante-post voucher at 66–1 for the horse that will win the Cheltenham Gold Cup. For a huge number of Welshmen it is beating England at rugby. Culturally and economically downtrodden, the Principality has every reason to cherish revenge on the rugby field, but even the countless appalling teams that crossed the Severn Bridge as sacrificial lambs to the mighty Welsh sides of the past harmed Wales in the long term. As other countries improved and developed, they remained stagnant, comfortable just to defeat the deadly enemy. Before the latest blood-letting, manager Robert Norster expanded on the theme. 'We have always said that Welsh rugby needs a vision beyond trying to beat England every year, but in this instance it will do very nicely.' Many Welsh critics, distressed at their national side's inability to use more than a modicum of good first-phase ball, thought the team lacked a vision to beat anyone. Yet such is their desperation to overcome England that the agonising about the overall footballing skill of Neil Jenkins, or the suitability of Alan Davies' bow-ties for a Welsh coach, was suspended as Welsh players drifted from the chapels of the valleys and the bars of Cardiff towards the longed-for Celtic heaven of victory at the Arms Park.

On the day that England's tidal wave flooded French defences it appeared that at least some Welsh prayers had been answered. Cardiff, in their latest defiance of my prediction, beat Llanelli 30–26. More important than that irritation were the names on the scoresheet: there were tries for Ieuan Evans, Nigel Davies and Emyr Lewis of Llanelli and Cardiff's Nigel Walker, all of whom had been recent international casualties. That was four more than Wales had looked likely to score in a whole month on their Paris showing. Further evidence of the distraught state of Welsh rugby was that Treorchy, more famous for their male voice choir than for their rugby, overwhelmed those legendary pantomime villains, Pontypool, by 31–8 in Gwent. What would the famous front row think of being steamrollered by a collection of tenors? The other Ponty, Pontypridd, continued to challenge as hard for the title as Pontypool were trying to descend into Division 2. They beat Newport 29–15 to keep alive my hopes of not looking like a total fool in Cardiff. On 8 February Pontypridd maintained the pressure on Cardiff with a victory against Bridgend, while Pontypool plummeted to a rare defeat at Abertillery. Cardiff scraped through 17–11 at home to the male voice choir, but for Alan Davies the most significant news was that Hemi Taylor, the Welshman from Morrisville, New Zealand, had proved his fitness and willingness to face his new old enemy, England. Wales announced their team the next day, and back came captain Ieuan Evans, Nigel Davies, Hemi Taylor and Emyr Lewis. It was an especially proud day for one man, Robert Jones. He was selected to join the exclusive club for Welshmen with over fifty caps. The only other members are J.P.R. Williams and Gareth Edwards.

It was appropriate that Jones should become the first 'modern' player to join this select band. Together with Ieuan Evans, he is one of the few current Welsh players with the wit, cheek and invention that was so commonplace in the 1970s. Jones seems to have been born to play rugby.

The career of the Swansea and Western Province scrum-half also illustrates Wales' steep decline. Despite his fifty caps, Jones has spent several frustrating seasons watching inferior players like Chris Bridges and Rupert Moon (an Englishman, God forbid) taking the field in the sacred No. 9 jersey. Strong and fearless they might have been, but neither possessed that Celtic touch of class. Jones had it; luckily for Wales, he also possessed an insane degree of national fervour, otherwise he would have chosen the delights of Cape Town over his beloved village of Trebanos in the Swansea Valley. If Wales were to have any chance against England, Robert Jones would need to play one of his greatest games.

Ieuan Evans celebrated his recall with the statutory statement of belief in the team. 'The ball is in our court – it is up to us to go out there and do it. We are still Five Nations champions. Within our camp there is a lot of confidence and we have our injured players back.' The subject of the injuries was a recurring one, but none the less rugby is as much about intent as execution and at least Evans was presenting a positive face. Massive doubts still loomed on the question of the negativity of a Welsh side which publicly expressed contentment with defeats they regarded as 'acceptable'. If an iron will is absent, it matters not which players are fit or otherwise.

Maintaining a perfect balance with Evans, as the players' spokesman, was Nigel Walker, who was becoming an unstoppable soundbite man. Before the French match he had proclaimed the Welsh tight five as 'the best in the world'; now he cast judgement on England. 'England are a good side, there's no two ways about that, but it's a bit premature to talk about them being a great side.' Welsh optimism, buoyed by the returning players, received a jolt just three days before the game when the experienced Cardiff centre Mike Hall withdrew. He was replaced by Mark Taylor of Pontypool, a man used to losing.

As match day drew near all the noise emanating from west of the Severn Bridge was positive, but it was almost too loud and too insistent to be genuine. On the eve of the showdown Nigel Walker issued a pithy battle cry: 'We can still win the Triple Crown.' Selector J.P.R. Williams, already rumoured to be a disaffected selector, added: 'England have been made odds-on favourites but I think it is going to be very tight. The key for Wales is to stop the English back row. If they do that then they will have a chance.' On the evidence of England's back-row performances against Ireland and France, there was more likelihood of the Queen and Paul Keating forming a deep and meaningful relationship.

More in touch with reality was the opinion of Wales' last great fly-half, Jonathan Davies. I bumped into him the day before the match in a car park behind the stadium. Asked about Wales' chances, he ignored the question and replied, 'If England can't win by ten points tomorrow, they have no chance of winning the World Cup.' A Welsh victory was not even a thought in his mind. Even the normally optimistic Welsh drinkers seemed drained of confidence. ''Ere, Barnes, Wales will stuff England! Give me 4–1 against and I'll bet a tenner.' In days past a Welshman would have taken Wales at evens against any side in Cardiff. I felt a twinge of regret at the passing of blind faith.

In Wales there was a surprising lack of tangible hope and expectation; in England, even more amazingly, the players opened their hearts for a Cellnet survey on Valentine's Day. The reward would be a substantial £100,000-plus deal for the squad fortunate enough to travel to the World Cup. Their romantic secrets were not of a sensational nature. They were probably of more interest to Delia Smith than the *Sun* newspaper, since food featured prominently. Tony Underwood's ideal Valentine's Day consisted of the theatre, dinner and a jacuzzi – I suppose the latter at least leaves something to the imagination. Kyran Bracken was even more commonplace: 'Have dinner, go to the cinema or for a walk.' I suspected Tim Rodber was rather more honest with his 'dinner, bed' one-two. Dean Richards painted the most unlikely romantic scenario, 'a quiet night in with a bottle of wine in front of an open fire – and if you believe that, you'll believe anything'. That was typical Richards, as was Nigel Redman's complaint: 'It's hard to be romantic when you're covered in mud.'

After this brief romantic interlude, the players were rudely brought back down to earth by a complete absence of planning on the part of the RFU. As we have seen, having had a mere four years to consider the World Cup season the RFU had resisted the temptation to look at the fixtures in the light of the commitments of the national squad. The result was that a series of crucial Courage League matches was scheduled between the French and Welsh fixtures. Jack Rowell claimed that it was not his fault such a mess had occurred and that his squad had agreed to rest. Assuming his best Machiavellian stance, he refused to budge. When Rowell was guiding Bath he would have had a slightly different point of view, but as England manager he stripped away all shadows of sentiment and followed a straight line, which led directly to Durban. What he did not need was the selection of Nick Beal, Justyn Cassell, Matt Dawson and Harvey Thorneycroft of Northampton for England's Hong Kong Sevens squad – such crass stupidity could only help to alienate the already disgruntled senior clubs. The secretary of Northampton, Roger Horwood, spoke for other clubs when he said: 'We were totally amazed they were selected with all that has gone on with the issue of club and country. It only shows you how much thought has gone into it by the powers that be.' It was hard not to agree with Louis Luyt's assertion that rugby was being run on 'an old-boys basis'.

Rowell, having justifiably divested himself of any responsibility for the shambles, called a squad session which must have ranked as one of the most miserable in the history of England. Northampton and Harlequins, providers of one third of the English team, came to grief in matches that left them tottering on the brink of relegation. Northampton, missing Bayfield and Rodber, lost all the line-outs, while Harlequins, narrowly beaten by Bristol, desperately missed their trio. Dick Best was absolute in his conviction that his side would have won with their England players. 'Moore would have made one or two decisions to change the game.' I thought it too cruel to point out that Quins were hardly surging up the table when Moore, Carling and Leonard did play. At the elite end of the table, Bath could only draw with Orrell, which was enough given that Leicester suffered a bitter loss in the mud of Kingsholm, where Mike Teague inflicted a rare personal defeat on an England squad member who was turning out for his club, Dean Richards. In the England camp only the half-backs, Bracken and Andrew, enjoyed their Saturday-night drink.

The implications for the clubs were profound; moreover, it appeared that the establishment were oblivious to the fact that top clubs are now a serious business. The likes of Ian McGeechan, Dick Best and Tony Russ are contracted to manage a commercial enterprise, not just a rugby club. The RFU seemed unaware that the financial lifeblood of most clubs, the sponsorship deals, are generally performance-related. Best cited a potential loss of earnings in the region of half a million pounds if Quins were relegated. His question 'Are the RFU going to compensate?' was savagely rhetorical. As the senior clubs can rightly take much of the credit for the re-emergence of a good national side, it is probably only a matter of time before they create an association completely independent of the RFU. It will present the union with a challenge every bit as big as the one facing Japan in the form of New Zealand in the World Cup.

The plight of the professional administrator was shown in sharp relief when Gloucester sacked Barrie Corless, their director of coaching, later in February. His predecessor, Keith Richardson, asserted: 'The game is going more the way of soccer, with paid administrators.' He was right. The corollary is that sport is becoming more commercial and the pressure to succeed greater. Corless joined Barry Taylor of West Hartlepool as the newest trend-setters – the rugby coaches who are treated like football managers. The one difference is the salary scale. The year of rugby revolution was starting to claim its share of heads, and there would be more.

13

The Battles of Hastings

W ales against England is a game guaranteed to put pressure on players and coaches alike. Alan Davies, mistrusted for those bow-ties (a sad indictment of factions within the WRU) needed more than a competent performance in defeat, while Jack Rowell knew that Cardiff had so often been the 'tube' that crushes the surfer on the crest. Rowell has long used humour to disguise his tension – in the build-up to Cardiff he probably needed the entire video collection of *Fawlty Towers*.

Rather than base themselves in the Principality, England set up camp, like an advancing army, just across the border in the general's quarters, Bath. Rowell dumped the usual protocol, irritating a large sector of the press corps. England normally have the one closed session on a Thursday. The manager, seemingly on the verge of a mild dose of paranoia, made both the Wednesday and Thursday sessions private affairs. His explanation betrayed the gathering tension. 'A couple of weeks ago at Richmond I noticed swarms of people there, including French TV. I'm not being over-sensitive about it, but filming and analy- sing what we do in our major practices could be very useful to the competition.' Perhaps his respect for Alan Davies' diligent analytical mind forced him to adopt such a defensive position; whatever the reason, the result was the commencement of the fortress mentality, so different from the days when Rowell could blame any faults on the 'inherited squad'. Where better for him to raise the drawbridge than Bath, the city that for so long had been his unconquerable domain?

One of General Rowell's most vital lieutenants would be Dean Richards. The Leicester skipper had answered the relevant questions concerning his fitness and re-asserted his importance within the team. For all the immense power and athleticism of Clarke and Rodber, it was the quiet policeman from Hinckley who produced the necessary shape for the side. The England back row was collectively a great unit, but

Richards stood out as its central character. The match against Wales would be his forty-first cap. Like Robert Jones, he had suffered at the hands of the selectors. His uniquely underplayed approach to the sport lost him some friends in high places. The folly of ignoring him (especially for the 1991 World Cup final) is graphically illustrated by England's record since the World Cup pool game against Italy in 1991, in which he did play. After that Richards participated in twelve games for England, all of which were won, while they lost five out of fourteen without him. Despite his modest protestations – 'I'm just an ordinary bloke sitting in a corner getting on with my life' – he is much more than that. To Wayne Shelford, the driving force behind the majestic 1987 All Blacks, he is 'the best No. 8 in the world'. To Rowell he is simply 'immense', despite his well-known aversion to blackboard, video and training sessions. Richards explains: 'Instant analysis on the pitch as situations develop is my style.' No wonder Rowell, the man who demands decision-making from his players, rates him so highly. It also accounts for his mystifying exclusion under the more autocratic Cooke regime.

One man Geoff Cooke did select was Martin Bayfield. Ironically it was Alan Davies, then coach of the Midlands, who discovered him idling in the Metropolitan Police side. Cooke ignored the school of thought which contended that Bayfield was 6ft 10in and little else and selected him. The line-out has become such an integral part of the modern game that even if Bayfield did nothing else, his ability to secure line-out ball is vital. If Richards is England's central cog, Bayfield is not far behind. If Wales were to have any chance of derailing England's gravy train, Derwyn Jones, the Celtic Bayfield, would have to prevent the giant from Northampton from winning good line-out ball. The glamour boys, Guscott and the Underwoods, might turn a match with a flash, but they could only do so if somebody of PC 546's stature could get the ball.

Occasionally a cliché can be entirely appropriate, and in the case of Bayfield, the description 'gentle giant' could not be bettered. Rarely irate, he is one of the most thoughtful of tourists with an enduring sense of humour which permeates even into the darkest depths of the Bedfordshire police headquarters where he sits in front of a work tray that his colleagues claim is empty except for messages from Tim Rodber, his Northampton captain. I met Bayfield there in February, the English monsoon season. A sign on the wall informed rugby-supporting policemen: 'Bedford v Rugby – OFF tomorrow'. Beneath it was a hurriedly scrawled addendum in Bayfield's hand. 'There hasn't been any rugby at Bedford for some time anyway.' It was 'merely good banter', according to the man who is legendary for pushing jokes to their limit on tour.

His geniality has led to frequent doubts about Bayfield's appetite for the game's harder side, although if you question him on the subject you get the impression that he is no soft touch. 'I am an aggressive player,' he bristled. 'So what if I don't throw punches? It's nothing special. But if someone hits me, I hit them back.' As in the title of Sartre's book, there is iron in the soul – and in Bayfield's case a focus: working solely for his team. In the early 1990s street wisdom had it that Bayfield could be destroyed by intimidation. That feeling no longer exists. He weighed just 17st when first capped; now he is a far more confrontational 19st. As he is a man who lists weight-training as a hobby, it is no surprise that none of the extra weight is around the stomach. In the line-out jungle 19st can be a real asset. Common knowledge suggests that weight could be a burden, but not half as much of one as a friendly shoulder holding a player down. For a player expected to do little but win line-out ball his inability to leave the ground is a fairly significant problem. It increased the pressure on Bayfield, labelled as a one-dimensional player; a line-out stag, but a 'Bambi' in open play. That tag infuriates Bayfield, who has always enjoyed the open game. In the French international he was mildly disappointed with his set-piece play, but his contribution around the field was massive. He had advanced a long way from the man nicknamed 'B.R.' – an abbreviation of ball-retention – after he was stripped of the ball by a back as he dived across the Welsh line in 1993.

Everything changed after his neck injury, sustained in New Zealand with the British Lions in 1993. England recalled him against Scotland and Ireland in 1994, but then he was dropped. Bayfield remembers a two-fold reaction. 'It hurt. It's a nasty experience. You feel empty,' but on the positive side, 'Being dropped made me realise that rugby was not the be-all and end-all. I realised there was life beyond rugby, so I decided how I wanted to play and what I should concentrate on most.' The combination of that inner resolve and the positive determination to contribute to the cause, rather than hide, was symptomatic of England in 1995, and nobody embodied it more than the laughing policeman from Bedford.

If Bayfield could provide ball, England would be looking to release the explosive running lines of Mike Catt from full-back. Catt was more concerned with defence. Against France he was surprised to find 'not much pressure from the French chasers. I don't expect that to be the case in Wales. I will need to work very hard to ensure a solid defence.' The anticipated bombardment of Catt was being discussed on a more regular basis than the fifty-year-old recollections of the flattening of Dresden.

Rowell, meanwhile, played his usual mind games, attempting to transfer the burden of expectation to clearly inferior opposition. He spoke about 'the adverse history and psychology of playing in Wales for English teams'. At the same time he balanced the morale of his own side in a more upbeat manner. 'The psychology is right. This team has got pretty excited with what they have done this season. This is a big opportunity for England. Are we emerging as genuine World Cup contenders or not? I want to see sustained improvement from the forwards. The next step up for the forwards is to perceive exactly when opportunities arise for the backs.' He did not add that the backs had still to master the decision-making process. His analysis of Wales appeared to be a deliberate distortion. 'When Wales were repairing their fortunes, Neil Jenkins was asked to kick the ball, but one of the strengths of this Welsh team is that they are able to play an all-round game.' Nobody will ever know on what evidence Rowell based this assumption.

Carling maintained Rowell's 'ultimate challenge' scenario, with some justification from the perspective of England's threequarter line – they had not crossed the Welsh try-line for a decade. He admitted to his side's potential but unknowingly assented to Jonathan Davies' question-mark over their mental approach. 'We have to prove to ourselves that we have the mental stamina and going to Wales is the ultimate test of that.'

'Ultimate' was joining 'awesome' as Carling's most common adjective for the entire England party. His increasingly shrewd statements revealed a fact that was obvious, but for so long had not been understood by the England captain. 'In the past England's Achilles' heel was that we had Plan A and only Plan A. But we have had so many sessions together that I am confident we can vary our approach according to the challenge.' If they could not, the World Cup would never be achievable.

In the mind of Rory Underwood, Cardiff was a place of nightmares. Twice his blunders had cost England chances to beat the Welsh, and the memories added a sombre, poetic tone to his voice. 'It always seems to be raining and parts of the ground are gloomy because the sun does not reach some corners at all in winter.' It sounded more like Milton's description of hell. As England trained in vicious, sleeting conditions on the Friday before the match, Underwood Senior could have been forgiven for feeling apprehensive.

Neither England nor Underwood need have worried. Despite all the hype, mainly of their own making, England proceeded to win, by 23–9, at a canter. If France was a decidedly soggy 'Crunch', Wales was hardly Y Ffydriad, the Explosion, even though Rory Underwood's long-awaited brace of tries was delivered. Another thriller was spoiled by those bullying killjoys, the England pack. Fate hardly levelled the playing field – two more injuries and a sending-off did not help their cause – but, whichever fifteen men Wales picked, it was clear that they could not survive the depradations of England's unforgiving white typhoon of a pack.

Martin Bayfield did not dominate the line-outs, but when he did win ball the quality was such that England produced three tries from them. As anticipated he was also irrepressible around the park. One crumb of solace for Wales was that Bayfield once looked as cumbersome as Derwyn Jones. Despite his ungainliness, however, Jones won plenty of squandered ball for Wales. The England back row were once more 'majestic', to borrow from Jack Rowell's lexicon. Richards played a monumental role. His understanding and strength seemed to be growing with every match. Ben Clarke complemented him with a brutal display of athleticism which eclipsed Hemi Taylor to such an extent that Clarke might not have noticed that Taylor left the field after 65 minutes. Leonard and Ubogu produced bone-jarring displays, and behind the scrum Carling emphasised his revitalisation with a break which set up Rory Underwood's second try. Mike Catt again looked accomplished beyond belief and Rory Underwood finally laid his Cardiff ghost.

It was a bleak afternoon for Wales. Tony Clement and Nigel Walker left the field injured; prop John Davies departed with a red card in front of his eyes. The Welsh pack again revealed itself as a good set-piece unit – especially in the line-out, so recently a weakness – yet they did not look like scoring. In their last four internationals they had managed just one paltry try. It was a record which bears comparison with England's most sterile phases in the 1980s. People in Wales were beginning to wonder if this was more than a coincidence. Coach Alan Davies had been one of England's foremost coaches in one of their least imaginative periods. In the same era Geoff Cooke took control of a poor team and remoulded them through organisation and discipline, but it was the vision of Rowell which produced the icing. In Wales, Alan Davies had inherited an even more demoralised team and, like Cooke, he had achieved wonders by making them competitive. Somehow, in 1994–5 he appeared to have reached the ceiling of his potential and Wales looked to be trapped in a damage-limitation rut. That they were satisfied to lose games by a narrow margin suggested that the scars of the heavy beatings of the late 1980s and early 1990s remained. Behind the scrum only the talents of Robert Jones reminded supporters of better days. His excellence also showed up the holes in the scrum-half skills of Kyran Bracken. His undoubted talent and youthful looks made Bracken an agent's dream – and true to form he had signed up with one of sport's leading agents – but his pass was becoming a nightmare for Rob Andrew. A scrum-half must be fast and accurate. Bracken was picking balls from the ground, rather than flicking with his wrists, then taking two or three paces before flinging the pass away. The lack of rhythm at half-back was England's most worrying facet of play.

For the moment, Rowell was happier to muse on the many bonuses of the day. The biggest, according to him, was the man whose selection had proved his vision and courage as a coach to be of the highest order. He said of Mike Catt: 'The full-back was superb in the conditions of the day.' If Rowell was delighted with Catt, and perhaps, secretly, his own judgement, Victor Ubogu was delirious with himself. Not only had he produced another world-class performance, but he had scored his first-ever try for England. That is always one of the highlights of a player's career. In Victor's case it had financial implications as well. In the next day's *Observer* we read that Ubogu had backed himself at 18–1 to score the first try. Sadly, the £100 Victor had asked his friend to lay did not make it to the bookie's, to the mirth of the entire nation, with the likely exception of his 'friend'. Even the racing papers relished Victor's embarrassment. Ubogu was quoted as saying that there must have been money on him as earlier in the week he had been 25–1. The *Racing Post* gleefully informed the world that on match day only one bookie offered odds of less than 20–1, and Victor found him. Never let it be said that the jovial Nigerian is interested in a 'value' bet.

On a more serious note, in the context of the World Cup the overall form of Bracken was becoming a worry. So, too, was the injury collected by his team-mate Simon Shaw while playing for England A in a 33–9 victory against their Italian counterparts at Gloucester the day after the international. Damaged medial ligaments ruled him out of the tournament. It was the first serious setback for England's likely World Cup squad. One man whose hopes must have been raised was the redoubtable Nigel Redman, who emerged as the most likely replacement. It would be a deserved reward for all those squad sessions when his eyes have been dazzled by the flash of cameras aimed at others.

While England and Rory Underwood buried the demons of Cardiff, Scotland crossed their own national Styx to face France in Paris, where they had not won since 1969, when Jim Telfer scored a captain's try for victory. The selectors had announced an unchanged team for the match, although it was rumoured that the frustrating talents of Gregor Townsend had come close to the keen edge of the axe. Duncan Paterson admitted that Derek Stark and Tony Stanger had been very much in contention and there was a small amount of discussion about the possibility of fielding Scott Hastings. Events would prove it to have been one of the more productive selection meetings of recent times.

Before the match France had displayed an amazing degree of composure in the light of their sporting massacre at the battle of Twickenham. The only change was enforced: Laurent Seigne came in for the injured Laurent Benezech. Berbizier held his nerve. 'We will keep our trust in the group and we hope the team will react against Scotland.' While the coach maintained his cool, there was a tense undercurrent running through his charges. The urbane flanker Laurent

Cabannes publicly denounced the French federation in the wake of the defeat by England. 'The players are held hostage by a system which is said to be still modern because ten years ago we used to win Grand Slams,' he said. Rumours of a disciplinary dropping circulated round France. The flanker remained in the team, but even captain Philippe Saint-André admitted that he 'lost sleep over Cabannes'. Berbizier, showing his good sense, as ever, said: 'We lost against one of the strongest teams we've met in the last twenty years, and it would not be wise to change everything. We lost far too many balls. Against Scotland we must be careful not to make the same mistake.'

France might have been battered by England, but their coach hinted that the old arrogance remained. 'I do hope they will respect Scotland, because if they don't, they might get a surprise,' he warned. But he boosted them with his final statement, 'I know they are still capable of playing great rugby.'

Scotland were less impressed. Rob Wainwright sounded one of the most belligerent Scottish notes since Robert the Bruce: 'History will be made by kicking France when they are down.' He spoke of Scotland's new-found confidence. 'We must unsettle them early on, and that means knocking them back from the kick-off. We are confident we can put Jim Telfer's try into the archives.'

Wainwright's assertion looked as insubstantial as we all thought it to be when France attacked from the kick-off and, within four minutes, Philippe Saint-André scored in the corner. The fault? Gavin Hastings' positional play. France continued to attack, but, critically, in their vaunting ambition these romantics failed to heed their coach's warning not to lose too many balls. Chances were missed and Hastings atoned for his positional fault with an inspirational 52-metre penalty. Scottish hearts pumped and belief returned as Gregor Townsend found an elusive gap 60 metres from the French line. Hastings surged on before the ball babbled back to Townsend, who side-stepped beneath the posts. Further inspiration from the boot of Hastings pushed his side into a 16–11 lead on the hour.

It was then that the real drama unfolded. Scotland's efforts seemed to falter in the face of the brilliance of Sadourny and Saint-André, who each scored a coruscating try to put France 21–16 in front. Reporters were preparing their 'brave in defeat' lines when, with a mere two minutes remaining, Gregor Townsend produced a flip from a French flair textbook. Thirty-five metres from glory was the figure of Gavin Hastings. Two months earlier a nation had wanted to drop him. Five seconds later he was re-affirmed as Scotland's sporting hero. At 21–21, Hastings nervelessly slotted the simplest of conversions. Scotland had won one of the most exciting internationals in recent memory, and Jim Telfer could happily retreat into the archives.

A year earlier Hastings had wept in front of the nation after Jon Callard kicked a last-minute penalty to snatch victory from Scotland's grasp. This time it was unashamed tears of joy in the dressing-room for the eighteen-point hero. Ever the team man, Hastings said: 'I thought that was an heroic effort by the team. We never gave in and I'm very proud of everyone. We showed just why we had been confident.' He ranked the win alongside the defeat of England in the Grand Slam decider in 1990 – it was that great a victory. Scotland returned to the pitch to salute their adoring public.

There was a typical piece of Gallic philosophy from Philippe Saint-André. An enquiring Scottish journalist asked if Scotland could beat England. He shrugged. 'Why not?' The only scar for the Scots was the injuries to Ian Jardine and Damian Cronin. Jardine, who played a beautifully organised game in the centre, fractured a cheekbone in the dying minutes, while Cronin ruptured a tendon in his elbow. Neither would be fit for the rest of the Five Nations. Hastings bore the setback with a smile for the wise journalists who had mocked the Scots' pre-match assurances. 'This sort of victory creates a different sort of pressure on us. It will be an even greater challenge against Wales in a fortnight. Confidence builds quickly when you win, and we go forward now with a lot of confidence.'

Berbizier's poise nearly lasted to the end of an inquisitorial press conference. Talk of 24 June seemed vainglorious in the wake of this disastrous defeat. His side had failed to retain possession; their much-vaunted back row had been outplayed by the rookie unit of Morrison, Peters and Wainwright; Accoceberry and Deylaud had shrunk almost to non-existence in terms of confidence. Even Sella had looked old. Only Saint-André and Sadourny looked capable of performing at the highest level. Berbizier was asked if France had any chance in South Africa after the two debacles. 'Of course we can still get to the World Cup final in June – after rain always comes fine weather.' Perhaps – but this was more of an electric storm than a refreshing shower. When asked who would win the Five Nations, he snapped, 'I don't give a damn.' Another coach was under pressure.

1a. On top of the world – Kobus Wiese demonstrates the art of the lift in the South Africa - Barbarians clash. The Springboks lost this match, but Wiese and his colleagues were still above the rest of the world when it mattered in June.

1b. Gareth Llewellyn proves that the Welsh line-out can reach the heights too. Yet their line-out excellence against the Springboks failed to lay the foundation for anything more than another honourable defeat. Wales were rarely to stay at even that modest level.

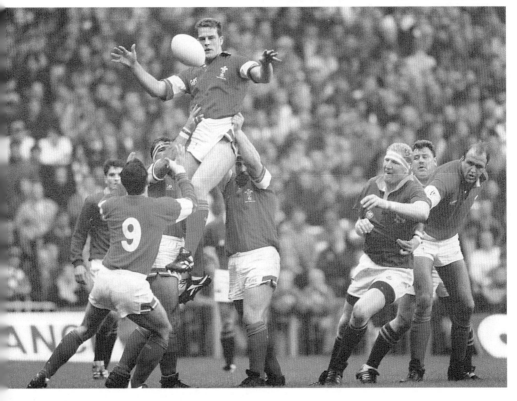

2a. Leicester hooker Richard Cockerill celebrates the end of Bath's four-year monopoly as England's champion club. It was a view that most neutrals, tired of the Bath stranglehold, shared.

2b. Unbridled joy as Brian Moore avoids the ignominy of leading Harlequins into the Second Division. The rest of the public greeted their survival with about as much glee as Northampton's scrum-half, Matt Dawson, displays.

3a. Not even the forces of Good can penetrate Bath at Twickenham. Wasps' flying theologian Damian Hopley is lassoed by Phil de Glanville.

3b. A Swift farewell. The oldest winger in town signed off with a superb performance in Bath's final triumph. The hat did not suit him.

4a. 'Spot, line, follow-through.' Dave 'Adidas' Alred shows Rob Andrew how it's done. Andrew nearly proved that practice makes perfect in the autumn campaign.

4b. Rugby is a religion in Wales. When you are national coach of a losing team the nation crucifies you. Davies' cross was too much to bear.

4c. The enigma on the outside. Jack Rowell contemplates the race against time in his bid to create a style to rule the world.

5a. Olivier Merle. Would you want this man as your school-teacher? The French second row provoked a storm in the British media by headbutting Ricky Evans during the Welsh clash in January. Upsetting people can be a thirsty business: why else would a second row drink water?

5b. Monsieur Merle dismisses the virtues of healthy living as he contemplates life as a pariah. 'I spit on the xenophobia of the British.'

6a, b+c. *Opposite:* The battles of Hastings culminate in one of the great Scotland triumphs in Paris. Hastings was the hero, but the subtle skills of Gregor Townsend were badly missed in South Africa.

7a, b+c. England's Grand Slam triumph. The men with the famous faces. Dean Richards (*top*), the tactical brains in the side; Rob Andrew, Tony Underwood and Jerry Guscott, the pretty faces; and the captain himself, Will Carling, the pied piper of the masses.

8a. Strained relations. This became a Will Carling specialisation both inside and outside the game. Dennis Easby now believes that their relationship will be stronger than ever, although Carling seems less than impressed with a bad odour that pervaded the air at this press conference.

8b+c. Shoeless Vic has the style to match the car. Rugby Union's first front-row playboy contemplates life in the fast lane. The famous red Versace jeans did not go with the car.

14

At Least Football Managers are Paid . . .

As the last two Saturdays of the Five Nations Championship loomed, the generals marshalled their troops for a renewed push in this arena of the war. Wales did not panic after the defeat by England. The team announced to play Scotland had four changes, three of them predictable. Wayne Proctor returned for the injured Nigel Walker, Mike Hall was recalled for Mark Taylor and Matthew Back of Bridgend was selected for his first start in a Welsh shirt. The one shock was the selection of Spencer John, the twenty-one-year-old Llanelli prop forward. His reaction to the news was a heart-warming reminder of how special a first international cap remains, especially to a Welshman. 'I thought it was just one big wind-up when my mum told me,' he said. The image of a giant prop forward sitting in his bedroom with his mother calling up the stairs, 'Mr Norster is on the phone for you,' cannot fail to bring a smile to any sports lover.

There were fewer smiles in France as the guillotine was dusted off at last. Olivier Merle returned for Roumat, a decision Rowell thought would strengthen France; Cabannes exited in favour of one of rugby's warhorses, Marc Cecillon. Sadly, the Tramp, otherwise known as Christophe Deylaud, was dropped. We had not seen the 'real Deylaud' as Berbizier had promised after France's opening match. His replacement was the hugely talented youngster Yann Delaigue, one of the many Frenchmen who explode on to the world stage and then inexplicably disappear. Thirty-three-year-old Franck Mesnel returned for Lacroix and Louis Armary made his comeback to solidify the scrum at the grand age of thirty-four. It was hardly long-term planning, but Berbizier's view was that France were not going to start discovering new talent with three months to go to the World Cup. He probably also guessed that the credit from the series win in New Zealand in the summer had run out. Defeat in Ireland could have been seeing Berbizier in south-west France instead of South Africa in May and June. Hence the recall of his trusty old guard.

Ireland's team to meet France contained the selection shock of the season: the golden boy, hooker Keith Wood, was dropped. Ireland were unhappy with his basics, but when men like Bob Dwyer and Jack Rowell rave about him it is hard not to wonder what Ireland thought they were doing. More predictably, Eric Elwood returned to kick the points. The Irish experiment with youth was over.

The one side who remained unchanged were England. Given such continuity, it was no surprise that the bookmakers made them 1–6 favourites for the Grand Slam. Scotland were only 6–1 at this stage, a world away from the generous 50–1, 66–1 and 100–1 available in the New Year.

On the club scene, Neil Jenkins became the first man to pass 1,000 points in the Heineken Leagues. The sponsors presented him with 1,000 cans of their brew in recognition of his achievement. If only his handling of a threequarter line possessed as much fizz as all that lager. Meanwhile, in England Jon Hall announced that he would retire at the end of the season as expected, but not before leading Bath to a comfortable quarter-final victory against Northampton in the Pilkington Cup. His coach Brian Ashton described him as 'a massive man – one of the greatest English players since the war'. Few experts would disagree.

In the other quarter-finals, Harlequins beat Wakefield 13–8, Wasps went through by 31–0 at Exeter, and Leicester scraped home 14–12 at Sale. The Leicester–Sale tie ended in controversy when, minutes from full-time, Steve Lander, one of England's nominated World Cup referees, gave the Tigers a penalty for a collapsed scrum 15 metres from Sale's line. Common sense suggested that even the most stupid front-row forward would not drop a scrum at such a critical time. The resultant three points won Leicester the game. Sky's studio guest at Sale, the volatile former Sale and England scrum-half Steve Smith, suggested that Mr Lander should consider hanging himself. It was colourful television, but it did not amuse the RFU.

Jack Rowell, for his part, was not amused by a semi-final draw that sent Bath away (their ninth consecutive away draw in the series) to Harlequins and paired Leicester with Wasps. There were likely to be far too many of the World Cup squad in Cup final action for the selectors' comfort.

For Rowell and his fellow coaches, Shakespeare's warning about the ides of March had a contemporary ring to it. Of those latterday Caesars of the Five Nations tournament, Rowell and Scotland's Doug Morgan had already achieved enough to plan their summer around South Africa, but others must have sensed the sharpening knives among their respective committees and federations. Gerry Murphy had guided Ireland to a pair of defeats; Pierre Berbizier's extravagant 'roads to the World Cup' seemed to be leading nowhere and, worst of all, under Alan Davies, the most demanding and introspective of all rugby nations, Wales, had lost three consecutive games without seriously threatening their opponents' try-line.

The Welsh management trotted out the familiar excuses, all of which had some validity. The players were under too much pressure; Robert Norster declared that the Welsh public should 'get off their backs – all the criticism doesn't help the team's performance'. Six thousand Welshmen were to travel to Edinburgh on the first Saturday in March. Such a monumental Celtic migration undoubtedly made it difficult to 'get the players to relax and enjoy it', which Norster described as a primary function of the manager. The 'absolutely staggering' injury list should be taken into consideration by the less than adoring public, as should the fact that the three defeats had been against South Africa, France and England, all major world powers. Yet Wales had played with no imagination and, in their two victories, over Romania and Italy, they had failed to impress. These inescapable facts rendered Norster's claim that 'all you need is a little rub of the green', because 'we've shown that we are capable of beating sides like South Africa, France and England', fanciful in the extreme.

Norster may have been implying that, with the boost provided by the returning players and the tougher games already played, things could only get better. Scotland's Parisian triumph and the fresh memories of the previous Murrayfield encounter between the two sides convinced the players to expect no respite. Gareth Llewellyn recalled the 20–0 beating. 'They didn't just beat us at rugby, they gave us a good kicking as well. They really went to town on us and I've been told they are rucking quite ferociously this season. That means it will be as hard as it was two years ago.' Alan Davies boldly stated on the eve of the match: 'I do not think there is much between any team in this year's Championship.' From the wine bars of Toulouse to the boozers of Twickenham, the sound of laughter filled the air. But it was pride that filled Wales' dignified captain, Ieuan Evans, as he was to join J.P.R. Williams, Gareth Edwards and Robert Jones in the Fifty-Cap Club. Evans recognised that Wales would have to overcome Scotland's granite captain, Gavin Hastings, if they were to resume what he called their 'winning habits'. His generosity towards opponents has always typified the fraternity of Rugby Union. 'Gavin has been the rock of so many Scottish and Lions victories over most of the last decade.' The strength of his voice reiterated the honesty and affection of his words.

His was not the only voice being raised in praise of the man Scotland had nearly dethroned before Christmas. Hastings' former Scotland and Lions coach, Ian McGeechan, doubtless delighted to talk about winners from his depressing position in Northampton, added: 'Gavin Hastings' role in the resurgence cannot be overstated. He's led from the front, he's kicked goals and scored vital tries, and he's playing with such confidence. I think Scotland's success can be directly linked to Hastings' contribution.'

Scotland's captain would be rejoined by a familiar face for the Welsh international: brother Scott was recalled in place of the injured Ian Jardine. If Scotland would miss the unfussy role that Jardine had played in his country's recovery, the infectious enthusiasm of Hastings Junior would keep their mood buoyant. All uncomplicated smiles, he admitted, 'I've fifty-one caps but I feel like the new boy again.'

Undoubtedly Scotland's confidence made them favourites, but a side that has recent memories of nine consecutive defeats has far too many nightmares to fall into the lair of complacency. Gavin Hastings warned his team about the likely ferocity of the Welsh start while Scotland's coach, the once unsmiling Doug Morgan, emphasised that any side featuring players of the quality of Ieuan Evans, Robert Jones, Gareth Llewellyn and Derwyn Jones must be good. That was an opinion reiterated by Jack Rowell and others throughout the season. It was bound to throw question-marks in the direction of the Welsh management if performances could not match their billing.

Barely had Hastings delivered his warning before the 6,000 travelling Celts began planning the taking of Edinburgh. Clearly Hastings was a better player than he was a lecturer, or his class were far from the top stream. The howls of derision in Toulouse and Twickenham became startled chokes on Ricard and bitter as Wales made the start of the season. Scotland gave away a penalty and Neil Jenkins stroked the ball to their 22. The ensuing line-out saw Derwyn Jones stretch to Olympus for a clean catch, as if to justify the praise of Doug Morgan and Jack Rowell, and Wales released the bullish Emyr Lewis into Scotland's midfield. Gregor Townsend showed rather too great an inclination to drift in defence and Lewis stormed to within 5 metres of Scotland's line. The Welsh pack rucked with collective vigour; Gavin Hastings scampered left to defend against the Welsh backs and up popped the ball for Robert Jones to gather, barely breaking his stride, and deposit between Scotland's posts. The long wait was over. Wales had not scored a try in three internationals, but in the fourth it took less than three minutes. How appropriate that it was scored by the one Welsh back who impressed everyone, Robert Jones.

So it was 7–0 to Wales in the opening minutes. In the Sky studio I scratched my head and wondered how bad France could be. If Scotland's rugby team were athletes, they would have little future over 100 metres. Against France they had stumbled out of their blocks, conceding an early lead; at Murrayfield there was no confirmation that the side were even out of the changing-room by the time Neil Jenkins kicked his simple conversion.

Whereas in Paris Scotland's response had been emphatic, Gavin Hastings cleanly striking a 50-metre penalty, on this occasion he missed two eminently kickable opportunities. The omens were looking better for the Welsh – once they could quell the pace of Scotland's pack. Despite 6,000 prayers they never managed this feat. Scotland's pack handed them a beating every bit as severe as the one inflicted by England. The England pack broke Wales through power; Scotland's weapon was pace. Stewart Campbell and Doddie Weir, both potential understudies for Damian Cronin and Andy Reed, more than matched Llewellyn and Jones and the result was a game played at a cracking speed. Wales arrived upright and in dribbles to loose ball; Scotland low, hard and united. The vision of Jim Telfer and his rucking stick sprang to mind. In training, Telfer had a habit of forcing his players to run beneath his stick as they attacked the ruck; anybody too upright would hit it and receive a fearsome whack. It was a humane version of the disgraceful barbed-wire fences with which showjumping horses are reputedly trained.

The Scottish pack maintained field position like an army defending its capital, and Hastings found his sniper's range. After twenty-five minutes they had clawed their way back to 6–7; by half-time they had charged into a 20–7 lead, effectively killing the contest. Scotland's superior organisation was evident for seventy-eight and a half minutes, but it was the brief spell before half-time that illustrated the critical psychological difference between the teams. Scotland, so often denigrated as the kick-and-rush merchants of international rugby, found a loose Welsh tactical kick bouncing on their 22-metre line. Rob Wainwright picked it up and passed to Hastings. He had aeons of time to plant a kick back to halfway. Instead he looked up and measured the Welsh defence. There was space to his left and he passed – to Doddie Weir. That was real confidence! Weir did not disappoint, showing a pair of centre's hands to release Kenny Logan against Garin Jenkins. He skipped mockingly outside Wales' bellicose hooker, inside Robert Jones and headed towards the Welsh line. Defence finally arrived, but so did Eric Peters on his inside, and the man-boy of international rugby lost the 'boy' half of his label as he strode 20 metres for a try which was greeted by the loudest cheer Hastings can remember.

Six minutes later, Scotland's pack produced an almost exact replica of an English driving maul, with another Bath player, David Hilton, the lucky man to cross the line. Eric Peters, known ironically in Bath as

McNasty because of his placid temperament, and McChop, the butcher from Bedminster, Bristol, would reflect how far and how fast they had travelled since joining Bath under the tutelage of Jack Rowell.

The second half did not produce the excitement of the first. Scotland sensed they had done enough to win the match, and when Wales did rally, Hastings would retaliate with the boot. It brought him another sixteen-point tally and, more importantly for Scotland, another impressive victory, by 26–13.

Scotland had made the long journey from 100–1 to 5–2 for the Grand Slam. England remained hot favourites at 1–4. Rowell would not be able to make his opponents favourites at Twickenham and England would have to face the sort of test Scotland had overcome against Wales. 'Wales presented us with a new challenge,' said Hastings after the Murrayfield win. 'Nobody expected us to win in Paris, but today we were expected to win. Now that's behind us we can look forward to Twickenham.' His fifty points had guided them to the Grand Slam encounter, but the immense confidence generated by a string of victories was another huge contributory factor. Hastings confirmed the role of this most vital of allies in the wonderful Eric Peters try. 'If we hadn't won our last three games in the way we have, I am sure we would have kicked that ball to touch rather than running it back at them.'

As Scotland, armed with their confidence, prepared to take the high road to Twickenham in their bid for an unlikely Grand Slam, Wales slunk back to Cardiff for the wooden spoon decider with Ireland, no longer burdened with the necessity to defend their status as Five Nations champions. Scotland had played with abundant pride and pace; Wales looked a lost and aimless ragged army. Rumours linking Neil Jenkins with Wigan Rugby League Club persisted, but it was hard to see why. As Wales retreated from another metaphorical massacre, Jenkins was not so much a Napoleon leading the retreat from Moscow as just another rank-and-file broken spirit. On the field the fly-half should marshal his side. Jenkins looked like a lost soul away from Pontypridd. The pack did not breathe the traditional fire of the Welsh dragon as St Andrew joined St George in putting them to the sword.

Alan Davies' earlier assertion that there was little to separate the competing teams in the tournament looked like the desperate last throw of a gambler. Despite having seen the roulette ball claim his last chip in Edinburgh, he was able to face defeat with integrity and honesty. 'We were comprehensively beaten in all phases of the game. Full credit to the Scots. We are in desperate need of a confidence boost.' Neither could Robert Norster suppress the reality of this dire situation. 'We regressed a bit today and I think we lost a bit of self-belief. Our match at home to Ireland is now doubly important.'

The Welsh squad and management were not the only rugby people under pressure. Neither Ireland nor France were exactly delighting their respective unions. Ireland, like Wales, had not won a match so far and France had lost two out of three from a base camp that was pitched halfway towards the top of the world before the Championship had even started. Berbizier's men were back in the foothills for their decider. Defeat against Ireland would probably result in the absence of Berbizier and Laporte in South Africa. It would be a bitter blow to the journalistic fraternity, who thoroughly enjoyed their refreshing wit and honesty, not always among the most obvious characteristics of international sports managers.

France were certainly more low-key in their approach. The trace of arrogance that Berbizier had introduced to the pages of our press before the tournament had been overcome by the smoke from the cannons with which Scotland and England had blown France apart. His moralising about the lack of positive rugby emanating from Britain no longer prevailed. An irate French national press questioned the recall of six ageing players to face Ireland. Guy Laporte spoke for Berbizier as well as himself when he replied: 'The six changes we made were specifically for the sort of match we expect to play in Dublin, where you have to keep it tight, as England showed.' The teachers had openly espoused the philosophy of the pupils. How Jack Rowell's eyes must have glinted in malevolent glee. The school of subtle diplomacy was also burned to the ground by Berbizier. He might have gained an edge in tact over England by dropping Merle after the Welsh match, but for this game all he wanted was a result to steady a boat which was close to sinking. Like Rowell, he believed Merle had a role to play in France's best team. 'Merle is a first-choice player and it is good to have him back.' Merle, in his other life a social worker dealing with juvenile delinquents, is clearly not the ogre many have portrayed him as, although I suspect few of the youngsters in his charge would like to face the potential repercussions of his behaviour. Merle admitted: 'I did something wrong, but there's no need to go on and on about it.'

Merle had been recalled to help France tighten their game and apply more consistent pressure, but there was real doubt over their ability to convert pressure into points without Thierry Lacroix. There is an appealing charm in the idea of selecting a national team first and then finding a goal-kicker. To be a slave to a kicker can be debilitating, as Wales seemed determined to prove, but to stroll on to the pitch for an international without one is quixotic in the extreme. It illustrates both why a French World Cup triumph appeals to sport's more romantic elements, and, sadly, why the side seemed unlikely to reach that level. Flair is a vital commodity, but efficiency is even more of a priority. England had an abundance of the latter and were frantically trying to release the former, but the French had no balance.

In the week prior to an England international Rob Andrew will spend up to seven or eight hours practising his goal-kicking in the pursuit of perfection. France's best selected kicker was probably Yann Delaigue, but the management wanted their young fly-half to concern himself with the overall demands of the position. The kicking duties fell to the lithe Toulouse winger Emile Ntamack, not even first-choice kicker for his club. Laporte thought the matter serious enough to spend thirty minutes with him to help him practise his kicking on the Wednesday before the game. Nothing could demonstrate more lucidly why England were on the threshold of another Grand Slam and France on the threshold of the abyss.

Pierre Berbizier was in no mood to pull any punches before the match. 'We haven't met our goals in this tournament. It's a failure and everybody is responsible for it, including myself. Now we must put a halt to this mess and get back to work. I still believe we have the right to be ambitious.' Le Petit General's ambitions would be pounded and left in the dirt of Dublin if his side could not finish the season with a victory. That was why age became irrelevant. He needed players with appetite, and as the thirty-three-year-old Franck Mesnel said, 'I haven't played for France for two and a half years and I'm hungry.'

Ireland had not shirked from recalling veterans, either. Keith Wood, blessed by one of rugby's most respected voices, Bob Dwyer, had been omitted for Terry Kingston, who would be in a position to travel for a third World Cup. The news was good for Kingston, but it questioned the vision of this ailing rugby nation. Irish hopes were not lifted by the withdrawal of Ben Cronin through injury. The lack of depth to Irish rugby was illustrated by the call-up of Davy Tweed of Ballymena for his first cap at the grand age of thirty-five. It did not matter to Tweed that he was joining a side in terrible trouble – it was his chance to represent his country. Consider a Ballymena man travelling to Dublin for that honour and the not inconsiderable healing strengths of sport are validated. His selection resulted in the move of Paddy Johns from second row to No. 8 – until the day before the match, that is. He, too, was forced to withdraw through injury and Eddie Halvey of Shannon, Ireland's champion club, earned a late debut cap. Across the Irish Sea there is a romantic fallacy that the 'good old Irish' do not take their rugby too seriously. Gerry Murphy, another beleaguered coach, scotched this nonsense on the day before the game. 'If you see me hanging from a goalpost you know something has happened.' I assumed that he was not referring to an Ireland victory. Unnerved by his suicidal tone, I was relieved to see nothing but a lick of paint on the Lansdowne

Road goalposts after Ireland had fallen to their twelfth consecutive defeat at the hands of France. Gerry Murphy did not hang himself and Pierre Berbizier would be aboard an aeroplane bound for South Africa.

France proved to be as good as their word – and nearly as efficient as their English masters. The game was played in a far tighter context. They did not move first-phase ball wide with grand ambition and lateral direction; instead the pack maintained a tight cohesive drive and Franck Mesnel played the role of a highly efficient battering-ram. He crossed the gain-line and remained on his feet. This allowed France to unleash their giant back row of Cecillon, Benazzi and Benetton, whose role was to charge into the Irish midfield before releasing France's elusive strike force. This tactic, which mirrored England's approach, was based on gradual corrosion rather than incision. In the first half Ireland held on, and only one try was scored, by Emile Ntamack, but France's glittering potential revealed itself from the re-start. The forwards, imperiously driven on by Jean-Michel Gonzalez, merged with the backs to create a dazzling try for Yann Delaigue. Ntamack's conversion was among the worst attempts of recent times. But another recalled player, Marc Cecillon, pounded over the try-line after a French forward surge and Ireland were in disarray.

The siege was briefly lifted by Simon Geoghegan, who found the Achilles' heel of the admirable Philippe Saint-André. He outpaced the French captain on the turn just as Tony Underwood had done at Twickenham. In theory Ireland had a chance, but Bradley and Elwood failed to offer any shape at half-back and it was no surprise that France scored two late tries to clinch a conclusive win by 25–7. Ntamack scored a second, and, appropriately, Saint-André added another. He had been the most impressive threequarter of the Championship. His fellow winger Emile Ntamack had proved himself the worst kicker of the Championship, leaving France with severe problems as they prepared for the World Cup. In the short term, however, relief at victory over-whelmed concerns for the South Africa. Guy Laporte, himself a great kicker in his prime, covered up the inadequacies in this area by claiming 'Ntamack kicked the two we needed.'

Berbizier's gratitude was obvious. 'In a way, this was the first match of the World Cup. I'm still convinced that this team is not so far removed from England. The main difference is that they are more con-sistent than we are.' England's level of ball-retention and goal-kicking were also 'slightly' better – with his relief finally came some justifiable kidology.

For Ireland just a visit to Cardiff remained, and few scraps of conso-lation can have been drawn from their loss. The one man who played with courage and not inconsiderable skill throughout was Davy Tweed.

Even in defeat this big man would remember 4 March for the rest of his life. Gerry Murphy was left to reflect that, with three failures each in the Championship, either he or Alan Davies would be counting the days to the end of life as an international coach.

15

Grand Slams and Bullets

W ith little more than two months to go to the World Cup, players and managements alike dreamed, with varying degrees of justi-fication, of becoming the champions of the world. But before the thoughts at the backs of their minds could be brought to the forefront, the small matter of which team would go to South Africa as champions of the northern hemisphere remained to be settled. So, too, did the less palatable question of who would travel as Five Nations losers. While England and Scotland licked their lips at the prospect of the multiple prizes of Championship, Grand Slam, Triple Crown and Calcutta Cup there for the taking on 18 March, Alan Davies of Wales and Gerry Murphy of Ireland contemplated the possibility of early retirement.

At least Murphy was spared the claustrophobic pressure that so burdens the Welsh camp. In Ireland there is always Jack Charlton, Gaelic football and hurling to divert disappointed sporting minds. Wales had a football team that were ground-breaking in terms of the woeful results that left them anchored among the worst sides in Europe. 'Wales is like a big village in rugby terms and things can get a bit too intense,' confirmed Norster in the wake of the Scottish defeat. The absence of any originality in the team had hardly helped the mood in the Principality. Wales had been understandably disappointed with the drive and mobility of their forwards in Edinburgh. Andrew Gibbs of Newbridge replaced Hemi Taylor of Cardiff and New Zealand, while the controversial decision was the recall of veteran forward Phil Davies instead of the Celtic beanpole Derwyn Jones. That and the reinstatement of Tony Clement for Matthew Back would provide the stimulus for knives to be drawn. Davies' choice reflected the short-term need to obtain a result, but in the long term it was a mistake which would hurt the selectors more than the players. The dropping of Jones was the only selection decision to challenge Ireland's treatment of Keith Wood as the most ill-judged of the Championship.

Ieuan Evans remained in determined heart, however. 'We have to prove to the public we aren't as bad a team as the results suggest,' he said.

They also had to convince the more dangerous sceptics within the ranks of the Welsh Rugby Union. Norster proclaimed that the side were 'looking forward to the opportunity on Saturday to get back to their best'. The articulate and honest utterances of Alan Davies implied that the coaches needed the win even more than the players. 'It's obvious that the performance of the coach is reflected by the performance of the team. You have to accept that. But it has not affected my confidence as a coach. You always accept the fact that if the team plays well, the players get the credit; if they play badly the coach gets blamed. The players can relax knowing they will be in the next team. I'm the one who's going to get the bullet if we lose.' His last comment revealed the sort of vision that his side had desperately lacked on the field throughout their autumn and winter campaigns.

Davies might have been depressed with the form of his team, but he could not criticise their loyalty. Of all the Welsh players, Robert Jones had the most reason to resent Davies, whose conservative strategies had cost the scrum-half countless caps as the lesser talents of Rupert Moon found favour in Wales. Yet even Jones stood firm behind the coach. 'Everyone is aware of the pressure Alan is under. He doesn't transmit it to the players, but he must be feeling it.' Jones also spoke of the rumours ringing round the valleys. 'I've heard people say he should go now, but to drop him before the World Cup would be a crazy decision. We are going out to win for a number of reasons, but one of them is for the management.' Clearly, Davies was more popular with the players than with the WRU.

Ireland could prepare for Cardiff with a degree more confidence, despite their equally atrocious season. Of their previous five Arms Park encounters, they had won four and drawn one. The psychological grip of a particular fixture is one of the mysteries of sport, and for some reason in Five Nations rugby these mental blocks seem even more prevalent than elsewhere. England and Scotland had laid the respective ghosts of Cardiff and Parc des Princes, but Wales' appalling record in Scotland had continued. Cardiff would be a test of Welsh, rather than Irish, nerve. Yet evidence of panic could be discerned from the decisions of the Irish selectors. Michael Bradley, the much-criticised scrum-half and captain, finally paid the price for a service far less smooth than the affable man himself. Niall Hogan was given another chance to atone for his disastrous debut in January. The axing of Bradley was a terrible blow for Keith Wood as well. Terry Kingston, who had replaced him against France, was now appointed captain to boot. It slammed the door in the face of Wood's World Cup chances. Behind the scrum, the choice of

Richard Wallace to replace Niall Woods and Jonathan Bell's return in place of Phil Danaher were more logical.

Ireland's immediate hopes were further dashed when Jonathan Bell (again) and Denis McBride withdrew the day before the match. Danaher and Halvey returned. Welsh hopes, too, nose-dived when Tony Clement cried off on the morning of the game. Gerry Murphy, having decided not to hang himself after the French defeat, even sounded a note of optimism on the Friday. 'I believe if we play like we are capable of we will win.' Ireland spoke of their capability, the Welsh talked of their need. It was a sign of an almost uncontrollable tension within Davies' squad.

The match itself was a stagnant affair. The mystique of Cardiff was replaced by mundane mediocrity, and only watching New Zealanders and Japanese can have enjoyed the sad spectacle. It was the sort of game that made me wonder what price Japan to finish second behind New Zealand in their group. If this was the best Wales could offer, they deserved to be based in Bloemfontein. They played without any confidence and as if paralysed by fear. The only moment that merited a mention as worthy of an international rugby match was Ireland's try, which was created by a combination of Richard Wallace's pace and poor Welsh defence. Brendan Mullin, Ireland's record try-scorer, finished it off. There was nothing else to celebrate. Once again Wales relied solely on Neil Jenkins' boot, and once again Jenkins failed to offer Wales any direction or variety. He can run, pass and kick but he cannot read the game. He had not grown into the Welsh No. 10 shirt. Victory by 16-12 was greeted with relief, rather than ecstasy, by the Irish. Gerry Murphy admitted that neutrals would be asking for their money back.

Wales had been incapable of providing the win needed to stabilise the future of their management. Even as the final whistle brought down the curtain on one of the saddest days for Welsh rugby, the WRU committee were preparing to don their togas and pick up their knives. Davies, even in defeat, sounded defiant. He vowed to fight on as coach, adding, 'I would hope there is no immediate threat to my position.' If his claim that there was little gap between the Championship teams had been wishful thinking, this was complete fantasy. The dark cloud of gathering vultures grew on the Monday after the debacle. Edward Jones, the WRU secretary, announced that Wales would delay the selection of their World Cup squad in order to allow the general committee to consider 'recent performances by the national side'. The pressure intensified as J.P.R. Williams and Geoff Evans, two of Wales' selection advisers, announced their resignations. Both were unhappy about the dismissal of Derwyn Jones. Even worse, having left the selection meeting early, they did not find out that Tony Clement had been recalled until they read the news in the papers the next day.

It is hard not to sympathise with Davies. He was the man in the paid and pressurised position – as he said, it was he who received the brick-bats in defeat – yet the WRU had appointed 'advisers', with no responsibility, to assist him. Critics could argue that tactically Davies made mistakes, but in the structure they adopted the WRU seemed intent on hindering rather than helping the man. Davies wanted to re-organise the crumbling edifice of Welsh rugby in order to strengthen the worn apex that was currently the national team. That aim stepped on too many toes and on too much self-interest within the administration of the game. There was a feeling that his paymasters were waiting for his fall.

Davies continued to play his cards with a straight face. 'I have been informed by the WRU that they don't wish the selectors to meet this week to choose the World Cup party. I am waiting to hear further when they wish us to proceed.' It looked as if he was waiting to be pushed. On the Tuesday after the international, one of the much-touted possible successors to Davies, Cardiff's Australian coach Alex Evans, signed a new one-year contract with his club, apparently ending 'speculation that he was being lined up as the next Welsh coach'. One week later Davies looked at the glint of steel surrounding him and resigned. The WRU had rid themselves of him without bloodshed. His management partner, Robert Norster, was left with no option but to exit left.

Their replacements were Cardiff's Alex Evans, as coach, in spite of signals to the contrary; Mike Ruddock and Dennis John (coaches of Swansea and Pontypridd respectively) as his assistants and Geoff Evans as manager. Alex Evans had clearly left the Cardiff ship at a fortuitous time, and not surprisingly, he was in upbeat mood. 'I think there is a fantastic amount of ability in Wales, and there is no reason why they should not do well in South Africa.' He had made a poor Cardiff team into likely Welsh champions, but to make this demoralised Welsh side into world-beaters looked like a trick beyond Houdini.

Alan Davies, meanwhile, voiced the pain of leading a poor side in a fanatical land. Whatever the turmoils of the club coaches such as Barry Taylor and Barrie Corless, this was a real pressure point. He was uncertain of his willingness to coach again. 'I very much doubt I will put myself or my family through that agony again.' An exile in Nottingham for so long, he saw with the clarity of the outside observer the myriad problems besetting Welsh rugby. 'Some of the things I learned coming back to Wales were things I knew as a boy. There is far too much infighting and chapel rivalry. What we have to do is pull together and try to drive the country forward. England and Scotland had settled sides, but Ireland and Wales were bedevilled by injuries.' It was a lame excuse – Scotland had lost Sharp, Reed, Cronin, Nicol and Jardine, yet still achieved stirring feats. Wales' problems were beyond those of the physiotherapist's table. One man Davies singled out was Mike Rayer. His loss had been a blow, not only to himself and Wales, but to the rugby world. A wonderful counter-attacker, Rayer also has a ready line in wit. He joined the players in their 'wake' after the defeat by Ireland. They sat in understandable silence until Rayer mused, 'All that's left is the Graham Taylor documentary.' He was right. It was not the end of the world. Not quite.

An evaluation of Davies has parallels with the story of Icarus. As Welsh manager he had a specific role. In order to improve the quality of players he unfortunately exceeded his remit and tried to reform Welsh rugby. From that moment onwards he was doomed: the WRU thought he flew too high. It was the antagonism he stimulated within the highest circles of the WRU that led to his downfall, not Wales' barren season. After all, he had taken an almost lifeless carcass and regenerated it to transform Wales into Five Nations champions in 1994. In 1995 he did have some legitimate excuses, but it would be wrong to absolve him completely. Injuries or not, Wales were a negative side. They were efficient in the set pieces, they were generally organised defensively and they worked for one another, but what they lacked was vision, the spark that ignites the fuse and creates celestial rugby. Davies, like Geoff Cooke, with whom he briefly worked with England, was too structured and too rigid a coach. It could work up to a certain level, but not the highest one. Davies lacked the inspiration himself to inspire greatness. Like Cooke, he should take great credit for his early work, but Wales, like England, needed another dimension to advance further. By the end of the Five Nations Championship Jack Rowell had proved he was that man for England; Wales were praying that Alex Evans could do likewise for them.

Jack Rowell had supplied England with the opportunity to expand their game. Their cohesive blend of pace and power left them on the verge of the Grand Slam and a mighty morale boost for the World Cup. Predictably, England had announced an unchanged side for the Calcutta Cup game, and their run of rude health had been a major bonus in the development of the side. One interesting addition to the twenty-one was Paul Hull, previously frozen out by Mike Catt. His inclusion in the squad preparation for South Africa must have convinced him that his name had been pencilled in for the World Cup.

England must have been impressed by Scotland's performance against Wales, full of the traditional national characteristics of fire and brimstone but occasionally laced with an attractive touch of adventure. As ever Jack Rowell was full of praise for the opposition, but for once it was justified. 'They are on a roll and the performance is greater than the sum of the parts. They are collective and are in the job together. They look sharp and they know what they are doing,' he said. Rowell is a man who will compare himself and his sides with famous predecessors. Such was his success at Bath that this was the only method he had of gauging the evolution of his side. In his quest for advancement he often cited the improved form of traditional rival clubs. It was a comforting way of convincing himself and his team that another victory would be unarguable proof of their development. Rowell was not to change the habits of a lifetime as he prepared for a Grand Slam decider. 'Scotland kick and chase better than anyone, but they are using their backs effectively and I believe that the pack is playing as well as ever – better than in 1990.' The message was clear: this will be a highly prized Grand Slam. If he were a racehorse trainer every Classic winner he trained would have raced in a vintage year.

Will Carling, meanwhile, had other reasons for wanting to grasp a third Grand Slam title, not least among them revenge. In 1990 England had been firm favourites to trample the flower of Scotland into the dirt of Murrayfield. Carling was perceived in some patriotic pages as a new golden St George, which placed a ridiculous pressure on both England and the captain. When England's wheels came off, the hyperbole was replaced by glowering criticism. Carling's tactical naïvety had always been a gossip point in rugby circles, but it was defeat in Edinburgh that resulted in the first widespread criticism of the man. Carling has many strengths, but a thick skin is not one of them, and the memory burned. Scotland, and Gavin Hastings in particular, became more than a simple traditional foe, especially when Carling lost the Lions captaincy to Hastings in 1993. Clearly he thought the Scot had been coach Ian McGeechan's choice, but he rarely reflected on others' perception that he, too, had a powerful benefactor in Geoff Cooke, manager of the Lions. Thus there developed a personal rivalry between two of rugby's highest-profile personalities – it even made the gossip columns, celebrity indeed for rugby players. As early as seventeen days before the Twickenham match Carling was commenting on the impending collision. 'We learned a lot [from 1990] and it hurt,' he said. 'I hope a little bit of the hurt will carry on for the five of us who are still in the team and give a little extra edge to our play.'

He indicated that one of the most painful lessons was that of humility. 'Perhaps England's weakness has been when we are perceived to be favourites, as we were in 1990.' That year again. Certainly, the arrogance that seemed to haunt some of England's squads between 1989 and 1991 appeared to have been consigned to history by the 1995 side. Ben Clarke had been complimentary before the French match and his remarks now were in a similar vein: 'We have great respect for Scotland. They are on a roll and must have the same confidence that we have developed by winning their first three Five Nations matches.' Clarke may be one of rugby's most affable gentle giants, but on the pitch his game had developed an edge epitomised by his new-found ferocious rucking style. When asked whether he would like to put his Bath colleague Eric Peters in his place, Clarke hinted at his new resolve. 'He already is in his place. He's in Bath second team mostly and I am first choice.' Two years previously, 'my farmer friend', as Rowell once famously dismissed him at Bath, would never have spoken with such assurance.

The lofty manager talked with less assurance himself about England's season. Rowell needed the Grand Slam to issue as a personal statement to those who had questioned his ability. Used to success at club level, Rowell demanded it from his internationals. Once again he challenged his team. 'The jury is still out on whether we have a successful season. If we really are favourites, I would like to think that we can impose our skills and will do so on the opposition.' He continued to cast doubt on the fluidity of the side. 'We want to add more width to the power game and use the Underwood brothers, Jeremy Guscott and our attacking full-back, Mike Catt.' It was a justifiable concern for Rowell and Cusworth – the England threequarters were definitely not exploiting the majesty of their forward play. However, Rowell believes in victory first and then adjustment – a 'transition' period is anathema to him. To those who knew him it appeared unlikely that Twickenham would witness any significant evolution in England's back play. The manager was quite definite that 'Grand Slams are not littered around in rugby history for anyone; this match has to be an end in itself'.

Moreover, it was unlikely that the scarred memories of Carling, Andrew and Moore would allow a high-risk game plan. As early as 8 March Carling had warned the rugby public not to expect anything too pretty, arguing, 'You can't really rehearse for conditions on the high veld when you are playing in a gale in Dublin. But it must be an enormous benefit to us if we go to South Africa for the World Cup as Grand Slam winners, however far along the road towards our new style we have reached.' So the back seat allocated to back play in Cardiff seemed likely to be retained at Twickenham. Carling played down his quest for vengeance as the match drew nearer, a sign of maturing captaincy. On the eve of the game he said: 'What happened five years ago at Murrayfield when Scotland outplayed us has no relevance to this weekend. We want it very badly for this team. We will be bitterly disappointed if we do not win. The result is everything now, but within five minutes of the finish tomorrow we will be assessing our display in terms of the World Cup.' England, as they have proved countless times, are extremely professional in their mental preparation. The World Cup did not enter their collective thought process before the game. Carling's final words – 'If we play to our potential we will win the game and win the Championship' – were not the boasts of naïve youth, but a hard-nosed realistic assessment.

Scotland have long felt contempt for what they perceive to be English arrogance, and sadly, too often it is justified. On this occasion, however, such contempt was misplaced. Craig Chalmers, stoked up for the match, talked belligerently about silencing England's fans, claiming, 'Deep down, I think they are very confident.' Bath's Eric Peters would have recognised that any signs of confidence would not be excessive. He said: 'Jack Rowell is very good at keeping his players in check, so while England will be confident, they will still focus on the task in front of them.'

English confidence, then, would be pitted against Scottish determination. Nobody could have carried the fight south from Hadrian's Wall with more commitment than Gavin Hastings. A hero so often for Scotland, in many ways this had been his finest season. This was recognised by Jack Rowell. 'Hastings is a man in a man's world. He is majestic. It is a measure of him that he has come back even stronger as leader, player and man after the recent run of poor Scottish results and the criticism he received as a consequence.' Scotland's younger players had eagerly acknowledged the self-assurance that their captain spread through his team, but even Hastings was quietly confiding that England would be a step up from France in Paris. Scotland may have been trying to re-create the role of underdog that so inspired them in 1990, but realistically it was a status that existed already. Before the tournament Jim Telfer had remarked that two wins from four would constitute success: in those terms, Scotland had already exceeded expectations. Duncan Paterson and Doug Morgan had looked the most likely international management casualties back in the autumn, but by this stage of the season they happily mixed humour and relief. Scotland announced an unchanged team for the England match four days after beating Wales. Paterson joked: 'I even managed to get home on the same day as the meeting started.' Having sat in on hundreds of Bath committee meetings, I can testify that this is a real rarity in rugby.

Former Scotland coach Jim Telfer was equally upbeat, but revealingly honest. 'There are a lot of things going right at the moment, but also a few things wrong, like the way we are still leaking tries. Six in the last three games is not acceptable. England are rightfully favourites and could give us a big shock. But even if we lose I'm confident we will learn an awful lot from going to Twickenham.' He made it sound like a headmaster's report on a precocious pupil. It was certainly not typical of the eyeballing coach of legend. Finlay Calder, one of the great Scottish rugby men of recent times, made his side's task sound even more monumental. 'If Scotland win, it will be the finest achievement of any Scottish side, ever. That's the enormity of the task facing them.'

The ifs and buts were even rolling off the tongues of the current Scotland side. Craig Chalmers warned: 'We must tackle them first time and that has to be our priority on Saturday. If we do not put them on the deck, England will simply walk all over us.' Kenny Milne joined the doubting Thomases: 'We have been getting better and we know we shall have to improve still more if we are to do anything in the World Cup.'

Scotland's persistent comments on defence and England's tension, epitomised by a ban on players talking to the press the day before the match, hardly held much promise for the showcase for which everybody hoped. Rowell would have reminded England that the game was effectively a cup final and, like so many of those events, likely to be anti-climactic. True to their word, Scotland played the game they had prepared. They tackled till their tartan faded and consequently England failed to add to their impressive try count. While Gavin Hastings twice came desperately close to England's line, the moments of 'goalmouth' excitement were few. The match evolved into a battle of boots and packs. England, with Bayfield outstanding, again dominated and Rob Andrew almost proved that practice makes perfect. He kicked all of England's twenty-four points, missing just one kick near the end. Scotland had neither the nous nor the collective forward muscle to present Hastings and Chalmers with such a volume of opportunities. Thus England achieved a 24–12 win which earned them a deserved Grand Slam. Scotland had defended with all the vigour promised before the game and England had reverted to their shell, as had been expected. Rob Andrew was criticised for dropping back to his armchair position behind the scrum almost immediately. It was a negative reversion, but one undertaken on the urgings of Jack Rowell. The manager and his team would not concur with the American poet Emily Dickinson, who wrote: 'Success is counted sweetest by those who ne'er succeed.' This Grand Slam was coated in sufficient sugar for England. They had not answered the numerous questions concerning their ability or desire to expand a game under pressure, but burdened by such a level of expectation and the memory of 1990, it was hardly surprising. It was not any sort of form guide for the World Cup. It was, after all, a cup final.

Carling heaped praise upon Scottish heads. 'The Scots are always tenacious. They are always going to be hard to beat, always tough. They have played very well this year, but for us it's been a great season so far.' Rob Andrew, basking in a new England points record, was equally gracious. 'They played outstandingly well. We weren't allowed to get into our stride. They caused us an awful lot of problems.' Rowell was delighted with the Grand Slam, but not the performance. 'We were nervy and jittery, but we have a further foundation stone in our progressive plan. But we would have liked to have scored tries. We did not play the ball early enough in clearing the rucks so the backs did not have the chance to show their skill.'

Predictably, the one man who saw the game from a different perspective was Brian Moore. His views on France and Ireland had been well aired, and Scotland received his full-frontal attack on television, the sweat of victory still on his brow. 'I think Scotland ruined the game as a spectacle. They did what they came to do, which wasn't very much. Scotland were always trying to slow the game down, getting bodies on the wrong side, and I think that they too had some responsibility for trying to make a spectacle of the match. We tried to play all the rugby but the Scots just wanted to kill the ball all the time.' Moore did not seem so concerned with the crowd's entertainment level when Harlequins League points were at stake. There was general condemnation for what was seen as a display of bad sportsmanship. John Jeffrey, from the *Grandstand* studio at Twickenham, called Moore 'despicable'. Among his few defenders was the journalist David Miller, who thought the England hooker should be applauded for his honesty. Miller felt that the criticism of Moore stemmed from the old-boy network, so despised by South Africa's Louis Luyt. If that had been the simple truth, I, too, would have sided with Moore. He has a right to his opinion, but it should be balanced. England are not angels who do not infringe, and Moore knows this, as does everyone else. Whichever team was crowned world champions on 24 June, it was certain that they too would be versed in some of rugby's black arts. It was hard to take Moore's new-found purity with anything but the largest pinch of salt.

Carling was suitably diplomatic about Moore's remarks. 'He plays in a different position from me. He might see things differently. I'm enjoying a Grand Slam and that's all I want to do at the moment – enjoy it.' One wondered what had happened to the 'Let's concentrate on the World Cup within five minutes of the final whistle' philosophy, but the England captain's earlier comments were forgivable. Whatever Jack Rowell's earlier misgivings, he had forged a good working relationship with Carling. 'Whatever kind of captain he was at twenty-two, I find him first rate.'

It had not been the ideal end to England's season in terms of performance, but the results and consequent high morale left the team in confident mood for the World Cup. 'We are in better shape to win the World Cup than we were in 1991,' declared Carling. 'There was not a deep-rooted belief in our ability to win when we reached the final. If we can use our full power we could be awesome. We could be dynamic.' I wouldn't be surprised if the press men wrote down those adjectives before he said them.

Current world champions Australia were suitably impressed by England's campaign. Nick Farr-Jones rated England and Australia as first-tier nations, South Africa and New Zealand the second tier and France and Scotland third – high praise indeed. The Wallabies' guiding light, Bob Dwyer, was equally complimentary. 'They are a much more complete team and much less predictable in attack. Their back row shows great strength and ball-winning talent and their first-phase play is excellent.' Rowell, meanwhile, seemed keen to hint at the reasons for the improvement Dwyer singled out. 'I don't think it is a better squad than 1991 in individual capacity, but England have taken a major step forward in how to play the game.' I wonder who was acclaimed the architect of their new approach?

ACT III

T he interregnum. The battle of the Five Nations subsides as the armies prepare themselves for the great world war that will take place in the months of May and June in South Africa.

In the English club wars, Leicester, inspired by their yeoman captain, finally overthrow the once irresistible force of the Roman city, Bath, as external forces deprive Bath of such soldiers as Jeremy Guscott, Victor Ubogu and Jon Hall. The Scottish alchemist McGeechan cannot save Northampton.

Bath, however, win the Pilkington Cup, but the event is overshadowed by the national furore that surrounds a pre-emptive strike by the forces of amateurism against the new age. The RFU dismiss the England captain, insulting clubs, sponsors and the preparation of a nation awaiting sporting conflict.

In Wales, Cardiff win the League, Swansea the Cup and Pontypool bid farewell to the First Division; north of the border, Gavin Hastings takes his leave of his beloved Murrayfield.

On the other side of the world the battle for the sport's soul accelerates as the threat of Rupert Murdoch's millions combines with Rugby League to force Union to embrace a professional future. Meanwhile, New Zealand and South Africa and the world champions, Australia, are starting to make belligerent noises. The acrid scent of World Cup gunpowder is in the air.

DRAMATIS PERSONAE

Dean Richards	Captain of Leicester
Jon Hall	Captain of Bath
Will Carling	Prince of England
Dennis Easby	The Black President
Rupert Murdoch	The Great Fear/The Great Hope (delete according to hemisphere)

16

Falling Empires, Aristocrats and the Political Game

With the international season completed, it was time at last to focus on the quest for the Holy Grail, the 1995 World Cup. But for Jack Rowell's warriors, notably those from Bath, Leicester, Harlequins and Northampton, there were battles to be fought on the home front as they prepared for South Africa. As Rowell basked in England's success another Grand Slam coach, Ian McGeechan, was having rather less fun at Northampton. It was one of life's cruel ironies that McGeechan's new video, launched in Scotland, was entitled *Making It Flow*, because the unfortunate Franklins Gardens faithful had seen barely a trickle of open rugby from their heroes. Tim Rodber had warned: 'We must start winning now, and regularly, if we are to avoid relegation.' There had been a few sighs of relief when the Saints did just that with a 24–13 victory away at Bristol on 4 March. Northampton scored four tries and their joy was complete when they heard the news of Harlequins' 10–8 defeat in the wastelands of West Hartlepool. Poor Dick Best lamented: 'About 90 per cent of the conversations I have at the moment concern whether we're going to get relegated. It gets you down after a while.' It might have depressed Dick Best, but Harlequins' precarious League position was amusing most of the English club scene. Kyran Bracken and Mike Catt openly admitted on *Rugby Special* that they would like to see the Quins playing at venues like Waterloo in the autumn of 1995.

If Harlequins lost their next match, on 25 March, their descent to the anonymity of Division 2 looked all too probable: their opponents would be Northampton. It was the most unexpected relegation battle in the history of Rugby Union: Quins with their glamorous triumvirate of England players, Carling, Moore and Leonard, against the Saints, captained by Tim Rodber and featuring Martin Bayfield, arguably the world's leading exponent of line-out play. Even more staggering was the status of the personnel involved on the coaching staff. Dick Best and Ian McGeechan were both Grand Slam coaches, both are reputedly among the best-paid professionals in the rugby world, and both were having difficulty inspiring their sides. While Jack Rowell made the effortless leap from club to country, the two former Lions coaches were finding the return journey something of a mystery. A football manager at a similar level of responsibility might have been concerned about the famous chairman's vote of confidence.

Before the showdown Best said: 'The match is going to be about who makes the fewest mistakes, who doesn't freeze.' It was not an inspiring call to arms for his troops and the game lived down to expectations. The groans rang from Northampton to Waterloo when the news of 10–9 in Harlequins' favour crossed the wires. The Second Division clubs grieved the lost opportunity for added revenue that a visit from the famous Quins would have reaped. Northampton, meanwhile, were three points adrift at the bottom of the League and set fair for the drop. So much for McGeechan's video. One man not confident of Harlequins' immediate future was their captain, Brian Moore. 'It's a huge sense of relief, but there is a lot to do to avoid relegation. I felt more pressure playing for Quins this season than for England.'

At the other end of the table, Bath seemed to be taking the familiar pressure of leading the League in their stride. Despite having failed to hit top gear, they were hot favourites to retain their title. Jon Hall was looking forward to retiring with another Championship. 'If Wasps win [at Leicester] and we defeat Gloucester,' he said before the 4 March match, 'we would be four points clear of Wasps and five ahead of Leicester.' His confidence was not shared by Gloucester coach Viv Woolley, who announced, 'Bath are there for the taking.' Not quite, but a 19–19 draw at the Recreation Ground at least supported the theory that Bath were not invincible. Worse still for Hall, Leicester beat Wasps 21–6, closing the gap to just two points. At Welford Road Rory Underwood scored his first two tries of the season, testimony to the tendency to keep the game tight in pressure matches.

It made for a sad comparison with the Super-10 series I was presenting for Sky from the southern hemisphere. Watching Queensland play reminded me that Rugby Union is more than a match for League when played with imagination. The failure of England's top clubs to illuminate televised rugby was an indictment of our coaching. The other area of persistent concern was the diabolical standard of refereeing that made so many games static. Even Ed Morrison, so highly respected by players, was far less fluent in his style than his southern hemisphere counterparts. Referees, like players, are ambitious to perform at the highest possible level, and the only way to get there in England is by following the letter of the law. Appointing Steve Griffiths to supervise refereeing standards was just one in a long line of mistakes, in my view. Instead the RFU should have appointed a former player who would at least have some empathy with the current players. Ed Morrison was to be appointed, along with Steve Lander, as England's panel referees for the World Cup.

Bath had more pressing problems. On 25 March Wasps beat them 11–10 at Sudbury to give Leicester the lead on points difference. The club had a right to complain about the demands placed on their international players, but that was a disadvantage of having such a strong squad. The problems went deeper than that. Bath has always been an argumentative club, but the overriding atmosphere is generally one of good humour. That was not the case in March, according to the rumours flying around the West Country. Jon Hall had been left out for the Wasps fixture due to a lack of mobility, a decision made while he was in Natal with England A. For seventeen years the Bath captain had had a major say in selection. The early meeting of the selectors was unique. Not only was it unique, it was stupid. The modern game attaches so much priority to fitness that it can occasionally forget about tactical guidance. Bath had always dominated opponents tactically, and the decision to leave Hall out represented the club's most regressive step of the decade. Leicester's back play proved that it was not that other clubs were catching up with Bath, rather that England's perennial champions were finally slowing down in their thinking.

Another problem for the club was the motivation of certain players, something which would have been just about unthinkable two years earlier. The harsh realities of being a top-class player trapped in an amateur game were steadily eroding the loyalty of the most committed players. Even though Wasps had always been perceived as a major threat, Jeremy Guscott had informed Bath of his unavailability for the match at the start of the season. It is easy to criticise the individual involved, but people should remember that the modern rugby player sacrifices a massive part of his life to a sport with little reward bar fun. It might be enough for a student or the landed gentry, but those two elements of society are hardly likely to nourish the game's future. However piously Twickenham talked of amateurism, the concept was starting to appear every bit as undesirable as the spectre of filthy lucre. If England's premier club were struggling to hold their players, the future for the amateur code looked rocky.

The absence of Victor Ubogu, away in Hong Kong as the Bath empire started to crumble in north-west London, was a bigger worry for Bath and, quite possibly, for Jack Rowell. The Grand Slam won, Ubogu duly informed Bath that he too would be unavailable for the crucial League encounter. The club had known about Guscott's commitments since August; they knew of Ubogu's with only a week to spare. To compound the problem, David Hilton had popped some ribs playing against his Bath team-mate for Scotland. The smiling prop was unrepentant: business must come first. At Bath the timing of Ubogu's visit to Hong Kong, which took him to the colony while the Hong Kong Sevens were being played, was seen as no coincidence. Players talked darkly of dropping him for the remainder of the season. The irrepressible England prop claimed he was collecting memorabilia for his new bar, Shoeless Joe's. The obscure name derives from a character who ambled into Caesar's Palace in Las Vegas with a welfare cheque for $273 and walked out with $1.6 million. As his nickname implies, he wore no shoes and dressed with no style. There were no obvious similarities with Victor, who is a hopeless gambler and a lavish dresser. The only thing they had in common was that Shoeless Joe lost his money and Victor lost a lot of respect. Unlike Shoeless Joe, Ubogu is certain to bounce back.

It was less certain that Pontypool would bounce back to the big time. Another fit of March madness saw them slump to a 29–3 defeat in the village atmosphere of Dunvant. Cardiff continued to irritate me with success upon success. Although Pontypridd remained level on points, Cardiff's try-scoring superiority gave them a clear edge. In Wales the authorities have displayed the good sense to make try-scoring the next most important thing to winning. The most notable match in the Principality was the quarter-final of the SWALEC Cup between Neath and Swansea on 8 April. Swansea appeared to have banished the ghosts of South Africa – they beat Neath in a thrilling 22–20 match at the unforgiving Gnoll. Doubtless followers of worldwide rugby in South Africa would remember their own battle of the Gnoll and raise a glass of Paarl to the Swansea Jacks. Meanwhile, events off the field made it look likely that many South African supporters would be returning to wet Wales earlier than they had anticipated on their departure in 1994.

While the players waited for further developments concerning the amateur – or otherwise – status of the sport from the IB meeting in March, the primary interest of the committee men was the venue for the 1999 World Cup. The wranglings that took place showed that whereas sportsmen might well be too focused to deal with political machinations, the authorities which control rugby are capable of acting with all the self-interest of the most cynical political party. Faxes had been winging around all parts of the rugby world as Wales and Australia prepared the ground-work for one of rugby's biggest battles, albeit one to be conducted on paper. The spectacle that unfolded was a convincing argument for making the sport professional at the administrative level to ensure that vested interests are secondary to the health of the sport. As it is, the IB seem as likely to resolve worldwide rugby squabbles as the

United Nations are to bring about universal peace and happiness.

On 1 March rumours leaked that Scotland and Ireland were going to vote for the joint Australia–Japan–New Zealand bid. The two Celtic countries were amazed that a prior 'verbal agreement' struck between the WRU and the RFU would grant England both semi-finals, one quarter-final and one and a half pools if Wales were successful with their bid for the tournament. Scotland and Ireland would each stage only one pool and one quarter-final. Vernon Pugh, the Welsh president of the IB, admitted that politics was playing a role. 'I cannot see the sense of splitting the tournament between three countries which are separate land masses. We are seeking to show IB delegates that it makes far more financial sense to go for Wales rather than Australia. But politics are entering the game. Individual unions are acting in their own interests rather than in those of the game in general and there is plenty of horse-trading.' Nobody ventured to suggest that Mr Pugh's vigorous support of Wales might be linked to his nationality.

At this stage Australia were the clear favourites to win, despite the protestations of Pugh and England selector John Elliot. Both were outspoken on the folly of a tournament that could send a player from the heat of Tokyo to the cold of Dunedin in the space of a week. Yet the logistics of the 1995 World Cup had already revealed that the interests of the players are of less consequence than the deadly combination of money and ego. By 11 March, the popularity of the Australian bid notwithstanding, the world had been informed that the Welsh bid had won. Plans advanced over a period of four years altered in ten days and the format of the World Cup was changed as a result.

The early indications were that many of the teams participating in the 1995 World Cup were not of a high enough standard. Poor Ivory Coast had lost 97–7 to Northern Transvaal, 62–9 to Griqualand West and 18–10 to an unknown but exotic-sounding team called Stellaland. The trend was against the so-called 'developing teams', yet suddenly we were informed that twenty teams would take part in the 1999 tournament. It was a decision made not in the interests of spectators or players, but for the sport's politicians.

Wales kept everything from the 1 March plan, bar half a pool. England lost one quarter-final and half a pool, but kept both semi-finals. Ireland and Scotland reclaimed their own pool and quarter-final, but suddenly, from nowhere, France appeared as a pool venue. There would be five groups of four with the winners of each pool qualifying automatically for the quarter-finals. The remaining quarter-finalists would be decided by three knock-out matches between the second-placed teams from each pool and the top third-placed team. For a sport projecting itself on the world stage it was a sad farce.

To compound the depression that hung over those who listened and

watched the antics of the IB, Vernon Pugh issued a statement as bare-
faced in its hypocrisy as anything could ever be – even in Parliament.
Ten days earlier he had poured scorn on the administrative problems,
the effect on the players and unfairness for supporters of hosting the
tournament in such diverse countries and climates as those advocated
by Australia. Magnanimous in victory, Pugh said: 'Either one of the two
unions bidding for the World Cup would have ensured a fine tournament.' Obviously he believed rugby followers had a memory span to
match those of voters at election time.

The IB made other announcements. They introduced a universal suspension policy for the 1995 World Cup. A player sent off for kicking or
butting would receive a ban for two months; for punching, one month;
for abusing an official, four months. Anyone striking an official would
be banned for life. I hoped for the sake of the players that the standard
of refereeing would be higher than the fiascos being witnessed every
Saturday in England. If the abuse-of-an-official ban extended to the
media, there would be a few rugby writers on the dole queue next
season.

Of course, the most eagerly awaited statement was that relating to
the IB's position on amateurism. Australia's contracts system had
already laid down the gauntlet, and the IB know how serious the implications of their decision could be for the future of the sport. Chairman
Vernon Pugh said: 'Amateurism is such an important issue. We've got
to get it right. We want players to be able to hold down a proper job
and a career, but it is a possibility that internationals will be paid for
appearing for their countries.' Australia were virtually doing this
already. Rugby Union desperately needed a clear lead, as Pugh recognised. 'The major threat to the game is its potential takeover by commercial interests.' The IB were hardly showing the requisite degree of
solidarity and strength to deter any such predatory moves. Instead of
making a bold statement, they fudged the issue. Their official statement
concluded that professionalism was 'inevitable' unless pressures on
players were reduced or controlled. A report would be made in August.
So much for their position.

Their procrastination was unsatisfactory to the more progressive
southern hemisphere, whose rugby was under siege by Rugby League.
New Zealand's RFU were so disappointed with the failure of their chairman, Eddie Tonks, to achieve anything other than an impersonation of
Neville Chamberlain that they pressurised him into resignation. His
replacement, Richie Guy, was perceived as a more conservative force,
but times were changing in New Zealand.

The Home Unions may have been more complacent over the future
wellbeing of the sport, but if the southern hemisphere was split over
money, the game would revert to its elitist and antiquated ways. Rugby

Union is too big a business to regress. If it does it will die. The northern hemisphere had undeniable concerns over the disadvantages of full amateurism on the playing side. Ireland's manager, Noel Murphy, said: 'We will have to define amateurism and professionalism. Our players are workers with full-time jobs, but they are expected to perform to the standards of other countries, some of whose players have more time to develop their game without the constraints of a daytime job.' In Rugby League, only two teams, Wigan and Leeds, were fully professional in the 1994–5 season. Murphy had a point. To underline it, Phil Danaher and Peter Clohessy withdrew from Ireland's squad for the World Cup in order to pay their mortgages.

There was disappointment in England, too, when the World Cup squad was announced on 27 March. Despite his inclusion in the twenty-two for the Scotland match, Paul Hull was sidelined, Jon Callard – who had enjoyed a superb all-round season for Bath – claiming his berth as back-up goal-kicker to Rob Andrew. Nigel Redman was distraught at the news that Richard West had won a battle for height over experience, while Jon Hall was equally disgruntled that Neil Back had shaded him for the final back-row spot. With a lack of tactical cover for Dean Richards, this decision was regarded by some as Jack Rowell's first bad tactical faux pas. Both Hall and Redman had sacrificed so much time for so little reward. Rugby's international failures are as good a justification as its successes for serious recompense for players. The normally unlucky Ian Hunter won selection and the twenty-sixth place went to Damian Hopley, perhaps England's most obvious amateur in the face of growing professionalism. When the theologian was asked where he would be on the Monday morning of the announcement, he replied, 'Probably the church or the pub.' The London grapevine suggested that he did not quite make it to church that day.

17

The Last Amateur Champions

T he age of mammon, rather than morality, had arrived – at least, that must have been the perception of the powerbrokers who had for so long defended the unique amateur status of Rugby Union. Those players, like Nigel Redman, who had ultimately sacrificed so much of their personal lives in vain, doubtless thought otherwise. Money is not the prime motivation for 99 per cent of rugby players, as Vernon Pugh asserted, but it would help to soothe the wounds of the hundreds of players who would not make the trip to the World Cup with their countries. A fortnight in the Caribbean re-acquainting themselves with partners who had played second fiddle to sport would be some consolation for the majority of players. The Home Unions committee do not share this view. How could they? Only a few of them have performed at the higher levels, and most of those who have did so when the game really was amateur.

Elitism has been the fence separating Rugby Union from the 'barbarian world of commerce'. Some people prefer to call it the real world. The Australians and New Zealanders, worried by the whispers of Rugby League, were already dissatisfied with the hedging of the IB. The rumbling advance of professionalism in the southern hemisphere must have sounded like the thunderclouds that drove Noah to the Ark – except that this time the players were not going to follow their administrators two by two. A sensible majority worried about the effects of stonewalling; one set of extremes generally leads to another. Nobody wants to see the sad sight of mercenary sportsmen striking for even more exorbitant salaries, as occurred with baseball in America, but the more stubborn the authorities, the greater the likelihood of a commercial coup – the very thing that Vernon Pugh feared most: the potential takeover of commercial interests.

On 5 April the storm broke – not over Rugby Union, but Rugby

League. Rupert Murdoch's News International Group were to set up a Super League in Australia to replace the existing ARL. Murdoch had the resources to buy the best from both codes, and the governing bodies knew it. Critics complained that there was an element of panic, but with the World Cup only a month away, it was perhaps understandable. Richie Guy of New Zealand was the first to comment. 'We're looking at ways of protecting our players from the League scouts, and we've been working very hard to free up the amateur rules. We don't want our players sitting there like lambs to the slaughter. The advent of Super League could force us to move to professionalism much quicker than we were going.'

The Australian reaction was even more clear-cut. Greg Thomas, the ARFU's media and communications manager, said: 'We are very keen to ensure that Rugby Union players stay with Rugby Union.' As Australia has a limited Union infrastructure compared to that in Britain, they had reason enough to worry about losing significant numbers of their stars. According to the *Australian* newspaper, the top fifty Union stars there would be offered around £150,000 per season to remain in the sport – a considerable advance on the sums mentioned earlier in the year. Such figures would clearly tie this elite to the sport, and the dreaded word 'professional' would no longer be banned from the rugby bible. Thomas admitted: 'At the moment the Wallabies can generate income from the game or around the game, so we shouldn't be talking amateurism any more.' In fact, Dudley Wood had made similar references to the unsuitability of the word 'amateur', but there the agreement ended. The direction in which he wanted to proceed veered sharply away from that of the southern hemisphere countries. Terry Doyle, the Queensland Rugby Union executive director and one of the world's most respected rugby administrators, opened out. 'Let's be honest, it verges on the professional now.'

Yet for all their ostrich attitudes, England, along with Ireland and Scotland, were one of the few countries that were not guilty of this hypocrisy. The high media profile of a few of its personalities convinced many otherwise, however. The Labour MP for Macclesfield, Ian McCartney, stated: 'Rugby Union has been found guilty and sentenced to capital punishment.' An element of spite was evident. He was referring to a report by the National Heritage Committee recommending that the government ceased payments of £70,000 a year to the RFU until they dropped their 'discrimination' against Rugby League, that is, the freedom of players to return to Union after a spell in 'the north'.

Dudley Wood was at his dismissive best. Safe in the knowledge that every home international nets a profit of £1.5 million, he said: 'The committee has little credibility and is obviously influenced by the Parliamentary Rugby League Group.' The professional politicians were reminding their Union equivalents that others could play power games too. Wood's evaluation of this group found favour with even the most commercially minded of Union men. Because Vernon Pugh had acknowledged that a few players were already making money from the sport, there was a conviction in certain quarters that rugby's high profile in England guaranteed that everyone was rolling in money. Ian McCartney, displaying all the balance of the average British politician, ranted: 'The situation has become completely hypocritical. Over the last decade and the last five years in particular, there have been huge pay-outs, with top Rugby Union players earning as much as top League players.' It was interesting to note that no names were produced. The players normally cited as high earners are the likes of Guscott and Carling. Both have made a good living by marketing their appeal, but it has all been accounted for within the RFU laws. They, like the rest of the England side, have not earned income from the game other than the nominal sums from Playervision, the company set up by the players to distribute legitimate payments for off-the-field activities.

Vernon Pugh appeared to believe that the players were in no rush to be given a definitive clarification of the sport's laws – 'I am comfortable with the way things are going. The players will not struggle for options after the August meeting of the IB' – but New Zealand were in more of a hurry. Richie Guy re-stated their position. 'I think it is our idea, our attitude, to convince the IB that the game should go professional.' His words were echoed by some of the world's great stars. Jason Little commented, 'They are saying after the World Cup, but personally, I'd like to see it sorted out beforehand. I realise the tournament can't be jeopardised, but some sort of commitment would be good.' Rod McCall, the recalled Wallaby lock, agreed. 'The players aren't unhappy with what's happening, but are probably glad that this [the Super League] will speed things up.' The British body might have been complacent in the face of the feuding millions of Rupert Murdoch and Kerry Packer, but the Australians were determined to protect their smaller player base. The ARU backed their two prime state bodies, New South Wales and Queensland, in their assertions that Union was no longer amateur in any case. 'The position of the state unions, namely that amateurism as a concept is outmoded, will be endorsed and communicated to the IB.'

The Australians, rather like the group of northern MPs in England, were wrong in some of their thinking. They proclaimed that 'those associated with the game around the world have been for some time receiving remuneration for their activities in various ways'. This misconception was born from the condescending attitude of the Home Unions, especially England. Leo Williams, the gregarious racehorse-owning president of the ARU, observed: 'Paradoxically, the unions which have benefited most from the intrusion of commercialism are the group that describe themselves as the Home Unions.' If Williams was implying that the RFU had made a fortune in recent years he would be correct, but the young men who generated that wealth, the team, were jealously protected from the corruptive powers of money, and not to the satisfaction of them all.

The hyperbole surrounding the future of the sport was not only detracting from the build-up to the World Cup, but endangering the preparation of some of the key individual participants. As news broke of a 'Super Union' competition being organised by the former Auckland coach John Hart, from which, it was said, players could earn NZ$33,000 per man, a frantic money mania seemed to fill the minds of some players. Not everyone was as sanguine as Australian captain Michael Lynagh, who showed the admirable focus needed for a team determined to win the World Cup. 'We are certainly not sitting in our hotel rooms every day worrying about our future. Our job at the moment is just to go out there and play.' The professionalism of the attitude of Lynagh and company was illustrated at the end of the month, when he led his side to a 53–7 victory over Argentina, a trouncing which suggested that Italy rather than the Argentinians would be favourites to qualify alongside England from Pool B. Lynagh helped himself to twenty-eight points in a display described by coach Bob Dwyer as 'a good start, something we can build on', although he added, 'We need to be a lot tighter.' The Australians were preparing for war like true world champions.

In England, however, hardly a day went by without the appearance of a newspaper article quoting a leading player on the temptation of money. Both Tim Rodber and Victor Ubogu announced that *if* an offer of £300,000 was laid on the table, they would certainly consider it seriously. There was no hard news – neither player claimed to have been approached – yet this stuff was being churned out as lead stories. Jonathan Davies remarked on Radio 5 that Rugby Union players and their agents frequently create such stories to stimulate interest. Both Rodber and Ubogu have agents. Jack Rowell was a worried man. The 'corruptive power of commercialism' seemed to be diverting heads at the very moment when England needed to concentrate most intensely. At the final squad gathering before England departed for South Africa, the players were treated to the sight of a man whose feet had left the ground, Mr Ubogu, naked except for headband, boots and a ball in front of his vitals, in the feature section of the London *Evening Standard*. Obviously his short-ripping antics on the field were part of a careful marketing strategy for 'Shoeless Vic'. The entrepreneurial prop forward was due for another of Rowell's rockets directed towards his over-exposed rump. The other issue being raised by the shenanigans of players like Ubogu was the loss of liberty to act in such profitable and frivolous ways should the game adopt a degree of professionalism after the World Cup. Whether Dudley Wood would prefer a paid Ubogu or a naked one must be a moot point.

Thankfully, there was more to April than nude prop forwards and money. The skirmishing in the Courage Leagues was drawing to a close at both ends of the table. Before the Championship was settled, there was the small matter of deciding the finalists for the Pilkington Cup. The Sky route took me to Welford Road, where Leicester met Wasps. In the other semi-final Harlequins faced Bath, who produced a predictable performance in the wake of the Wasps defeat and crushed the struggling aristocrats of the game by 31–13. Brian Ashton declared it the best Bath display of the season. From a purely televisual point of view, I was delighted that my old club would be gracing Twickenham on Cup final day. As Bath and Leicester had produced such a poor spectacle in 1994, there was a feeling among the Sky crew that the best scenario would see Wasps win a vibrant thriller at Welford Road in front of the massed and noisy ranks of Tigers supporters, as the locals in this part of the Midlands call themselves. That wish was granted when Leicester's Stuart Potter dropped a pass with the line at his mercy in injury time. Potter was devastated, but the real reason for Leicester's defeat went much deeper. Without the injured Dean Richards, they were tactically shapeless. Their pack won a steady stream of possession, but Jez Harris and friends failed to use it. In contrast, Rob Andrew kept his cool to fire over three dropped goals in the first half which, combined with a try from the flying vicar, Damian Hopley, was enough to enable Wasps to hold out in the tense final minutes. At full-time it was a rare silence that descended over England's pre-eminent club stadium.

So Leicester's hopes of the double were dashed along with the hopes that Neil Back would force his way into the England side on the hard grounds of South Africa. It was his missed tackle on the bigger Buster White that led to Hopley's decisive score. The Wasps were in ebullient mood as Rob Andrew confirmed. 'Confidence-wise, the players now know that they can live with the likes of Leicester and Bath. They're the ones who have set the standards. We have made significant strides, now we must aim to overtake them.' Wasps would have their chance on 6 May at Twickenham.

The Midlands had no more interest in the Cup, but the League was a different matter. Leicester were locked in battle with Bath at the top, while their local rivals, Northampton, fought for survival. Franklins Gardens was the next port of call for me as the Sky team travelled to Northampton for their clash with Orrell. Defeat for the home side would almost certainly consign them to Division 2. It was only the second time I had seen Orrell live. At full-time I was grateful that it had only been the twice. If Orrell and Leicester had produced the worst match of the season in September, this game challenged the Quins versus Saracens Cup tie for second place. There were no tries and little excitement as Northampton secured a sterile 15–3 victory a million miles removed from the exhortations of Ian McGeechan's video, *Making It Flow*. As Leicester produced their own yawn-inducing win by 22–8 at home to the hapless Quins and Bath ravaged West Hartlepool 53–17, there was still a glimmer of light for McGeechan's side. They remained within one point of the other two stragglers. For Bath the light appeared dazzling once again. Their margin of victory put them back at the top of the table on points difference. Jon Hall was a confident captain. 'We are on top of the League and in the Cup final. We are on top of the world.' Dick Best, not surprisingly, was rather more downbeat. 'The dogfight at the foot of the table continues. We cannot rely on Northampton and West Hartlepool losing.'

The dogfight turned nasty for those Northampton mongrels the following week. Someone must have misinformed Harlequins that the away trip to Orrell on 15 April was a Cup match, for they proceeded to slaughter the Lancastrians by 28–10. Carling proved his ability in a tight corner, producing a splendid display. In the north-west, West Hartlepool won 23–17 at home to Sale, leaving the Saints stranded once again, three points adrift of everyone else, after a controversial 14–13 defeat at Kingsholm which left Gloucester safe. Meanwhile, I wished Sky had travelled to Kingsholm rather than made the familiar journey to Leicester for the game that would probably decide the outcome of the League, Leicester against Bath. The home crowd created a magnificent atmosphere which clearly inspired Dean Richards' team. At half-time they led 18–6, controlling the game through the efforts of Richards and Martin Johnson. The second half was memorable for a Bath fightback which was a showcase for their superior footballing skills, but Leicester held out in a fabulous and breathless finale when Gareth Adams tried to throw the ball, quarterback style, in front of his posts. Instead of creating a counter-attack, the move resulted in the ball flopping into the predatory arms of Rory Underwood and the try was a formality. The Bath dream of a fifth consecutive title had disappeared in the highly charged atmosphere of Welford Road. The jubilation of the Tigers at full-time revealed how much the victory against Bath meant to the efficient Midlanders. The reaction of the Bath camp, meanwhile, was typical of the spirit of amateur sport. Poor Gareth Adams was distraught with himself after gift-wrapping the score that sealed Leicester's victory. There were no recriminations from his team-mates; instead they gently teased him with the new nickname of Joe Montana. It is difficult to imagine the game maintaining such a sense of perspective should the club scene become fully professional.

The Leicester victory made rather a mess of my social life. I had planned to stay in London with friends the next week, anticipating that my presence would be required at the Stoop for Harlequins versus Bath. The prospect of watching my former club taking a step to another title and at the same time pushing back the Quins into the snarling dogs of relegation would have delighted me were I not so scrupulously impartial. Instead the Leicester pack had re-directed our cameras to Manchester, where the Tigers were to face Sale. The match was another turgid affair, the champions elect prevailing 20–10. When one of the sport's romantics, Tony Underwood, admitted that results and not performances mattered, I knew that Dean Richards' burning desire to overthrow Bath was about to be fulfilled. Bath themselves came back from a 19–3 deficit to beat Harlequins, a result that was received with rapturous acclaim by both sides at Northampton, where the Quins' deadly rivals, Wasps, surprisingly lost. Cynically, I recalled Dick Best telling me that the Harlequins would lose £500,000 if they were relegated. I wondered whether any of this surplus would find its way round the North Circular. Bristol, the worst team in the 1995 calendar year, turned the battle for the drop into a two-horse race with another inept display which presented West Hartlepool with a rare away win. The following week Damian Hopley bumped into some of the Quins in the City and generously offered them some parachutes for their impending descent to Division 2.

On 29 April, the last Saturday of the League season, Northampton had to make the longest journey of all, to West Hartlepool. As they had kept alive their hopes of survival largely through their five home victories, it looked like a daunting fixture for the Saints. But just as the local rivalry between Wasps and Harlequins might have conspired to aid Northampton the previous week, so transfers earlier in the season could have an adverse effect on the Quins. West Hartlepool had been deeply distressed by the loss of Mick Watson and Simon Mitchell to Harlequins in December. Now that they were safe from relegation, West could seal the fate of their former comrades who had left for the bright lights of London. A rugby side would not throw a match and there is no question of fixing, but psychology has a part to play and doubtless the news of Watson and Mitchell being consigned to the Second Division would have afforded a few smiles in the clubhouse. The home side played their part – Northampton secured the win they needed – but the news from Kingsholm that Harlequins had won 28–17 banished McGeechan's squad to Division 2 and visits to Blackheath.

McGeechan must consider himself a lucky man. In a year which claimed two First Division coaches and an international coach, his record was disastrous. For all the excuses about international commitments, Northampton played the bulk of their matches with Bayfield and

Rodber. Even without them, the pack performed creditably; the real problem was the startling inadequacy of their backs. As McGeechan was a distinguished midfield player himself, it is difficult to fathom how a talented player such as Paul Grayson remained so unchannelled. Doubtless the Saints will bounce straight back, but the standards are so low outside Division 1 that this will hardly represent an achievement to a club the size of Northampton.

The loss of one former Lions coach was another's gain as Harlequins hung on by the skin of their teeth to their status in the top flight. Before the battle of Kingsholm, Brian Moore announced that he would retire from rugby after the World Cup, prompting his longstanding rival, Graham Dawe, to muse: 'Even terriers have to be muted at some stage.' The timing of Moore's announcement (which he was later to reconsider), just a day before the last match of the season, surprised many, including his club-mate and England captain, Will Carling, who knew nothing of the plan. But there was logic to it. Moore rightly reasoned that if his side lost, people would accuse him of jumping ship. The Quins skipper stated that he expected his club to win and stay up, despite the fact that they had never beaten Gloucester away. Carling himself informed me that the Quins would win comfortably. Neither man was embarrassed by their confident assertions. Gloucester, without their impressive second row of Sims and Richard West, who was hidden in cotton wool before his trip to South Africa, failed to provide the Londoners with any sort of test, and to the chagrin of so many fans, the aristocrats survived. Not quite the day the music died, but a sad one none the less.

Nor was there any sign of happy news at Bath. Worse still, the West Countrymen went down not with a bang but a whimper. An 18–13 home defeat at the hands of those free spirits from Sale was testimony to the excellence of player-coach Paul Turner's influence, but it also ended the Recreation Ground careers of Tony Swift and Jon Hall on the most anti-climactic of notes. Hall left the pitch with a shoulder injury that threatened his farewell Cup final appearance the following week. In 1995 Bath had won just six of their nine League matches at home. England's four-times champions had finally been dethroned by the efficiency of Dean Richards' Tigers.

Welford Road, then, was bathed in the sunshine of success. If Harlequins thought that West Hartlepool were their worst possible allies at the season's climax, Bath must have shared similar feelings about Leicester's last opponents, Bristol. Not only were they the worst team in the League on 1995 form, but they will always be Bath's biggest enemies. It was hard therefore to envisage Derek Eves winding up his team for one last superhuman effort to save the pride of the west. The quality of Bristol's play suggested that it was irrelevant whether they tried or not. Playing with the direction of headless chickens, they did not once threaten the Leicester try-line. It was depressing that Leicester themselves could manage only one try, but the dearth of flowing rugby epitomised the limitations of the champions. They were deserved champions because the game is as much about grind as glitter, and, quite simply, this side ground their opponents into sporting oblivion. Behind the scrum their inadequacies were revealed by their season's try tally of just twenty-seven, compared to Wasps' fifty-eight. Bridesmaids to Bath for so long, the Tigers rightly cared little about style, but even as his side celebrated their victory, director of rugby Tony Russ admitted that they would need to improve dramatically if they were to challenge Bath's incredible decade of success.

So the Courage Leagues finished with a sense of anti-climax, but speaking personally, the thought of being spared the journey from Bristol to Leicester for at least four months brought a smile to my face. In the last month of the season, Sky had visited Leicester on three occasions. Each time we stayed in the Stakis Hotel, and each time the atmosphere of the bar was ruined by a playerless piano which spewed out the worst imaginable musak. If the AA could install one of these contraptions in every bar in the land, the country would soon be teetotal.

18

A Bad Smell on Bath's Day

Although the Welsh would be packing the wooden spoon for the trip to South Africa, and despite the presence of numerous chapels, Wales remained a far from sober place in April, especially in Cardiff, where Mike Hall's team wrapped up the Heineken Leagues. My mind strayed back to early in the season when I had forecast that Cardiff would not win the League. Poor Jack Brown, the 'leading rugby book-maker in these parts', must have taken a serious pounding from the army of Cardiff supporters who ignored my advice. In three years Alex Evans had taken Cardiff from the threshold of relegation to the Championship. If he could fulfil his pledge to make Wales a world power by next month, many would start to wonder about the nature of his conception. He could not work the miracle of the double, however. Swansea, finally revived after the Springbok massacre, beat Cardiff in injury time of the semi-final of the SWALEC Cup. Their opponents in the final would be Pontypridd and the deadly boot of Neil Jenkins.

For Jenkins the final had added significance. Alex Evans had announced his World Cup party and the Principality was awash with the rumour that Jenkins would play inside centre. The Cup final would be his chance to prove that he had grown into the No. 10 shirt, as he had informed the public earlier in the season. Other players had no such chance. Ieuan Evans, the talisman of Wales for so long, was axed as national captain and replaced by Mike Hall. Alex Evans clearly wanted a Cardiff man who knew his systems to lead Wales. Additionally, wing is probably the worst position from which to read a game. Alan Davies' advocacy of Evans as captain encapsulated his philosophy as a coach: he believed that he should make the key decisions rather than the players. That classically English opinion was seen by many as the official reason for his downfall.

Players followed Davies into obscurity, for the summer, at least, when the tour party was announced. Matthew Back, Nigel Davies, Phil Davies and Richie Collins were all left out of the provisional thirty-two, but the biggest shock, to the world's rugby media as well as to Wales, was the omission of a Cardiff player. Nigel Walker, the flying wing and incessant talker, was out. Who would provide the press with those pearls of wisdom? Walker was left out because Evans doubted his fitness for the hard pitches of South Africa. In the light of Walker's injury-riddled season, the coach may have been correct. Nevertheless, it was a brave and confident decision. But spare a thought for Dennis John, the assistant coach, who had to inform his own son, Paul, of his omission. What a cruel task for a father-coach.

There was cruel luck, too, for Gregor Townsend and Scotland. Townsend's subtlety had been a cornerstone of the Scottish revival, but he had damaged his cruciate ligaments and would have to miss the tournament. Doug Morgan acknowledged how big a blow to Scotland his absence would be. 'This season he has been in remarkable form and he has brought the best out of a number of players around him.' Another disappointed Scotsman was Andy Nicol, potentially their best scrum-half. Even though he had been absent for the entire season, the Scottish selectors travelled to Bath to watch him in a second-team match. A place was clearly being held for Nicol – until he damaged his other knee. He would be another player who would not enjoy the 1995 World Cup.

There was more misery for the French. Before the Five Nations Championship, Pierre Berbizier had scrawled a note on the board at the team's training camp, 'Be there on 24 June,' the date of the World Cup final, of course. Now that they had struggled to a 24–15 victory against the Romanians in Bucharest, it seemed more likely that Bill Beaumont would be recalled as England's captain. The man who seemed a better bet to captain England in the tournament – at least, he did until 4 May – Will Carling, was also disgruntled, despite England's continued luck as far as injuries were concerned. He was angry with the South African-dominated organisation of the World Cup. Carling was annoyed that his side, the runners-up in 1991, would be meeting the winners of Pool A, either Australia or South Africa, in the quarter-final, instead of the legitimate seventh seeds, who, on form, would be Ireland. There was definitely something more appealing about that fixture. Carling sighed, 'There is no point in spitting your dummy out. There is nothing we can do about it. But there is no doubt that the organisers have put as many hurdles in our way as they possibly could.'

Other England players had rather more lighthearted worries. Carling might have been delighted with the preparations of the squad, but others were not so enthusiastic. The captain eulogised about the training suits that 'cover our whole body except for a visor that keeps in the heat'. The idea was to simulate the heat and humidity of Durban, or, as Rex Hazeldine put it, the suits created 'a micro-environment close to the skin which replicates the local conditions'. In short, the training wear looked ridiculous. Unfortunately Damian Hopley was pictured in the *Daily Mail* wearing his Dr Who reject suit, and the next day his telephone was ablaze with mockers. To look on the bright side, it meant a spate of business for the smiling Wasp.

Hopley and the rest of the England camp did have something to smile about: the form of their group rivals. Western Samoa were touring South Africa, ostensibly as part of their preparation. Instead they became sacrificial lambs to a Springbok slaughter. South Africa beat them 60–8, inspired by the form of Gavin Johnson at full-back. He collected twenty-eight points in a performance which made one wonder whether André Joubert, one of the brightest stars of the rugby constellation in the autumn, would regain his Test berth after injury. As goal-kicking was one of South Africa's concerns, Joubert must have been a worried man at full-time. Yet while Western Samoa looked a shadow of their 1991 selves, the form of the hosts was a greater fear. Powerful and pacy, they appeared to be peaking to perfection. Even worse, from the English perspective, was the form of Queensland in the Super-10 series. At Ellis Park the Australians produced a performance of such clinical efficiency against Transvaal, who boasted the core of the South African Test side, that even Capetonians, normally the Transvaal's most bitter rivals, were depressed about the broader implications for their country. In the centre Queensland's Jason Little proved how much he had blossomed outside the shadow of his friend Tim Horan. He looked the best centre in the world and his partner, Daniel Herbert, appeared to be the natural replacement should Horan lose his fight for fitness.

The Super-10 series was not a pleasant experience for New Zealand, either. Their provincial sides were outplayed by Transvaal and Queensland. The All Black supremacy of recent times had been linked to the dominance of Auckland, who, in 1995, were a poor imitation of previous sides. The tournament did not augur well for a Rugby Union nation under duress, as 1987 World Cup-winning captain David Kirk explained. 'If the All Blacks lose, there will be some acceleration of interest in the [Auckland] Warriors [Rugby League], there will be an acceleration [in the number of] players playing Rugby League and there will be a general degradation of people's belief in and enthusiasm for the All Blacks. If they win, it will limit any further movement and hopefully give the game a shot in the arm.' In a country where rugby has long been a religion, the incumbent team were being placed under huge pressure to keep the sacred flame burning.

The one man in New Zealand who did not regard the sport as a religion was the great flanker Michael Jones. He informed the squad that he would not play on the sabbath. As the All Blacks were scheduled to play both their quarter-final and their semi-final on Sundays, Jones joined the list of non-attendees. Meanwhile, Andrew Mehrtens, the Canterbury fly-half, cemented his position for the tournament. He made his Test debut against Canada, another of the teams offering themselves as cannon fodder. New Zealand eclipsed England's 60 points, leaving the depressed Canadian captain, Gareth Rees, to declare, 'They were more threatening than England and played it wider and more often than I had expected.' Nobody enjoyed the romp more than Mehrtens, who collected twenty-eight points. Before the game, Laurie Mains said: 'You'll get the general idea of the style of the game we want to play.' If New Zealand planned to take this frenetic and highly individualised style to South Africa, they would be the great entertainers of the tournament, but they might lack the precision to conquer the world. One wondered whether this was how the All Blacks really wanted to play, or if it was simply a reaction to the threat of League.

Scotland were well aware that to avoid New Zealand in the quarter-finals they must beat France in Pretoria. For that reason alone their international at home to Romania was a critical form line. As Gavin Hastings said, 'This is the first game in our build-up to the World Cup.' It actually meant a lot more to the Scots, as Hastings had announced his retirement two days before the match, which would now be his Murrayfield farewell. For those not travelling to the southern hemisphere it would be the last chance to see Scotland's rock of a full-back in action. To Doug Morgan, the national coach, 'his efforts and productivity for Scottish rugby have been quite phenomenal'. Romania, buoyed up by their performance against France, were bullish. They had spotted Scottish weaknesses in the Grand Slam match with England which they hoped to exploit. Unfortunately for Romania, they did not quite possess the same task force as England and Scotland were able to offer Hastings a rather happier send-off than Bath had managed for Hall and Swift. Hastings started his career with a mistake against France; he began his final Murrayfield appearance with a try after ninety seconds. Having left the field just before full-time as a precaution, he returned on the final whistle to receive the crowd's acclaim. Hastings and his young side could head out to South Africa in good heart. As for the Romanians – well, at least the wine of Stellenbosch is better than their own.

While Gavin Hastings offered a stinging riposte to his critics and walked from Murrayfield a national hero, his longstanding, and at times bitter, England rival, Will Carling, was to discover that some fairy tales have vicious twists. As rugby journalists started to prepare for a brief interlude before South Africa, with only the season's premier club match, the Pilkington Cup final, to anchor the memory, all hell broke loose in the newsroom of every newspaper in England. Writing now about the events of the weekend of 6–8 May, it is still hard to believe that even the RFU could commit an error of such magnitude.

The battle lines between Carling and the RFU committee were drawn during the filming of a television documentary entitled *Fair Game*. The subject matter was nothing unusual for the average rugby supporter – the hypocrisy of the sport's administrators in an age when most neutrals believed that amateurism was dying on its feet. Ironically, the country that has always been savaged over the issue is England, seen throughout the rugby world as the final stronghold of the sport's traditional spirit. In England, Rugby Union lives in a paradoxical world where administrators are the great advocates of 'rugby as recreation', and the players are the most affluent beneficiaries – or so Leo Williams and the rest of the world believe. Due to the relative economic strength of the country and the density of population that makes it an adman's dream, the English have remained among the world's most prominent players in terms of hype and media exposure. Excluding David Campese, England has the most manufactured superstars in the sport – and the highest profile of them all belongs to Will Carling.

During his tenure as captain, England has become a great power on the rugby field and Carling, together with Brian Moore, has spearheaded the drive for financial compensation for the commitment that has elevated the side. In addition, Carling, with the shrewd assistance of his agent, Jon Holmes, has used his high profile to create a comfortable lifestyle for himself. He also left the army at an early stage, which would not endear him to the imperialistic element within the RFU committee. In short, despite the fact that his stance is not a particularly rebellious one, Carling found himself the symbolic enemy of the guardians of amateurism's flickering candle.

This can be the only explanation for the draconian reaction to a documentary in which Carling and Rob Andrew delivered the usual and justifiable criticisms of the establishment. Carling rounded off the thirty-minute programme with a metaphorical raspberry, calling the entire RFU committee 'fifty-seven old farts'. Quite how the thirty-four-year-old Cambridge don Mark Bailey took to being thus described is unrecorded. Knowing Bailey, he probably laughed – indeed, it deserved no more serious treatment than that. However, the England captain must have started to feel concerned when Dudley Wood said that the comment was less a reflection on the committee than on Carling. As long ago as 1991, one sympathetic committee man had informed players that a substantial element within the RFU did not want England to win the World Cup as 'the players are getting too big for their boots'. In their eyes, nobody wore bigger boots than Carling's size 9s. Four years later, the hasty actions of six undemocratic men confirmed the suspicions of the players: that egos were more important than the tournament. Wood may have condemned Carling because of a few immature and ill-chosen words, but the entire nation sat in disbelieving judgement when, just hours before the Pilkington Cup final – not to mention less than two weeks before England's departure for South Africa – the official announcement of Carling's dismissal from the post of England captain was made.

The Pilkington Cup final, the highlight of the club season, was relegated from a worthy headline to a mere postscript as the Carling controversy raged. At a time when clubs are increasingly flexing their muscles with bellicose mutterings in the direction of Twickenham, politically it was not a good option to insult Bath and Wasps, two clubs who had brought far more to the game than the beleaguered committee. The insult has further heightened the likelihood of a breakaway in the style of football's Premier League. Not only did the RFU display contempt towards the clubs, but they treated Pilkington, the most loyal of rugby sponsors, with utter indifference. The sun shone, Bath and Wasps produced a fine spectacle and Pilkington were justified in expecting valuable coverage on both national television and in the newspapers. It was not forthcoming. Stephen Jones, the rugby correspondent of *The Sunday Times*, did not even watch his beloved Bath – I use his words. Instead he filed the Carling story. Jones later confirmed that the paper gave the match the space that had initially been dedicated to the final of the Pilkington Shield, a tournament for junior clubs played as a curtain-raiser to the Cup final. The rest of the Sunday newspapers followed suit. So much for special relations with sponsors. At full-time that Saturday, the relationship between the RFU and their prime sponsors was roughly on a par with that between the Ulster Unionists and the USA when Bill Clinton met Gerry Adams.

Worst of all was the RFU's obvious indifference to England's World Cup hopes. Former England prop Jeff Probyn, an increasingly embittered opponent of anything to do with Carling, thought that a change of captain would have no effect on England's chances; Jack Rowell, who was not consulted about the decision, thought otherwise. As the six men who sat in surreal star-chamber justice on Carling and agreed with Probyn possessed just two England caps between them, and those dated back to 1955, it is hard to fathom why they felt they were qualified to judge. Dudley Wood, whose tenure as secretary of the RFU was to end after the World Cup, said: 'It's a very unfortunate time for a change of captain, but I think they had no choice. Will has lost the confidence of the committee.'

Voices were raised in indignation. The press corps, far from universal fans of Carling in private, were firm in their condemnation of the sacking. Dennis Easby, the president of the RFU, responded that the committee were 'past the stage of rapping his knuckles. As England captain he should know how to behave,' but the public were less than convinced that a panel of six men, only one of whom had ever played senior rugby, knew what they were doing. The nation had finally lost what confidence they had in the conservative forces that had fought so long against the inevitable arrival of the twenty-first century. Even politicians jumped on the bandwagon. Labour MPs such as Tony Banks called for a motion to condemn the RFU. Carling's previous support for Margaret Thatcher was not held against him as politicians accurately gauged the national groundswell of opinion to be in his favour. The political games of the RFU had turned against them as the country united in a show of contempt that almost eclipsed the nostalgic celebrations and commemorations of VE Day.

By Sunday night the 'star chamber' were so concerned about the reaction to the vendetta which compromised England's World Cup hopes that rumours of a U-turn of a magnitude to make John Major look consistent were being discussed. Carling was backed up by his team-mates, led by Dean Richards, who announced that in such circumstances it would be impossible for him to accept the mantle of captain. Rob Andrew followed suit shortly afterwards. Then the entire squad issued a press release in support of their captain. Even Dennis Easby must have realised that it would be an untenable situation for England to travel to South Africa without a leader.

Solidarity was the first proof to the people of Poland that the oppression of the Soviet Union's distorted form of socialism could be cracked. Similarly, the admirable unity of the England squad exposed signs that the elitism of the RFU would not last forever. On Bank Holiday Monday, the news of Carling's reinstatement filtered on to the airwaves. The squad could resume normal focused preparation after the events of a weekend which turned Carling into a national hero and threatened the very people who had sought to protect their position by sacking him so savagely. It was a political manoeuvre of such insanity that for a brief moment I thought the RFU was run by the Tory party. That might explain Labour's support for a man who would rather leave the left wing to Rory Underwood.

By the Tuesday morning Carling had undergone a transformation from darling of the establishment – excluding the RFU – to national treasure. Suddenly the ex-army officer and upstanding Conservative was the man of the people. Jon Holmes, his agent, could never have done such a wonderful PR job. The main concern for all English rugby supporters was the resumption of the previously excellent preparations for the World Cup, once the media circus of the Monday-night squad session at Marlow was completed. Yet while this episode may be the axe that finally breaks the anachronistic thinking behind the RFU, other questions remain unanswered. The man who first discussed the Carling crisis with Dennis Easby was Jon Holmes. If financial loss for his client was a serious possibility, then that is understandable from both his and Carling's points of view. But what right does an agent have to broker on rugby matters? Amid the euphoria of Carling's reinstatement, nobody seemed to be concerned with the fact that the man paid to promote and manage his client, not the team, was such a key negotiator. The connection between Carling's personal affairs and the position of England captain seemed uncomfortably close. Only days from the World Cup, everyone with England's best endeavours at heart welcomed the decision. Carling was the right man to lead England, but the role of Holmes cast him rather less in the role of the selfless champion.

Other heroes, all with their own particular faults, bade farewell to rugby in the early days of May. The grumpy king and captain of Bath, Jon Hall, did not receive the fairytale end for which his many friends had hoped. He did not recover from the injury sustained against Sale the previous week in time to lead a resurgent Bath to the 36–16 Cup triumph, and it was a big decision for him to omit himself. Bath did allow Hall to receive the trophy in splendid isolation from a bemused Prince Edward, who cannot have expected to present it to a man who had watched from the stand. A bitter-sweet day for Hall, it was a wonderful end to Tony Swift's career. The deadliest try-scorer in the last decade of club rugby left his mark at Twickenham with a magnificent display, and of course, a try. The game will not only miss his lethal finishing, it will also miss his unique celebratory gloatings after scoring. What will British sport do without Swift and Jürgen Klinsmann?

Wasps had missed their chance to prove themselves a match for Bath under real pressure, and in Wales, Neil Jenkins failed to convince anyone outside Sardis Road that Alex Evans should not move him to centre for the World Cup as Pontypridd stumbled to defeat by 12–17 against Swansea in the SWALEC Cup final. The ghosts of André Joubert and friends were finally laid by the men of St Helens.

The Cup finals were the culmination of serious engagements in the domestic season, and appropriately it was left to the defending world champions, Australia, to play the final international before the great war of South Africa. They defeated Argentina by 30–13, having trailed 3–13 at half-time. It was the sort of performance that convinced me someone had informed them that Stuart Barnes had tipped them. It had been that kind of a season for my rugby tipping. I had predicted Bath would win the Courage Leagues, that Cardiff were not good enough to win the Heineken, that Scotland would win the wooden spoon . . . and that Australia would retain the World Cup. If the Wallabies maintained their form from the Second Test with Argentina, I stood on the threshold of my own tipster's wooden spoon.

ACT IV

May to June 1995

I n which the armies of the rugby world finally fly to sporting war in South Africa 1995. Amid a fanfare of media and television trumpets, Will Carling, the Prince of England, and Jack Rowell, the England Alchemist, leave the shores of their homeland in search of victory and the golden trophy.

Despite Gavin Hastings' inspirational leadership of Scotland and the renewed confidence of Wales, the British armies are not expected to conquer any but the weak. Ominous portents have been seen in the southern hemisphere. The defending champions, Australia, are confident, while the pieces of Kitch Christie's South African jigsaw, on the evidence of the sixty-point thrashing of Western Samoa, finally seem to be fitting together. The Dark Lords of New Zealand, considered by many undercoached and ill prepared, appear to have several secret weapons with which to wreak havoc and pursue honours.

A new professional age is on the horizon, and, mingling with the apparently volatile atmosphere in South Africa, it promises to make this the most dramatic ever of the sport's great conflicts.

As this year of living dangerously draws to a close, the stories of triumph, disaster, glory, tragedy and, yes, even humour, unfold in the climactic months of May and June.

Dramatis Personae

The Armies of the World, led by their Princes

François Pienaar, the Prince who has guided South Africa out of the rugby wilderness

Sean Fitzpatrick, the veteran leader of New Zealand

Will Carling, the hero of the English nation, survivor of the coup of the Black President and his extremely Round Table

Michael Lynagh, the Heir Apparent to the King of 1991, Nick Farr-Jones

Gavin Hastings, the Tartan Clansman respected throughout the world

Philippe Saint-André, the gifted leader of the frustrating French

Countless Warriors, Heroes and Villains from the World in Union

THE ALCHEMISTS

Bob Dwyer, the Australian Wizard, who has plotted the defence of the Crown

Jack Rowell, the Club Guru, who has raced against time to prepare England for their great test

Kitch Christie, the South African with a nation on his shoulders

Laurie Mains, the man whose head was wanted by a nation. The Alfredo Garcia of the southern hemisphere

Alex Evans, the man who has promised the mystic Welsh a return to greatness and a host of miracles

Pierre Berbizier, a worried Napoleon in a sharp suit

And finally the Narrator joins the action, armed with a laptop, a reputation as a poor tipster and an unquenchable thirst for truth and red wine

19

Arrival in the Cape of Good Hype

F light SA235 was three hours from take-off and Heathrow Airport could not be negotiated safely without a sidestep like Gerald Davies', so cluttered was the place with television cameras and crew awaiting the arrival of Terry Kingston and his Ireland team. The serious spotlights, however, were reserved for Will Carling, the new-found populist darling, and the confident English camp. It had been a long time since an English sporting team had carried such great expectations into a major tournament.

The airport, then, was awash with excitement, even as the stale smell of the old farts story lingered in the air conditioning. So many potential stories and headlines: it was frightening stuff for a novice like myself. Hell, I was even nervous about finding the right plane without the shepherding skills of a liaison officer. A life as a rugby player is not necessarily the best route into journalism. If my sanity was not to be threatened by my myriad concerns it was imperative to escape to somewhere where I could lay my hands on some free booze – I was determined to take my job as a writer seriously. Using a feature that I wrote for South African Airways' in-flight magazine as my lever, I bullshitted my way into their first-class lounge. It was a display of sufficient cunning and deceit to enable me to consider a political career should my pen dry up or my face puff up too much to continue as a TV sports presenter.

Street-smart and cool enough to be wearing Cuban heels, I glided thirstily into the lounge to be confronted by the sight of the Black President himself, the defeated and retractably-minded Dennis Easby. We exchanged pleasantries in the best English tradition as I briefly wondered whether he too had conned his way into the area. I doubted that greatly. It was no surprise to find the president travelling first class, but after the RFU's recent efforts to undermine the England side a few must have wondered if the luggage hold would not have been more appropriate. Sixty minutes passed, with little diversion bar the tinkling of wine glasses and the embarrassed coughs of the English race, before the fanfare that heralded England's arrival. Bashful greetings were exchanged between the side and the president, the sanctity of a private room saving the team from a fit of mock coughs. They were a focused bunch, some thought too focused. When they reached Durban, England watchers commented on their solemnity.

Most players had time for a quick hello as they wandered through the gateway to everywhere, ushered along by Colin Herridge, their liaison officer, but the overall tenor of the trip was set by Carling's initial press conference once they reached Durban. 'Now it is time for rugby.' Right on, Will. Some of us were feeling pretty pissed off about the tales of Murdoch's millions and noxious smells emanating from Twickenham.

But for now the World Cup and some real action was almost upon us; so were the ceaseless plaudits for England from Bob Dwyer. Bored by tabloid stories speculating on whether England would earn £1,400 or £1,500 per man, per week, during the tournament; uninterested in the generous SAA offer of a free World Cup Ostrich Egg, I grabbed a *Racing Post* newspaper. Searching for the latest Derby prices, I found Dwyer's words looming large on the back page. 'DWYER FAVOURS ENGLAND', trumpeted the headline. I yawned. All year the Australian coach had waged a campaign in praise of England, a deliberate policy aimed at striking to the heart of the perceived arrogance of the former master race – at least in British, or rather, English eyes. Before the Grand Slam decider, Eric Peters, of Bath and Scotland, had claimed to know Jack Rowell well enough to mock any 'arrogant' theories, but a majority of the southern hemisphere writers did not believe that even God could temper the conceit of the empire with the sagging waves and grey lifestyle.

If the southern hemisphere thought little of English modesty, I thought even less of British drinking on the plane. The spirit of the sport has been destroyed, as evidenced by England, and even the Irish, emerging sober after a flight of almost eleven hours. My regrets about the changes in the game were mingled with relief and excitement at being in the media rather than the playing corps as I watched England depart for Durban, Ireland for Johannesburg, and me for Cape Town. Sportswriting may not be the worthiest of vocations, but it beats the hell out of my previous incarnation as a building society manager. My former customers doubtless feel the same. So I admit I was a happy man as I circled Table Mountain and the confluence of the Atlantic and Indian Oceans. Shut your eyes to the horrors of Crossroads and all that inherent apartheid and the place is the nearest thing to my idea of heaven: a vineyard with free wine. I bounded off the plane. All those bars, all that scenery and lead-free air, were something to breathe for.

Yet my joy was outweighed by the despair of South Africa's most beautiful city. Since his release from nearby Robben Island, that sweet soul, Nelson Mandela, has been the numero uno in the country. But in Cape Town one man challenges him, and hard, for the title of main man: Chester Williams, the great Cape coloured king wing, who proves that white supremacy is a myth every time he dons the Springbok colours. The player who would win South Africa the tournament and worldwide popularity, according to the locals, was out. The city was shot to pieces and in despair. 'In the streets the children screamed/the lovers cried and the poets dreamed/not a word was spoken/the church bells all were broken.' A rugby nation was in mourning.

A more cruel blow could not have been struck against a nation ablaze with World Cup fever. The first sight as you left the airport lounge was a giant advertising hoarding. A pair of familiar eyes stared straight through the onlooker. Above the eyes was the message: 'The wait is over.' Not for you, Chester, I thought to myself. The hero of Cape Town seemed destined to miss his moment; another four years would be an eternity.

Chester Williams apart, the tournament was serious business in the country. Parliament announced it would suspend operations on 25 May to allow ministers and staff to watch the opening match. Political propaganda was replaced in print by rugby's version of psychological warfare. The newspapers were crammed with Springbok assertions that Australia were under greater pressure in the opener because of their world champions tag. Those column inches were countered by Aussie claims that home pressure placed the South Africans under more stress. Reading the press was becoming rather similar to watching a long baseline rally as both camps launched the same salvos back and forth.

Australia's assertion seemed the more believable, a theory endorsed by the nerves of the South African media, who prayed for, but did not expect, victory. Most of the sporting world reckoned that Australia were the most professional side in every respect, both on and off the field. Even Dwyer's propaganda offensives were a part of this ultra-professionalism. Taking the opportunity to grab the guru at an Australian training session, I questioned the sincerity of his frequently voiced opinions. Dwyer just twinkled his eyes in a most alchemical manner.

The Wallabies' great trans-Tasman rivals, New Zealand, also had their minds on things mysterious. TVNZ'S familiar commentator, Keith Quinn, hired a Zulu *sangoma* – a witchdoctor – to cast a spell on Australia. His televised prediction was a South Africa–New Zealand final. By 18 June this man would be in a position to name his price.

As I watched Australia train I decided that this Zulu would have to be a pretty powerful operator to stop the Wallabies. Given the success rate of my forecasts this year, I should have known better – or perhaps the *sangoma* really was a master of the occult. Australia looked every inch the masters of Rugby Union. They were relaxed and fresh, and their training was almost as impressive as Table Mountain towering behind them. Only David Campese ruffled the calm surface. He accused me of being an English spy. Even the trusty 'objective journalist' line met with a degree of scepticism. Campo fever was another early feature of the tournament. We read of his personal BMW, which had been delivered to the team hotel; we even read stories about Campese denying that he was a party animal. Nobody was in any doubt that he headed the list of world stars as the battles to come loomed ever closer.

Campo gathered with all the other World Cup warriors for the opening lunch on Saturday 20 May. The venue was South Africa's oldest and grandest vineyard, Groot Constantia, one of the few places I knew about in the dark days of apartheid. The estate is proof that wine can enhance as well as destroy the mind. Even a member of the Temperance Society would appreciate its beauty, but unfortunately that day the fairest Cape had turned foul and rain lashed through the giant marquee in which the event was held. Four hundred and fifteen players were rather less appreciative of the environment than the countless committee and media men who were able to celebrate the commencement of hostilities with the aid of God's greatest crop.

In fact, 416 players should have been present, but Dean Richards was nursing a worrying strain back in Durban. Jack Rowell masked his concerns well as he sipped champagne and listened to the opening speech made by his verbal sparring partner from a year earlier, Louis Luyt. The day before Luyt had been discussing the creation of a three-team international tournament in the southern hemisphere, a topic that would later rock the sport, but today the closing words of his address carried Churchillian overtones. 'The Rugby World Cup is not an ending . . . no, no, it is merely the beginning of everything.' Physical comparisons, too, between the SARFU president and the late English statesman were justified, but this was one war that Luyt would prefer to see England lose.

The England camp appeared tense. Only the effervescent Victor Ubogu seemed at ease. In their snazzy green-and-white boating blazers, the Australians stole the fashion show, but nobody was going to get the better of Victor in the decibel battle. From 50 metres distant I heard the familiar guffaw. The source of his merriment was Emile Ntamack, France's black wing. Along with the other French three-quarters, he had shaved his head completely. They looked more like characters from *Pulp Fiction* than rugby stars. Ntamack's appearance, though, was slightly different. 'His scalp is white!' shrieked Ubogu, in both horror and amusement. Few opponents would have the chance to laugh at Ntamack on the pitch in the next month of rugby.

The bald French backs provided classic footage for the intrepid Ubogu, who was videoing the lunch for background material for his bar, Shoeless Joe's. The one team who were less than enthusiastic to assist Victor were his English colleagues. One player felt that the recordings were a money-making scheme for Ubogu's company, and that therefore a token donation should be paid into the players' kitty, as is the norm – a bizarre way to demonstrate collective unity and a warning of the many debilitating effects of the new age of greed that prevails, even as you and I barter for our pay rise. Fortunately, Ubogu shrugged off the problem in his customary jocular manner.

Another potential star of the tournament, that throwback to Welsh greatness, Robert Jones, was finding it more difficult to accept a collective decision by the Welsh squad to refrain from all alcohol. As Wales were based in Bloemfontein for their first match, the odd beer was a must to stave off almost suicidal boredom. A team man to the core, Jones valiantly tried to follow the rules, but by 8.30 p.m. on their first full day in the Free State, some rum had mysteriously found its way into his glass of the Real Thing. The unfortunate Welsh had to leave Bloemfontein at 5.30 the next morning for the official function, so when Jones settled into bed it wasn't long before he had to get up. Such irreverence only days before the start of the war increased my affection for the scrum-half.

Jones might have brought a smile to my face, but the sight of Neil Jenkins leaving the function with a bottle of red and a bottle of white caused consternation.

'Hey, Neil, I thought booze was banned.'

'It is, but I want the souvenir labels.'

Did this man really pour the contents of those bottles back into the earth from whence it came? The full horror of what the answer might be forced me to shy away from asking the awful question.

The day drifted drunkenly on, and later I caught my first glimpse of players breaking camp when I stumbled across Adriaan Richter, Johan Roux and André Joubert hidden in the corner of a Cape Town bar. Putting two and two together, several of us deduced that the talented full-back must have been left out of the team to play Australia in the opening match because of his erratic goal-kicking. As we left, the wild man of South African rugby, James Small, arrived, looking for action. The South African team announcement the next day was going to be interesting.

Accompanied by my regular Sunday hangover, I watched the announcement of the Springbok team on television. I was wrong again. Joubert and Small were both selected, to the relief of many admirers. Both would need to be at their best to beat an Australian side with the strength in depth to omit Tim Horan, described by Bob Dwyer as 'ready to tear someone apart'. Poor Canada and Romania must have felt like Christians in the bowels of the Coliseum.

The tournament was not due to start for another four days, but the media had plenty to sink their teeth into. Following the naming of the teams for the first match was the confirmation of Jack Rowell's XV for England against Argentina in Pool B. Richards was not fit, and Rowell chose Ojomoh to play at 8, leaving Clarke and Rodber on the flanks and Neil Back in the shadows. The headlines, however, were reserved for the recall of Dewi Morris over Kyran Bracken. As Bracken had been out of form in the last month of the Five Nations and injured since then, it should not have come as a surprise to anyone. Yet it was another alarming indication that England were reverting to their old and ugly static style. Neither Rowell nor Cusworth were instinctive fans of Morris's 'forward-friendly' style. The inclusion of a pair of half-backs more popular with forwards than with backs suggested that Bob Dwyer's secret reservations about the decision-making skills of the side remained too accurate for English comfort.

Sections of the British media were more concerned about the social unrest in South Africa. Colin Price of the *Daily Mirror* described Durban as 'hell', adding tamely that he himself had been neither mugged nor harassed. The *Evening Standard* was even more sensational. 'WORLD CUP TERROR ALERT'. Alarmed readers were informed that travellers 'will be mugged in Johannesburg. They [the fans] have flown here to enjoy the rugby. Instead they will be robbed and probably beaten up.' From a society that has engendered such violent areas as Moss Side, to name but one, it seemed pretty rich to a very irate set of South African journalists. They had a point.

The headline in that Monday's edition of the *Cape Times* also worried me. 'WIND IS THE MAIN CONCERN FOR STRANSKY.' The British thought only Will Carling suffered from such problems. Neutrals were of the opinion that the hosts faced a whole galaxy of greater problems as the countdown to the tournament drew near. Newspapers carried pictures of relaxed Australians unwinding away from training alongside a shot of Balie Swart, the Springbok prop, evidently contemplating life on Death Row. Joel Stransky, the Western Province fly-half who had forced Hennie le Roux into the centre, called every Test 'a matter of life and death', before remembering to remind us that Australia were the team under pressure.

A state of paranoia appeared to have infected the South African squad. One innocent citizen stumbled, quite accidentally, on the Springbok training camp 10 miles out of town and was swiftly ejected by a bouncer he claimed had been told to 'forcibly remove anyone who objected'. An ugly mood was in the air. My own fears bordered on the paranoid when the normally affable SARFU liaison man and chief executive, Edward Griffith, warned us: 'We will do everything possible to enable these players, who are under enormous pressure, to concentrate solely on the task of winning the World Cup.' He sounded like one of the thugs Nixon employed to put off over-intrepid journalists.

Feeling the pressure myself, I headed for a bar and a Cape Town 'special cigarette' en route to Stellenbosch and a Danie Craven memorial match. The University town was the perfect escape from the increasingly tense city. Full of gorgeous gabled architecture set against the massive peaks of the Jonkershoek, it was a fairytale town . . . and of course, there were the vineyards. Mental stability was nearly restored. If only I had avoided the match. The Craven XV, captained by Naas Botha, smashed Nick Farr-Jones' World XV by eighty points on an afternoon during which the feeling of narcotic disorientation increased alarmingly.

To my horror there were two referees on the pitch. Even William Burroughs cannot have suffered such scary drug delusions. One is normally a nightmare, but two, Jesus! Things degenerated when Danie Gerber, that epitome of the old South Africa, appeared on the scene, still as unsmiling and powerful as ever at the age of thirty-four. I was finally driven over the edge as the terraces of students burst forth into 'Swing Low'. I stared at the rows of vineyards in the distance and inhaled slowly and deeply.

The madness was contagious. Attending a press conference in Cape Town the next day, I watched the usually diplomatic Springbok captain, François Pienaar, apparently flip. He launched a bizarre attack on the city of Cape Town. The rich diversity of targets ranged from the partisan nature of the local media to the weather and even the low standard of driving. Suddenly I was yearning for sane old Bristol. Cameramen deluged Pienaar with demands for different angles. The cameras clicked like crickets until he snapped. 'I am not an actor,' he complained. Pienaar's enemies in Cape Town argued that acting was his only forte. The man remained more respected outside his own country, where provincial jealousy plays no part in judgement.

As South Africa prepared in the manner of a live time bomb, the Australians were as laid back as ever. One or two Aussie writers, notably former Test player Peter FitzSimons, thought they were too laid back and lacked the requisite will and focus. I refuted his assertion. Surely I would not be wrong again. Around the country, team news filled the air. Neil Jenkins had lost his battle with Adrian Davies at fly-half; Laurent Cabannes was still in the cold for France; Eric Elwood was recalled to face New Zealand . . . But we were bored with teams and statements, we were ready for the sound of thunder, the start of the 1995 World Cup.

20

The Great White Dopes

I awoke early on the morning of 25 May. I felt sick with nerves; the adrenaline of an expectant nation was affecting bystanders from 5,000 miles away. It was too intimidating even to think myself into the position of Pienaar and his team. Were the Springboks looking at an early-morning Table Mountain, wondering, as I was, whether God, like President Mandela, was a recent convert to the team who were once the world's pariahs? There was a feeling abroad that something as intangible as destiny was protecting South Africa, the latest and most spectacular converts to democracy. I left the house of my friend and loyal bar cohort, and South Africa's sports journalist of the year, Louis de Villiers, and headed for the Newlands Stadium. Any pretence of objectivity was stripped bare as the historic and belated World Cup entrance of South Africa drew near. Sheer joy and ebullience were the themes; the triumphalism of the race seemed to have been tamed by the momentous and moving events of its recent history.

The smiling home crowd wore All Black, Irish and a host of other shirts as the atmosphere built up. The one common feature was the multitude of faces painted in the colours of the Rainbow Nation. In the spirit of democracy, street hawkers flourished. Everything from biltong to 'rugger rubbers' were being sold – the latter were perhaps the only way to express a 'fuck rugby' sentiment on this day when a nation ground to a halt. Smells from a nearby brewery wafted into Stoker's Bar, where I sat with an increasingly excitable Louis and his colleague from the sports pages of *Rapport*, Freddie Hendriks. The odds were stacked on Freddie, a notoriously emotional man, crying during the anthem. The opening ceremony left the hardest of men moved with its colourful and overt symbols of unity. The pageantry rattled on to P.J. Powers singing 'World in Union' and 50,000 voices roared in unison as South Africa's beloved father and leader, Nelson Mandela, walked on to the pitch. The chants of 'Nelson, Nelson,' echoed around Newlands as proof of renewed sanity in South Africa flooded the emotions. Such was the poignancy of the afternoon that even the slowest bar staff in the universe could not drive me to despair. That really is a special day. And, yes, Freddie did cry like an infant as 'Nkosi Sikelel' iAfrika' played. He was not alone.

It was a scene that belonged in a different and better world; infinitely more than just a game of rugby was being celebrated. That factor worked in favour of the nervous but inspired home side. Australia, in contrast, seemed prepared for a rugby occasion, but not something as monumental as this. During the anthems the bewilderment on their faces was evident – they had not been expecting to confront a stadium on speed. In the opening stages Australia found abundant holes within the organisation of the Springbok back row, but the failure of their back line, devoid of individual spark, to push them clear was to prove decisive. The Australian pressure slowly disappeared as Joost van der Westhuizen drove the Springboks into attack with a series of powerful surges. It was to be the Australian skipper, Michael Lynagh, who scored the first try of the tournament, but thereafter he was fully eclipsed by the Capetonian Joel Stransky. The man with the wind problem scored twenty-two points that will rank among the most memorable in the long history of Springbok rugby.

Even Pieter Hendriks, the man wearing the shirt of the beloved Chester Williams, became a hero throughout the country. The tournament would end sadly for him, but this afternoon he grasped his moment to swerve around Campese and score a triumphant try which might be regarded as the beginning of the end for one of the sport's greats. Neither Campo nor Lynagh looked like the same players who had so dominated the world in 1991; Lynagh in particular seemed burdened by the captaincy that he inherited from Farr-Jones. Lacking their expected inspiration, the Wallabies were well beaten. Even Bob Dwyer appeared jaded. His side played as if the sport were a game of chess. The wit and instinct that characterised the 1991 team were replaced by robotic rugby – minus Japanese efficiency.

Australia's magicians had been found wanting by the challenge of an entire nation's will. A day of eternal memories was scripted to end in South African triumph, and I made them the new favourites for the tournament. After just one game, only France blocked their path to Ellis Park on 24 June. Australia, on the other hand, faced the three peaks of England, New Zealand and either the Springboks again or France if they were to retain their crown. In a rare display of prophetic accuracy, I dismissed their hopes as I left the ground.

The night ended with the extremely inebriated preparation of copy for *Rapport*, the Afrikaans Sunday with enough humour to employ an

Englishman who had described Bloemfontein as the Fourth Reich only twelve months previously. I awoke with a substantial and impressive hangover, realising that a major rewrite of my eulogistic piece on the Springbok half-backs was required. Alcoholic inspiration is a myth. After repairing the night's damage I bade farewell to the wild excesses of Cape Town and flew to join the great northern hemisphere hopes, England, who were based in Durban, the Blackpool of South Africa. Arriving in the Sunshine City on the Indian Ocean was an overwhelming anti-climax. The high-octane energy of Cape Town was replaced by the quiet seriousness of an introspective England camp. The opening match of the tournament had had the aura of a wonderful occasion, but England were approaching their first game in Pool B in their customary 'just another international' style. There is nothing wrong with such professionalism, but it was a pity that so many players were deprived of the special atmosphere that surrounds a tournament like this.

The players, with the odd exception, cocooned themselves in the claustrophobic team room to watch a triple-header of rugby. I sloped off to my room, away from the temptations of alcohol. The first course was the debut of the Scotland side in Pool D. Their opponents were the Ivory Coast – or Côte d'Ivoire, as they preferred to be called. The match was an historic one, as Gavin Hastings continued his amazing exploits with a world-record forty-four point haul. The poor Africans looked as if they were rather too fond of the famous lager from which I would hope the region of Stellaland derives its name. The 89–0 result represented a staggering start for the Scots, but it was not my kind of rugby.

The main course promised to be more interesting, as France tussled with the erratic Tongans, an outside tip to reach the knock-out stages. This was a real international. After sixty minutes France were on the ropes and lucky to hold on to a 9–3 lead. The match turned on the first sending-off of the tournament, when a case of wrong identification led to the dismissal of the Irish-sounding Tongan, Feleti Mahoni. The victim was poor old Philippe Benetton, a man who obviously bore a strong resemblance to traditional Tongan doormats. Suddenly France found an assertive gear and rattled up twenty-nine points for a flattering 38–10 win. The most impressive Frenchman was the sinuously graceful Ntamack, whose performance was the exception in another disappointing French display. As with the Australians, there was too little individual brilliance – an insane problem, considering the instinctive talent of Pierre Berbizier's side.

Feeling full, I watched the pudding, Canada and Romania, with the mildest of interest. Romania won the line-out battle decisively, but the world's portliest fly-half, Gareth Rees, controlled the game and helped Canada to a 34–3 win. As far as the rest of the world was concerned, these sides could now revert to the roles of fall guys for the Aussies

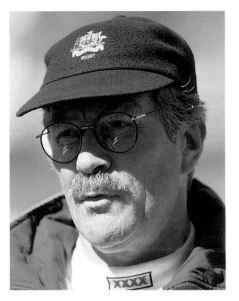

9a. *Above left:* Bob Dwyer, Australia's Alchemist, comes to terms with defeat in a disappointing World Cup effort.

9b. *Above:* South Africa's magician: Keith Christie was the man who guided the 'Boks to glory.

9c. *Left:* One of the great moments of the World Cup: Laurie Mains, coach of New Zealand, smiles.

9d. *Below:* The Irish admit to the world that 'We are not worthy' after victory against Wales in the most depressing game of the tournament. Eric Elwood appears to be wetting himself at the joke.

10a+b. *Below and below left:* Flashpoint. Gareth Rees offers a two-fingered verdict on his dismissal in the Canada–South Africa clash, while James Dalton heads towards a phone to cadge a tearful lift home from his dad.

10c, d+e. *Right and opposite page:* Happier times. Pieter Hendriks sets the country alight as he rounds Campese. The Aussies were on the way out as the 'Boks headed for glory.

12a. That familiar Carling pose – arms aloft in celebration. Australia were beaten, but the nature of the English win suggested that the end of the road was near. Not quite as pyrrhic as the Scotland game, but by now it was clear that England had conceded the battle to translate the Rowell vision.

12b. Jack Rowell walks away from the dismal play-off performance against France. Head down, he knew he had lost his race against time.

12c. The prime minister lets his hair down. He arrived in time to concoct his unique Midas touch before the New Zealand semi-final.

13a. So close to glory. Philippe Saint-André came within one wet slide of a World Cup final.

13b. Third place restored - temporarily - the damaged reputation of Pierre Berbizier.

13c. Swinging in the rain. South Africa had many reasons to thank their broken-handed lounge lizard, André Joubert. Neither the rain nor France affected the poise of this great player.

14a, b+c. The man who has changed the face of rugby – *on* the pitch. Jonah Lomu surges forward as the All Blacks march towards their Grand Slam against the best of British.

15a+b. (*Opposite*): New Zealand produces the lamb, but it was the British to the slaughter. 'Rob and Mike who?'

16a. Jonah Lomu is finally shackled. André Joubert ignores his broken hand to take on Lomu, and although this attempt failed there was always cover enough to ensure that in the game that mattered Lomu did not run away with the spoils.

16b. *Left:* Heroes Mandela and Pienaar celebrate the arrival of a new day in South Africa.
16c. *Below:* It ended in familiar fashion for the author and Chester Williams – in smiles.

and 'Boks in the group of death. The Canadians, however, had other ideas.

It was not one of the most memorable Friday nights of my life, but I suspect I enjoyed it much more than an England side growing increasingly tense in their self-absorbed isolation. No matter how much Jack Rowell smiles, anyone who was fortunate enough to play under him at Bath will laugh at memories of last-minute nerves before big games. In the final training session before a match he exorcises his own fears. Not this time. Carling informed Rowell that the players did not want a session. With that valve blocked, tension grew. On the morning of the Argentina match it strangled even the hotel residents uninvolved in the England camp. Jack Rowell preferred to talk about South Africa, calling them 'the greatest rugby nation in the world' and making them favourites for the Cup after their 'epic win'. That win had enhanced the respect he developed for them on the 1994 tour.

Rowell drifted around the public areas of the hotel, but the players lacked the freedom of an international morning in the Petersham Hotel before a Five Nations match at Twickenham. The Holiday Inn Garden Court was a meeting-place for the well-intentioned, innocent supporters, in their white shirts, who inadvertently drove the team into the stale air of the team-room. The 5 p.m. kick-off was another irregular feature. Instead of showing the deep focus for which they are renowned, the team were distracted by the match between the other sides in the pool, Italy and Western Samoa. When Rob Andrew, one of the most intense players, talked of alarming levels of disorientation, it became clear that the squad were not at a peak of readiness. It was not just another match, but a World Cup, played in very different circumstances. Perhaps the criticism that England do not have the ability to adapt on the pitch is also a valid comment on their mental preparation.

The players watched Western Samoa produce some superb running rugby to beat an Italy side labelled by the world's media the country most likely to surprise everyone. Quite how a team tipped universally can be a surprise package still confounds me. Anyway, in the process the Samoans also caused further embarrassment to me in my new guise as a columnist for the *Racing Post*. Stretching the punter's terminology to extremes in my Saturday column, I implored readers to back Italy to win 'for a slice of la dolce vita'. Sad, no? Brian Lima, the Samoan star who had remained immune to the lure of Rugby League, produced a great exhibition of wing play to silence the many who believed that the islanders' resources had been too far stretched since their glory days of 1991. Italy had chances, but suffered from poor ball-retention and appalling midfield defence. Neither side looked capable of shocking the England side, despite the deep impression that the Samoan running lines in the centre made on Rowell.

The next match from Bloemfontein was of superfluous interest to England: the first Pool C game between Japan and Wales. The Celts had been starved of tries all season, but against Japan they flowed like a swelling river. The confidence that Alex Evans had apparently instilled shone through as Wales scored fifty-seven points. The Japanese had recruited Pacific Islanders such as wing Lopeti Oto to boost their physical presence, but their lack of stature in the line-out allowed Derwyn Jones to celebrate his recall with a monopoly of possession. Gareth Thomas, an almost unknown lump of a twenty-year-old, scored a hat-trick on his debut and the deposed skipper, Ieuan Evans, ran in a consolation brace. It was a good start for the renewed Welsh.

As the Celts breathed a sigh of relief, their great rivals from east of the River Severn emerged on to a wet King's Park pitch in Durban. With a capacity of 50,000, the stadium was never likely to be full, especially as a rout by the England side that scared both Australia and New Zealand was anticipated. Minutes before kick-off, the ground was closer to being half-empty than half-full, another unnerving unfamiliarity for a team brought up on Twickenham and the Parc des Princes. Jack Rowell looked nervous as he checked his watch, buttoned and unbuttoned his blazer and tightened his tie. It was a sight I had seen so often. He was about to discover whether the reversion to static type during the finale of the Five Nations had been a blip, or a symptom of failure in his race against time to change the instincts of the side.

Carling led out England to a fairly insipid 'Swing Low'. The bloody song had followed me from Twickenham to Stellenbosch and now Durban, and this was the worst version yet. In retrospect it seemed like a bad omen. The players appeared tense and tired – there was scant sign of enjoyment. The atmosphere was funereal compared with the adrenaline of Newlands forty-eight hours earlier. Sure enough, the opening England play set a tedious tone for a cool Natal night. I remembered a first line from a corrupted Hot Chocolate song – 'It started with a kick.' Rob Andrew thumped the first ball he touched into orbit and proceeded to do little else for the longest seventy-nine minutes of rugby I can remember. It was the sort of game that made me wish that I was a croquet columnist – anything rather than watch this turgid stuff. The side gave themselves no chance to test the Argentinian defence from anything other than first phase as they repeatedly kicked the ball away. Only two big hits in the midfield were needed to destroy the most fragile of confidences. The questions raised in the wake of their performance against Scotland were surfacing again. The pressure was on, and England were reverting to type – at times beyond even the previous pale of static rugby. Rowell had his answer: he had lost that race against time. These determined dogs were not for being taught new tricks.

The crowd appreciated that early tension was inevitable and made allowances, but after twenty minutes their impatience began to surface. Andrew, entrenched in the game that is as comfortable as an armchair for trundling forwards, but so debilitating for a player like Jeremy Guscott, who needs some action, hugged the touchlines and kicked his goals with a sniper's precision, but Guscott looked indifferent, an artist frustrated in an artisan culture. Had it not been Brian Moore who had reminded Scotland of their duty to entertain? Presumably he would be the first to urge the side to make a public apology for a dismal match fit to grace the dinosaur age of rugby.

As the game progressed into its final quarter, England, via the boot of Andrew, led by a reassuring 18–3. The problems started when Argentina finally opened their eyes and realised that this England side were more frightened than frightening. Patricio Noriega (no relation to the deposed Panamanian dictator) crashed over for an old-fashioned prop's try and the Pumas were lifted. England's response was to revert to even more stolid rugby and by full-time they were fortunate to have hung on to 24–18.

The entire twenty-four-point haul belonged to Rob Andrew, but it was not a 24-carat performance. Headline writers were delighted with the easy 'one hero and fourteen old farts' storyline, but the truth, as ever, was far more complex. As a longstanding rival on the field, my criticisms of Rob Andrew are invariably tainted in the eyes of many, but this, my friends, is how I see it. His central and conservative role was the prime reason for the sad sidelining of any creative impulse. He was driving talents like Guscott's into obscurity. Andrew is a man of incredible virtues – commitment, will, nerve, he has them all in aces – but his heavy-booted tunes were the wrong melodies for a side with ambitions to win at the highest level. Any lyricism on the field of King's Park belonged to the men from the Pampas. At the final whistle, Latin faces of dejection mingled with English faces of depression. It had been a grim experience. At Newlands, I had crossed Australia off my list of potential winners; now England were scratched out too.

As France had not been on the list before the tournament started, I was down to South Africa and the All Black dark horses. New Zealand met Ireland in the final match of the day and stirred the dying embers of my rugby enthusiasm, as did the Irish, who revelled in that familiar underdog role and rocked the Blacks with their early passion. Garrett Halpin surged over for another prop's try and offered New Zealand the sort of two-fingered salute for which a footballer would be fined the entire Irish tour allowance. Not a good idea, Garrett, old chum, to wake up this side so rudely. No, let's rephrase that: it was absolutely stupid. Battling in the front row, Halpin obviously hadn't noticed a nineteen-year-old-kid who weighed 19st, ran the 100 metres in 10.7 seconds and failed to appreciate a request to fuck off. Garrett, you made a big mistake. The prodigy called Jonah Lomu scored two sensational tries in a forty-three-point Kiwi retort. The tournament had the star all major events so badly need, and the All Blacks as a unit were a lot better than most of the world expected. Laurie Mains' secret weapons had been revealed: from the nuclear force of Lomu to the tactical nous of Andrew Mehrtens at fly-half, the Blacks, to the concern of the rest of the rugby world, were back.

New Zealand and South Africa, then, looked the best teams after the first set of games, but that did not dissuade the local Natal press from concentrating on their seeded team, England. The Sunday paper the next morning upset the English heart-throb, Ben Clarke. He was rumoured to be disillusioned about his omission from a list of English 'hunks', the local preference being for 'the Oriental sexiness of the Underwood brothers'. More serious was Rowell's private verdict on the performance. The squad looked as tense before their team meeting as they had done before the match the previous day. Indoor fireworks were inevitable. Only the media men who headed for lunch on the ocean at the Oyster Box enjoyed the sunshine.

The Monday was even less enjoyable for Shoeless Vic. The England team announcement made it perfectly clear that Rowntree had been selected on merit for the Italy game and that Ubogu was axed. Big rocket, Jack. Brian Moore thought that Ubogu had been made a scape-goat. Victor's legendary aversion to scrummaging always leaves him vulnerable when the wheels fall off the scrum. Neil Back was a shock recall and Phil de Glanville replaced the injured Carling, Rob Andrew standing in as captain. The players looked miserable, despite the pres-ence of their wives and girlfriends nearby, and the training session, held behind closed doors, was apparently a tense affair.

I watched the Italian team train. Perhaps the England boys should have joined me. It was the sort of session to cheer an English team badly in need of some urgent karma. Instead, on the Monday night they booked an entire sushi bar. Quite what Jason Leonard thinks of raw fish is not recorded: Terry Cooper of the Press Association did bravely poke his head into the restaurant for a quick word with the Cockney sushi king, only for Rob Andrew to tell him to 'do yourself a favour and leave the premises in a hurry'. First the amenable Edward Griffith of South Africa, now the affable Andrew. The tournament was languishing in a limbo between sport and paranoia. Whatever else it did, the raw fish failed to spark a training session of anything other than indifferent quality. Les Cusworth expressed his concerns about the midfield's ability to play the flat game; Don Rutherford watched and criticised. Few people left the session with a spring in their step.

The session was most notable for the gathering of the 'barmy army', who were slowly arriving to add their support. They succeeded in heightening the already obvious siege mentality in the camp. Supporters often confuse the elusiveness of players with aloofness, but ceaseless back-slapping is not conducive to ideal preparation. The reason for England's reluctance to stay at a central hotel was clear and justified as they sought relaxation in vain. After training, the hotel was full of knowledgeable supporters trying to chat up the local waitresses by slipping in first-name references to internationals. Success, thankfully, seemed a rare commodity. The spurned Romeos eventually conceded defeat and left the hotel for the giant marquees which had been erected on Durban's Golden Mile. Large screens and cheap booze seemed as good a way as any to watch the Tuesday feast of rugby.

The day's hostilities commenced with a match of great significance for England: Argentina against Western Samoa. Jack Rowell was rooting for a Samoan victory that would automatically qualify them for the quarter-finals and perhaps dampen their raw aggression. To win they had to overcome the superb Argentinian pack. To their credit the Samoans achieved what Rowell and the England team thought was beyond them and won one of the best games in the tournament by 32–26. It was a game of wonderful contrasts. Argentina scored first, after eight minutes and seven awesome scrummages – an apt Carlingism. The Samoan response to this bludgeon was a quicksilver threequarter try that left Rowell asking, 'Why didn't we do that?' I think he knew the answer even before the final whistle against Scotland. It was a lack of ambition, not of talent, that was undermining England. Rowell allowed this negative grip to re-assert itself. There was something fatalistic about his attitude. If the Argentina game was the final proof that England were not ready to beat the best, it would explain why he became more relaxed as the tournament progressed. There was no hint of conservatism from the freewheeling Samoans, who had wheelbarrowed their way to the tournament. They were battered up front, but showed the resilience to fight back from 26–13 down to claim a quarter-final berth, to the relief of the England team.

The English relief was in stark contrast to the abject misery of an Argentinian pack that had once again played magnificently. Tight in the scrum and dynamic in the loose, they possessed at least four forwards who could have been considered for a world XV. But they were out. In the defeat against Samoa, José Cilley, the recalled fly-half, kicked six out of eight attempts. Rowell admitted that such statistics would have beaten his side at the weekend. But I have the feeling that Messrs Mendez, Noriega and friends would not be consoled by the fact that it was merely mindless selection which had cost them a place in the last eight.

The less impressive Romanians followed Argentina out of the tournament when South Africa's shadow side beat them 21–8. The thrill of Cape Town was missing as I watched from one of the beer-sodden marquees. South African scores were greeted with applause rather than rapture. The biggest cheer of the game was reserved for Joel Stransky, who joined the match as a temporary replacement. It was as dull as a wet day in Bucharest – and that is not a recommended experience – but at least Romania tried. They were a different side from the sad bunch who begged for mercy at Twickenham in the autumn. A consolation try for the Eastern Europeans was not resented by the host nation. It left England and the Ivory Coast as the only tryless teams in the tournament. This was not the table at which England had come to feast. Worse was to follow: by 7.30 p.m., South African time, England, much to the amusement of Scotland, were the last tournament try virgins. Something about practising and preaching floated down from the direction of the previously lambasted Scots. At the conclusion of the Cup this statistic remained a treasured one for Gavin Hastings. In fact the Ivorians scored two in a spirited 54–13 defeat by a complacent French side with all the dynamism of a sloth-bear. On full-time a TV reporter interviewing Saint-André suggested that he was pleased with the performance. The normally articulate French captain stared in astonished silence. Enough said, or unsaid. It was not just the Poms and Aussies who were worried.

French concerns were heightened by Gavin Hastings in the last game of the night. He followed up his forty-four points with another thirty-one as Scotland sank an ugly, ill-tempered Tongan side. The England camp had hoped that at the very least their old rivals would be rattled, but 41–5 reflected the remarkable renaissance of a team which had been the laughing-stock of the sport in December. Without the creative talents of the injured Townsend, there was no magic behind the scrum, but they were at least explosive; that was a lot more than could be said for some of the northern hemisphere countries thus far. Their chances of beating France looked good. That would mean avoiding the Kiwis in the quarter-finals and playing the Five Nations flops, Wales or Ireland, instead. Scotland were enjoying themselves.

Poor England, burdened by expectations, both external and self-imposed, looked as if they would rather be anywhere than South Africa. The betting companies still predicted a victory of twenty-seven points the next day against Italy. My advice in the *Racing Post* was to bet against such a wide margin. The mental strain appeared to have transformed the side which had enough dynamite to blow up Parliament back in February into a fat fall guy set up for good ole Frank.

My itinerary dictated that I would not stay in Durban for the rest of the group matches. I was delighted to escape an atmosphere that drifted from occasional flatness to more tangible tension. I was bound for the city under siege, Johannesburg, and the Welsh squad as they prepared for their crucial pool games over the following five days. I would soon find out if Alex Evans was a coach worthy of a place among the great alchemists of the game.

Booking myself into the Sunnyside Hotel with the Welsh was a deliberate decision. No nation tells you so much about themselves through their body language. Some people claim to be able to determine whether Wales will win a match by the way they walk the day before a game. Call me a sucker for romance, but I was hoping that all the swagger of which I had read was a reality; the sport loves a cocky Welsh side, even if it is just for the satisfaction of beating them.

Before I could find out whether my hopes had any basis in fact I had to negotiate the drive from the airport to the hotel through the Hillbrow region of town, where cannibals, white-slave traders and a militia of muggers were supposedly waiting for me. Yes, I am a trendy lefty, but two weeks of horror stories had seriously messed up my right-on posture. My mind recalled Tom Wolfe's *Bonfire of the Vanities*. One wrong turn would ruin my life at best, leave me dead and mutilated in a downtown gutter at worst. Every red light brought fear; the sight of four black faces in a minibus was a moment of profound paranoia. Concentrating totally on my route I arrived at the hotel without drama. Relief, embarrassment and shame flooded over me as I parked up and strolled with insouciance, every inch the world traveller, into the hotel reception. The horror story that never was was over.

One or two of the Welsh squad were in the lobby, but with a Test against New Zealand only six or seven hours away, the majority were ensconced in the dreaded team-room. No clues for an amateur psychologist could be gleaned here, so I departed, by taxi rather than risking another fearful drive, heading for Ellis Park, where Wales would play that night.

Before the live match there was a daunting glut of 240 minutes of international rugby. The three battles were expected to constitute a sporting slaughter – tedious fare for a fan. The world champions were first up in Pool A. Surely a Canadian side humiliated by England and New Zealand in recent times would allow the gold to flow from the green this time. The Australians needed a convincing display to stimulate a campaign that had taken a turning far worse than any I had so far made on 'the streets of fear'. The locals of Port Elizabeth, Shakespearian to the nth degree, came to praise Australia, but left wondering how Canada did not bury them. It was the start of a strange day's rugby that re-awakened my hallucinogenic fears. Christopher Hill wrote a Marxist critique of the sixteenth century in England entitled

'The World Turned Upside Down'. Until New Zealand intervened, that was how this tournament was shaping up.

Yet all was normal after fifteen minutes. Tim Horan was reunited with Jason Little and Michael Lynagh and the magic was back. Australia raced into an unassailable 17–3 lead. We awaited death in the afternoon, but by half-time the big-hitting Canadians had tackled Australia out of their rhythm and the lead had not progressed beyond 20–6. All the harmony in the second period emanated from a dominant Canadian side. Only a fumbling display by scrum-half John Graf prevented Canada from pushing Australia to the limit. The final score was 27–11, but Dwyer's men had been outplayed for an hour. Canada had revived memories of their 1991 form, but for Australia, the rediscovery of the magic appeared to have been a mirage.

The next game was even more bizarre. In Pool C Ireland scored fifty points yet were taught a real rugby lesson by a Japanese side which won the hearts of Bloemfontein. Ireland won because they were bigger. There is no more to be written. When the Irish management arrived at the post-match press conference, Gerry Murphy was asked how he thought Japan could improve. He smiled and suggested that Ireland were not able to teach Japan anything. Correct. The Japanese (and the Pacific Islanders) played all the creative rugby. In footballing terms, their performance stamped them as one of the teams of the tournament, hampered only by their physique. It was no coincidence that, for all their pretty patterns, the men who could break tackles were invariably their foreign imports. Sinali Latu and Lopeti Oto were outstanding, but they were about as Japanese as Ford motor cars. They battled back from 19–0 to 26–21 with just twenty minutes left, and only two penalty tries resulting from collapsed scrums secured Ireland's win. Poor Japan. To use boxing parlance, they produced all the combinations, but what price the greatest Mexican flyweight against even the most wooden of heavyweights, know what I mean? Japan will never be a rugby power unless a handicap system is invented.

If Japan's problem was their size, England had no such concerns. Unfortunately, their bulk was apparently matched by the burden of pressure, worn like some crazy badge of sporting status. All Jack Rowell's broad smiles could not hide the obvious angst in the wake of the opening performance. Never had I seen Rob Andrew and Mike Catt looking so gaunt as when the tournament's final try virgins ran on to the pitch to face an equally dejected Italian side whose hopes of qualification had been squashed by Western Samoa.

It was a special day for Graham Rowntree, who had escaped from the horrors of life on the bench. As the rain lashed down during the anthems, Brian Moore stood alongside his new colleague and offered a warm pat on the backside, a veteran's thoughtful welcome. Rowntree was smiling after eight minutes when England finally lost their tryless status. Ball-retention, such a problem in their first match, again undid Italy. A good attack broke down near the English 22, and with De Glanville and Catt running textbook lines, Tony Underwood was offered a rare early pass in space. His response was to sprint 50 metres for a try. 'Remember me, lads? I'm a winger. Run fast, score tries, that sort of thing.' The tournament would soon turn sour for him, but against Italy, Underwood reminded the world that he can play with the ball in his hands.

Martin Bayfield dominated the line-out and we all awaited the onslaught, but a television close-up of Mike Catt's face emphasised the frightening degree of strain and explained why such a skilful player had struck the word 'counter-attack' from the English rugby dictionary. Catt, to the delight of South Africans, who had given him the 'Judas' tag, gifted Italy a try from a charged-down kick on the stroke of half-time. At 16–10 after a damp squib of a half, it was all pretty desperate.

The second half was little better. Still Bayfield excelled and Rory Underwood scored a well-executed try, but the full-time score was a mere 27–20. A successful *Racing Post* column for me, but for England another performance to be greeted with contempt in the press and on the terraces. The most recent soccer World Cup had seen a side managed by a tall, sharp-witted Geordie called Jack bore the pants off supporters. It was happening again as the Great White Hopes continued to look like the Great White Dopes. Rob Andrew offered the usual post-match patter: 'A good Italian side . . . difficult conditions . . . bit by bit we're getting there.' I scratched my head at that. Along with many other people, I had no idea where England were going, bar back to the comfort of set-piece dinosaur days.

Those early days of dynamism were buried under a cloud large enough to hide Table Mountain, but the depressives of the domestic season, the Welsh, were as bright as the sun that defied the mood of the English to rise over the Indian Ocean at Durban most mornings. As the reputations of Rowell and Dwyer wavered, it was Alex Evans, the Aussie alchemist of Wales, who seemed to be the coach in the ascendant. The mere act of lifting the morale of a Welsh team left in tatters at the end of the Five Nations Championship was a minor miracle. Yet who would have believed that the proud rugby nation of Wales could be uplifted by victory against the team Max Boyce once jestingly mocked, Japan?

On the eve of battle with their great nemesis of forty years, the All Blacks, Robert Jones had been bubbling with confidence. Champagne or spumante? Speak to a sportsman the day before a contest and the assertions are nearly all bullish, but there is a chasm between sounding confident and feeling confident. The Celtic assurance of Jones positively resonated with inner conviction. Those close to the Welsh since their arrival in Johannesburg reckoned that the strutting arrogance of the 1970s, if it did not exactly fill the air in their hotel, at least 'curled once around the house' like T.S. Eliot's fog in 'The Love Song of J. Alfred Prufrock'. 'We're in a brilliant mood,' Jones had declared effusively. 'There was a real buzz when the team was announced. We've a new coach, renewed enthusiasm and a lot of players making it competitive.' On the theme of their new coach, he continued: 'He's coached Australia and has more respect than anyone else on the scene. He keeps telling us how good we are.'

It was a pity that Evans was quite so convincing. The Welsh manager, Geoff Evans, caught the infectious mood and told a quizzical world: 'We are bigger, faster and better than the All Blacks.' It is sensible to beat New Zealand before making such claims.

Under the lights of Ellis Park, the team looked confident enough as they emerged on to the pitch. New Zealand laid down their challenge with the *haka* and Wales advanced forward to meet it. Great psychological stuff. They came off the blocks well. The 6ft 10in Derwyn Jones won the first three line-outs and from the third, Neil Jenkins, playing at fly-half due to a slight injury suffered by Davies, dropped a goal. It was 3–0 and the dragons were unfurling in the stadium.

But not for long. The Ellis Park night was transformed into another false dawn for the Welsh. Andrew Mehrtens started to drill 70-metre diagonals into the heart of the Welsh and they cracked under the weight of the renewed Bunce–Little centre combination. Wales, remembering their ancestors at Rorke's Drift, defended valiantly, but they were doomed. Mehrtens' probing kicks punished them like a heavyweight boxer softening up an opponent with blows to the midriff, assisted by Kronfeld. Marc Ellis crossed near half-time to open a 20–3 lead and all the old fears returned. On half-time Neil Jenkins cut the deficit with a penalty goal and the tannoy voice in the stadium declared: 'Striking a big blow for Wales is Neil Jenkins.' If a fly colliding with an elephant is a big blow, I agreed with him.

The second half was a mute affair, as in most dead contests. The greatest roar was for a dropped ball by the brilliant young full-back, Glen Osborne. The All Blacks, chillingly effective, were at least mortal, but they looked the sharpest team in the tournament with a great deal to spare; worst of all, at least for everyone else, was the majestic control of Andrew Mehrtens. Grant Fox had at last been replaced – and this kid could run as well. Neil Jenkins' winter form was a sad comparison. Wales did not capitulate, but there was nothing they could do to prevent one last New Zealand score. The talents of the new sensation, Jonah Lomu, had been caged, but suddenly he exploded into life. He hurtled 60 metres down the touchline, a cross between a cheetah and a bull elephant. He barely noticed the Welsh defenders until Tony Clement somehow checked his stride long enough for Josh Kronfeld to carry the move across the Welsh line. Lomu, the knock-out punch, was delivered and the final score was 34–9. Thus Welsh boasts were proven to be of little consequence, but at least humiliation had been avoided.

Wales were absolutely shell-shocked in the changing-rooms, according to Dewi Griffiths, their media liaison man. It was proof that they had believed in their chances. When they re-emerged into the real world they departed for a club called Caesar's Palace. Even in defeat, they seemed more positive than an English camp full of Faldoesque introspection. It was an old-fashioned booze-up. Athletically, the effects were surely detrimental, but the psychological benefit of escaping the growing tension of the tournament offset that. Despite the glaring sterility of the Welsh threequarter play, I confidently asserted that Ireland would be beaten, leaving Wales in the quarter-finals. My notebook read: 'Will this be another Barnes curse?' Sorry, boys.

21

The Dragons' Fire Doused

As Wales prepared for their destiny on Sunday 4 June, I concentrated on breaking away from the siege mentality that appeared to be gripping the majority of overseas visitors. The Welsh team saw little of Johannesburg, bar the Sunnyside Hotel, the training pitch and Ellis Park. The same applied to the other teams. I decided to plunge into the maelstrom of the city and found whole sections of the place full of energy and life. The pleasures of the late-night bars of Rockey and Raleigh Street, the restaurants and second-hand bookshops of Melville, so many good areas that players, surrounded by excessive numbers of armed guards, would never discover. Poor Jo'burg will suffer a distorted reputation on the dinner-party circuit of British players and, worst of all, sections of the media, who treated their respective hotels as havens from the mass degeneracy believed to be awaiting the unwary on every street corner.

What a difference from the countryside, so vast and open. On the Saturday I left Jo'burg for the pleasure of a day in the conservative Northern Transvaal, where it has, for so long, been a case of black fearing white. I had no fears – I felt wonderfully alive on the open road, earning a living from travelling and writing on sport. It was fun for a daydreamer.

On the drive to Rustenburg, where Tonga and the Ivory Coast were playing their final match of the tournament, I fantasised about those André Brink novels in which the anti-apartheid heroes race north for freedom through the conservative heartlands of the country. Rustenburg rather than freedom was my destination, the chance to visit the home of the wonderfully named Stellaland team. My mind lingered too long on the memory of the taste of a decent beer, a rare phenomenon in South Africa, and I flew a hill to be met by a large policeman with a gun. I did not think it was a speed gun, either. My

Brink dreams suddenly turned into delirium. He was a speed cop. I walked hesitantly to a roadside van and was told to get inside. Christ, what if they knew I was the bastard who abused Bloemfontein in 1994? Luckily, they were either not the sort to bear grudges or, more likely, not regular readers of the *Daily Telegraph*. A polite admonishment and a savage £20 fine was as ugly as the scene got.

Despite my unscheduled stop I arrived in Rustenburg at least two hours before kick-off. Also present were Clement Freud and Ian Wooldridge, more in the capacity of feature writers than of spectators. I suspect that we were all there for the 'let's rubbish the redneck Afrikaners' article – it was certainly not to report on the match. What a joy to see a Mafeking Rugby Club tent pitched inside the stadium perimeters. It was just what we wanted, a bit of Boer mentality to provide some colourful racist material. Certainly the group already at the bar were not interested in polite conversation with myself and Ian Wooldridge, a good sign for everyone. But then it all went wrong. A singer grasped the microphone and started the Eddy Grant song 'Gimme Hope, Jo'Anna', whose words plead for harmony in the dread city before the ominous-sounding 'morning come'. Apartheid duly crumbled and here, in a supposed AWB stronghold, drunken slobs sang along in unison. The next song was the Fleetwood Mac number 'Don't Stop (Thinking About Tomorrow)'. I returned my poison pen to my pocket.

On the terraces the mingling races further destroyed the story. All chanted 'Elephants,' the nickname of the hapless Ivorians. A fat white man in khaki passed the grassy bank where the sunshine was better than the rugby. He carried the old flag of the republic. If he anticipated moral support, his expectations were as wild as mine had been earlier. The crowd shouted, 'Your flag is the wrong colour for the Ivory Coast, you old fool.' Their next target was the extraordinarily huge police cordon that surrounded the pitch, complete with dogs which were trained to growl at black faces. As stupid as their handlers, these mutts remained oblivious to the new spirit at large in South Africa.

The evil of apartheid might have been fading, but in another and unexpected way this was to be the most tragic day in the history of the World Cup. Ivorian Max Brito, a twenty-four-year-old wing, married with children, broke his neck as a result of a freak accident which, we were to learn later, left him with total quadriplegia. It was the first time I had seen such a disaster on a rugby field. When I became aware of the extent of his injury the next morning it was difficult to regenerate my enthusiasm for the tournament. Accidents will happen, and the show must go on, but this tragedy emphasised the stupidity of anyone who subscribes to Bill Shankly's oft-quoted philosophy. Football, rugby, cricket – forget it. None of it is a matter of life and death. It made the overburdened mien of the England squad look pathetic. At least RWC and the South African hosts rallied quickly in financial support: contrary to some reports, sport does have a heart.

Brito's condition would not be disclosed until much later that evening, by which time France and Scotland were locked into one of the most important matches so far witnessed in the tournament. To the winners Wales or Ireland, to the losers New Zealand. It was like asking whether you would prefer a holiday in Clacton or the Caribbean. Scotland were playing the best rugby of the British teams. Unlike England, they were savouring the event and this joy was transmitting itself on the pitch. What the Scots lacked in star quality they compensated for with their organisation and heart. The rucking of the pack was impressively ferocious, and at the epicentre of the effort remained Gavin Hastings, defying logic and his opponents.

Scotland's great concern was still the creative gulf left by the absence of Gregor Townsend. Subtlety was the missing ingredient, replaced by an avalanche of high balls from the boot of Craig Chalmers. After two minutes Hastings and Saint-André collided under the first of them and the scene for this titanic struggle was set. Scotland's pack blasted the French backwards in the first half; only the odd blistering break by Laurent Cabannes, back in the side, lifted the siege. Brilliant with the ball in hand, he was utterly outplayed in the 'dog' stakes by the sheer determination of Morrison, Peters and the man who must surely be the next Scotland captain, Rob Wainwright. He scored a try on half-time to ease Scotland into a 13–3 lead. The semi-finals were beckoning and the head of Berbizier seemed set to roll in the grand manner of French rugby.

The tactical appreciation of the French coach had been changed by the tight excellence of England in the winter and the appalling laxity of his own side's Parisian performance against Scotland. Today they attacked tight, but Scotland hammered them back. Olivier Roumat's increasingly dominant presence in the line-out and a glorious display of pressure kicking by Thierry Lacroix offered a vestige of hope. But fifteen minutes from the end Loftus Versfeld forgot 'Die Stem' and echoed to the sound of 'When the Scots Go Marching In', a marginal improvement on 'Swing Low'. Their lead was 16–9, but because of points differential a draw would win them their 'Caribbean dream'. France lacked the midfield punch to hurt Scotland; only the boot of Lacroix posed a threat. He kicked another penalty to close the gap to 16–12, but a mere eight minutes from time Hastings replied in kind for 19–12.

But still France, now dominating through the efforts of Roumat, fought back. Berbizier's dogged spirit shone through. With two minutes left Saint-André spurned the chance to run a penalty and asked Lacroix to kick them to within one try of victory. Another immaculate strike, and then what had so recently been unthinkable became reality and broke the brave Scottish hearts. Fittingly, it was the mesmeric skill of Emile Ntamack that pierced the almost impenetrable defence. Only seconds remained when he dived over in the corner to give France the lead on the finishing line. By the time Lacroix bisected the posts from the touchline it was over. The late drama of Paris was surpassed as French flair slipped the coach's noose to win a match that logic and Scotland's irrepressible spirit seemed to have denied them for seventy minutes.

In unashamed delight, Philippe Sella raced up the touchline like a twelve-year-old; Gavin Hastings stooped like an old man filled with sad memories. The Scotland captain could not articulate his feelings beyond 'pretty shell-shocked'. Berbizier, as unruffled and diplomatic as ever, admitted that 'Scotland deserved the victory as much as we did', and on the question of their quarter-final added, 'Scotland have a big heart and anything can happen in a one-off.' Whatever he said, though, Scotland had the draw that nobody wanted – the All Blacks. If Gregor Townsend had not been missing, I believe it would have been the French who lined up against the metaphorical wall in the last eight.

France still looked to have too little pace or precision to trouble the big guns, but the Welsh and Irish hardly constituted an elite. Their semi-final place seemed assured: even my curses could not prove strong enough to mess up their progress. The prospect of another three games from Emile Ntamack was a real treat for the game's connoisseurs. At last the tag of the 'new Blanco' became comprehensible. He seemed to enjoy the South African climate more than a wet Cardiff afternoon, and who can blame him.

French, Scottish and neutral all agreed that the match had ignited the tournament. The final encounter of the night would create even more headlines, but for all the wrong reasons – if political correctness is your kick, that is. The locals ran for the giant screens erected in every bar as the South Africans faced Canada. Kitch Christie had taken a calculated gamble by not selecting his best side. Against Romania, the majority of this team had been as unimpressive as the Canadians had been impressive against Australia. Defeat would leave all three teams with two wins (Australia having beaten Romania easily as I drove from Rustenburg to Pretoria earlier that afternoon) and the possibility of an early exit. If that happened, Christie would need a reinforced ambulance to save him from the public. He was emerging from the alchemical coaching gang as the poker player.

Gareth Rees and his re-galvanised Canadians met the hosts in the Boet Erasmus Stadium in Port Elizabeth, a ground with a 'history'. It was here that Jon Callard and Tim Rodber respectively had suffered near-mutilation and a dismissal with England the previous year and it was this stadium that witnessed the infamous 'ninety-nine' battle cry from the 1974 Lions, the signal for everyone to join the fray. There were great beaches in the area, but seriously bad vibes; not a setting for a Beach Boys song. Against Australia we had seen the power of the Springboks on the pitch; here we saw its failure off it. The lights went out during the anthems, leaving Louis Luyt less than ecstatic. As a result the match kicked off forty-eight minutes late. The Canadians began in attacking mode. The Springboks were more cautious, but the perceived weakness of their scrum was a massive strength. After thirty minutes the No. 8, Adriaan Richter, dived over for his second try from a push-over. All the ambition of the Canadians seemed in vain as the hosts ground their way to a 17–0 lead.

But Canada responded heroically, as they had in adversity against Australia. Their potent combination of power and excellent close-quarter handling forced South Africa to defend for the entire second half. More poise near their opponents' line and a shock, or even two, might not have been beyond a side who proved irrefutably that money and regular rugby, not a lack of raw talent, were the major obstacle to further development.

The 'noble losers' headlines were already being written when a masculine confrontation of a game boiled over into real violence. Whether it was in the worst or the best rugby tradition I will leave you to judge, but God, it makes your heart beat – and those with a marginal interest in the sport love it. Pieter Hendriks, the Newlands hero, was now the villain. He instigated the fight with some petty face-shoving. The Canadians, already on their way home, had little to lose and piled in. It was no place for a UN peace-keeping force. The battle escalated into war when the fearless full-back Scott Stewart recklessly short-armed Hendriks from behind.

When the mayhem ended we were left with the spectacle of three sendings-off and two citings. Gareth Rees, leading from the front, was dismissed with the cult Newfoundland prop Rod Snow. South African supporters watched the No. 2 shirt of their hooker, James Dalton, heading for the early bath. For the Canadians, suspension could be spent on a beach somewhere; for Dalton, on the other hand, it signalled the end of the World Cup. It was a tearful farewell to the tournament for a man who publicly admitted that he cried, 'Dad, come and take me home, my World Cup is over.' He was a truly pathetic sight, a match for Gazza in his last soccer World Cup.

More controversial was the punishment of the two cited players by the disciplinary committee of RWC after they studied the video of the incident. Nobody cared about the Scott Stewart ban, but the one on Hendriks caused a sensation. Under the existing rules, it was the individual, not the team, who was responsible for 'unbecoming conduct', and a replacement for the banned player was allowed. In South Africa's case, the ruling was a cause for national celebration. The most famous symbol of the new South Africa after Nelson Mandela was back: the king of Cape Town, Chester Williams. Like the man in the David Bowie song, Pieter Hendriks had been 'a hero, just for one day'. Once again I had been wrong: Chester's wait was a lot shorter than I anticipated.

Williams' return diverted media attention from the mock outrage at the violence that is a part of rugby which many people love. Admit it and enjoy the confrontations – this ain't synchronised swimming. Kitch Christie offered hope to the silent majority of the bloodthirsty. 'There will be more [violence] to come in the knock-out stages.' The World Cup had really lifted off.

After a sterile and excitement-free Saturday night trying to find a res-taurant open at the outrageously late time of 10 p.m., I awoke feeling unpleasantly sober. I had spent the previous evening in the rich suburb of Sandton, a world for human Barbie dolls with a fear of city air. This is what hell will be like. 'If you want to stay healthy, Barnes, it's an eternity amidst the calorie- and alcohol-free, white-teeth world of Sandton, with a string quartet playing badly and the jukebox forever broken.' I vowed to be a good boy and drink more often.

Not that I would have chosen East London as a good place to drink. A set of very big and grouchy *amigos* from Argentina must have wan-dered the town pouring anything down their throats that would help them forget the existence of their backs. England had been outplayed by the Pumas' pack, so had Western Samoa, yet on a sad Sunday, their last hope of a consolation victory against an Italian side which had failed to live up to their billing as the surprise package foundered. The Pumas won the battle for the loose ball by a staggering 60:25 ratio, yet the Italians won the match by 31–25. Even the most fleet-footed and artistic-ally minded of wingers would have felt sympathy for a pack which had earned universal recognition. The Argentinian fiasco led to a revolution within their administration: Hugo Porta would be returning home from his post as ambassador in South Africa in an attempt to lift Argentinian rugby to a loftier position. They have the talent.

All my sympathy belonged with Argentina for precisely the interval between their exit and New Zealand's kick-off against Japan, the side some labelled the best technical team in the tournament. Garrett Halpin told the All Blacks to fuck off and the response was forty-three points; Wales told the world they were bigger, faster and better and thirty-four points followed. Japan did not offend the All Blacks in any way, but the media claims on their behalf did, and the proof that Japan were not the best footballers was one of the most ruthless and beautiful per-formances of rugby that I have ever witnessed. Earle Kirton, the New

Zealand coach, thought it was their best match of the Cup. Japan scored seventeen points to blight the perfection, but the All Black total of 145 was some consolation. Never had slaughter on the sports field been so riveting.

This was a different animal from the old stone-faced sides of yore, epitomised by the brilliant Marc Ellis, who scored six tries from centre that afternoon. Before the kick-off he had checked the record of Test tries in a match for an All Black, which stood at four. When Eric Rush, who, to the relief of everyone, finally made his Test debut, had scored three tries to Ellis's two, the Otago back bet Rush that he, and not Rush, would break the record. The centre did, and he was to move to the wing for the quarter-final, much to the relief of the men outside him.

The lopsided match was also notable for the match commentary of John Eales. New Zealand had registered in excess of ninety points when Hiroyuki Kajihara scored. Eales, a fine cricketer, mused, 'I think they're in their nervous nineties.' Humour – God bless John Eales.

Rugby's most famous rugby humorist, Max Boyce, was also in town. The man who made us laugh to 'Ahso, Ahso Yogashi, me Welsh-speaking Japanee' was touring the country. He was in Jo'burg for the serious business on the night of 4 June. The media were just as nervous. A lot of Welsh or Irish journalists could be on the plane home if their team lost. In the press box at Ellis Park there was an attitude of 'Objectivity? Fuck it.' Or at least, there was until the final whistle. I too had a reason to root for Wales. Not only had I tipped them, but I was still in their team hotel. After the hell of Sandton I was eager to find a bar-room heaven, but please dear Lord, not alongside a nation which can display its despair with the most depressing clarity. Think what you may of their rugby, but few can outmourn Wales.

Ellis Park was only half full for the match, a fact that prompted one South African journalist to boast about the profound good sense of his countrymen. The tannoy voice urged each set of supporters to cheer. The Irish, bolstered by drunks who think that regular attendance at McGinty's bar makes them Irish, were the more numerous. The Welsh supporters were the more confident. It was time to discover whether Alex Evans was an alchemist or a con man. His crash course in psychological rehabilitation had worked with the players – the 1970s swagger had not been completely destroyed by Lomu and Mehrtens. Only one small fact spoiled the party: Barry John, Gerald Davies and Gareth Edwards, all in the stands watching, were not on the pitch. The imitations on the field were less than convincing.

Wales puffed themselves up like peacocks, Ireland rolled up their sleeves and attacked. Nick Popplewell scored from a line-out after just four minutes. Worse followed when Denis McBride, a 14st flanker, burst through the ineffectual combined tackle of Adrian Davies and Neil

Jenkins, who looked as if they were arguing over who should play fly-half rather than trying to stop him. Wales were 14–0 behind and bewildered. Hadn't their coach told them they could win the tournament? So how could they be fourteen points adrift so early and what should they do? They did not have a clue.

The Mexican wave, that 1990s sign of tedium, lifted the crowd in a way that the third-rate rugby of both sides could not. Thirty minutes had passed and two of the best players, in the eyes of the crowd, Ieuan Evans and Simon Geoghegan, had not touched the ball. Come and get me, sleep. At half-time Ireland led 14–6, and I wanted to be anywhere rather than Ellis Park. Except, perhaps, living in Sandton.

The second half was of equal quality. Mike Hall waved his arms around in despair, a sure sign of tactical wisdom. When he was given the ball he ran straight back into the Welsh pack. Were Wales suffering from collective agoraphobia? But gradually the Welsh forwards started to dominate. Neil Jenkins scored a penalty to narrow the gap to five points and Adrian Davies kicked the ball dead from 30 metres. A good guy, but not a good international, his nerve was lost. Ieuan Evans clutched his head on the touchline; his team-mates were unlikely to give him much ball to clutch.

Ireland struck back with an Eddie Halvey try and Jonathan Humphreys, another Cardiff newcomer, scored for Wales, but when Eric Elwood kicked a penalty with two minutes left the Irish were eight clear and home. Yet so tired were they that they allowed Hemi Taylor another try for Wales. Good Lord, it was nearly exciting. The clock ticked into injury time as Neil Jenkins prepared the lengthy conversion ritual from in front of the posts. A hasty dropped goal might have forced Ireland to re-start and offered Wales one last throw of the dice, but Jenkins ran the clock out. It typified the Welsh performance – thoughtless and unadaptable. The mourning in the valleys began in earnest as Alex Evans joined Alan Davies on the Pantheon of False Prophets.

Robert Jones stood alone and distressed at the final whistle. How could his talent have been buried so deep in the Welsh doldrums? In the stands, Gerald Davies could not grieve. The performance of his side had driven him beyond blind patriotism. Ireland performed a lap of honour. Wearily skirting the pitch, the players bowed in the 'we are not worthy style' adopted by Matthew le Tissier's adoring Southampton FC public. They were right. It was the only good decision either side made. To Ireland, then, a match with France in the quarter-finals, but the lasting memory of the tournament should be deep embarrassment for two proud rugby nations. Argentina, Canada and Italy were all more deserving of a place in the last eight. Ireland's celebration at qualification suggested that they too could see the end of the road. At the post-match press confidence, Terry Kingston said: 'Against France we have nothing to lose.' True, but they also had precious little to offer.

And so, once again, my curse destroyed my fancy. In retribution, that celebratory drink became a wake. Robert Jones called Wales 'so parochial and introverted', hinting that he might retire from international rugby. Several other distressed Welshmen offered exclusive retirement stories between internecine criticisms of the loading of Cardiff players in the squad. In the despair of the Principality, the chasm between east and west Wales was as glaringly obvious as ever, exactly as Jones had said over his tenth Guinness and Alan Davies with his parting shots. It will take a long time for a Welsh coach to make his team strut after the despondency of this night.

As the Welsh tried to come to terms with their undisputed status as the worst international team in Britain, the European champions, England, sought an improvement from the static start they had made to the tournament. The pressure was off in the match against Western Samoa, as both teams had safely qualified. That was the official line, but when you meet Samoa, the fear factor alone is sufficient to generate tension. Jack Rowell, normally a conservative selector, as his early-season choices for England had revealed, actually surprised most people with his side. In the wake of the sixty-point beating the 'Boks had administered to Western Samoa, François Pienaar predicted that England 'will win, but it will be hard'. Rowell decided to heed that advice and key players such as the points-scoring Rob Andrew were rested. It was a wise decision, as in the event the Samoans lived up to their reputation and maintained the exodus of opposition players from the field. England finished the game having used five replacements, including Brian Moore and Kyran Bracken in the strangest ever England back row. The novelty of Bracken's cap as a forward was scant consolation as Dewi Morris, thriving under the physical challenge, cemented his place for the knock-out stages. It had turned into a sour season for the glamour boy from Bristol.

The match, however, was England's brightest display of the tournament. The reason for the difference between this and the other two games was a serious worry for Rowell. It was no coincidence that the presence of Mike Catt at fly-half and Phil de Glanville in the centre had sharpened the side's determination to play with the ball in hand. Jon Callard produced another calm and measured display to leave some wondering whether England would regret Catt's failure to throw down a serious gauntlet to the more conservative Andrew. Catt varied play well; high balls, a dropped goal and probing runs offered the centres rare scope to attack, but whatever the quality of one performance, Rowell would not risk him after a season of inconsistency with Bath. Carling and De Glanville benefited to such an extent that the media considered the unthinkable: the demise of Guscott. Yet few questioned why Guscott's appetite seemed so diminished. Neil Back scored a debut try for England from a rolling maul, which was not a fair reflection of the playing style. The team found its dynamic shape and England raced into a 21–3 lead just after the interval.

The Samoans responded in their typical fashion, a mixture of free-flowing brilliance and physical intimidation which eventually tires even the fittest teams. England's Ian Hunter finished the match looking in need of some bamboo and wore sunglasses for the next week. He described the Samoans as 'not like Europeans. They want to hit and hurt people.' Despite the world's romantic obsession with the Pacific Islands, I found the game of the Samoans one of the most frightening aspects of world rugby. It is impossible not to admire their achievements, but these people are fearsome – and they were only warming up.

The final score was 44–22. Overall, it was an excellent performance by a young and hungry side. John Mallett and Damian Hopley earned their first caps from the replacements' bench, the latter because of a faked injury by Carling, a gesture appreciated by the entire squad as well as a grateful Hopley. Richard West also made his international debut as Rowell protected his line-out ace, the excellent Bayfield. It was a relief to hear Carling finally use the word 'awesome' with some pride. The match was perceived as the one that would lift England; it could certainly do morale no harm, but as the team for the quarter-final with Australia would be substantially different, it was difficult and unwise to draw many conclusions from the game.

One fact was certain. England would have to beat their 1991 nemesis, the world champions, Australia, if Carling's dream was not to end.

22

Rob Andrew MBE – Hero of
Eng-er-lund

As the eyes of the world focused on the knock-out stages after the
hurly-burly of the pool rounds, the troubled England and Australia
squads polished their armour for their quarter-final showdown. The
Aussies knew that they were past the second-chance stage. One defeat
already had consigned them to the wrong side of the draw; one more
and it was au revoir to the Webb Ellis Trophy. England were barely
more comfortable. Their stuttering pool form had deprived them of the
face-saving 'glorious defeat' angle. 'Build them up to knock them down'
is a very British motto, and one that rugby players find hard to accept.
And why should they? I'll tell you why. The player who phones a writer
to say, 'Hey, that glowing article is over the top,' is a rare species.
Everyone likes the guy who writes the nice stuff. But newspapers have
to sell, and when the hero bombs the people want to know about it. It
may cost a player an appearance fee or a speech, but the press are not
agents. When rugby becomes fully professional, watch this space. There
will be some ugly scenes that only the likes of Ian Botham and George
Best have experienced up until now. When the agents start to manufacture images, the sportswriter is obliged to desert the role of the defender
of sport's magic and to debunk the mystique. The truth is often unpalat-
able, but when the diets of lies come around it's time to tell it like it is.
The money factor makes sport a business, and who talks about romance
in business? The players want the money, and there is nothing wrong
with that, but the boys will have to pay a price.

Before the tournament started there was widespread concern that
England were more concerned with finance than with winning. That
nonsensical notion disappeared during the tournament, but nevertheless morale had seemed poor in Durban. Even the social trips flopped.

Dean Richards organised an excursion to find sharks entangled in the nets that protect the Natal beaches. A five o'clock departure resulted in zero sightings and much lighthearted abuse of Richards. England might have topped their group, but otherwise little had gone to plan since RWC had dictated that they stay in a central hotel and had thereby created a siege mentality for a team with much support.

England arrived in Johannesburg and checked into the Sunnyside, Wales by now having been exiled to an airport hotel along with the other 'down-and-outs from Japan, Tonga and Romania', as Cardiff scrum-half Andrew Moore described the sorry scene. With space at a premium, I moved to the Parktonian in the run-down district of Braamfontein. Paranoia was everywhere. The media conducted a sad existence of lobby-living relieved only by the odd taxi to Ellis Park. As the bar was appalling, the atmosphere was tense, to put it mildly. As a bunch of journalists, we were not too intrepid. It was a pity. I found the city an intoxicating mix of pleasure, life and fear. Stroll in the wrong area and bang, but that can happen anywhere. Jesus, when I was a building society manager my branch in Bath was raided, but I saw no trouble in Jo'burg. So from my personal angle I would advise you to avoid dangerous Georgian cities. At the very least check that anyone who tells you horror stories of Jo'burg made it past the hotel lobby.

England, like Wales before them, were also cautious in the city, but they were relieved to have escaped the well-meaning claustrophobia of supporters in Durban. At training on the Tuesday before the quarter-final there was a definite sense of calm perspective which had been absent in Durban. Dean Richards was to play in the match after his worrying early injury. According to three younger members of the squad, his leadership qualities were 'shining through', despite his shark-net failure. The confidence that was missing before the Samoan match, but now seemed to have miraculously re-appeared, was illustrated by a conversation I had with Rory Underwood at the end of the session. He told me that he would be thirty-two while England were in the country. His birthday was 19 June, two days after the semi-final – to still be in South Africa by then England had to make the last four. There was an edge during training, the sort that recognition of a real battle adds. Perhaps pressure had co-existed with complacency in the group stages; maybe Dwyer's attempts to make England complacent were grounded in more than wishful thinking.

But not against Australia. For all Campese's baiting, the England players believed that Australia were the ultimate test. Before the Aussies played the Springboks, Mike Catt had confessed that England expected the Wallabies to win by twenty points. The respect stemmed from the fact that both New Zealand and South Africa had been beaten in the previous two years. England had not met Australia since 1991, and the world champions were the benchmark for the squad and for Jack Rowell. His personal duel with Dwyer had been anticipated for a year. The fact that both sides were not playing well only added to the intrigue of the game.

Training finished with a relaxing game of football. The arch-trainer Dean Richards was goalkeeper. Mike Catt shot; Richards did not move and the ball hit him. He read the round-ball game as well as the oval one. Less calming was the sight of Rex Hazeldine, the national fitness adviser, carrying a set of scales around the hotel at all times to make spot checks on weight loss and dehydration levels. Some players with an appetite became very fit by changing direction as Rex approached. Even more serious was a players' meeting which raised the subject of a complete alcohol ban. Only Jason Leonard raised his voice in defence of rugby's great tradition. His reward was the 'Dick of the Day' jersey. Uniform bans – be they imposed on booze, subtitled films or the Bay City Rollers – seem a throwback to schooldays, when children are judged too immature to know what is for their benefit. Two pints and a good night's sleep for Leonard would far outweigh the benefits of a perfect body but a troubled mind. Great teams need individual variety and such draconian rules should not be a part of their scheme.

England were a collective group, rather than a coherent mix of individual genius, a reason for the shadowy, rather than dazzling, presence of Guscott. His form was such a topic of conversation that a few of the media were surprised when Rowell named him in the team to face Australia. The Australian assistant coach, Bob Templeton, was less surprised, but he was pleased with the conservative selection. The youngsters who had beaten Western Samoa all gave way to the experienced core.

On the day England flew to Cape Town, forty-eight hours before the match, they held a packed press conference. David Campese was again the media hero. The previous day he had asked some English press men why nobody had highlighted Carling kicking him in the head in the 1991 final (sorry, Campo, no memory of that one). Better still, when asked about the then impending retirement of Brian Moore, his retort was 'Good.' The tabloids sniffed blood, but Carling showed the tact that had marked his captaincy throughout the season, bar the one occasion, and laughed it off. Only in public, though. Both Carling and Rowell praised Australia, both said they were beatable, and I wondered what the hell I was doing in the middle of such blandness. I did detect a note of excitement in Rowell's voice as he said, 'We're just getting our feet under the table of RWC.' There was a definite feel that the gloves were off, the question that mattered was could they, and did they, have the will to deploy their full attacking arsenal?

Yes was the answer, according to Will Carling. 'We have the knowledge that we have beaten the southern hemisphere sides recently, so there is more belief than there was [in 1991]. There is more of an intent to play a style that will be successful.' According to Jack Rowell, England aspired 'to that talent being exercised on the field'. If this was to be a repeat of the form that had trounced France, England had a chance, but if it was the staid approach witnessed under pressure, forget it. One big effort from the forwards might carry them through one match, but they could not beat Australia, New Zealand and South Africa in successive weeks without fifteen men. Too many players seemed partial to ten.

Later that Friday I asked Bob Dwyer if he would be surprised to see England play fifteen-man rugby. His 'yes' was unequivocal. He continued: 'Do not necessarily equate good with open rugby.' His real fears were transparent. 'England shut you out of the game for long periods, either ball in the air, or in the hand, and if we can't impose our pattern we're at the mercy of the opposition.' Where Rowell had been relaxed and confident earlier in the day, Dwyer was all tension. The Australian pledged a more expansive and varied game. Michael Lynagh assured us: 'We can move in three, four, or five areas. If one fails we can revert to the others. We will move it wide, but if it doesn't work we'll go elsewhere.'

The only place left for Australia by 2.30 p.m. on Sunday 11 June was the airport. Bob Dwyer's worst fears were realised as England's inspirational pack deposed the world champions, depriving them of the ball for two-thirds of the match. England's attacking scheme involved just ten men, as Dwyer had anticipated, but his own side, overcoached and tired, could not find the resources to unlock the seemingly impregnable English defence. The match was memorable in terms of excitement; in terms of adventure, it was sterile. England won the quality of ball that has allowed them to pulverise Five Nations opponents without exhibiting any ambition. The tactics shut down the Australians through the driving maul and the high kick. Eventually pressure leads to a penalty, and then it's the kicker's job. And what a kicking job Rob Andrew did again, another twenty-point haul, and with the best dropped goal of all time thrown in for good measure.

This is the beauty of sport. An event may be mediocre for its entirety, as this match was for a neutral, yet one moment can change your perceptions completely and render it unforgettable. The moment is worth recalling in detail.

'My head was down, and the next thing I knew the ball was soaring through the posts.' Those words belonged to Martin Bayfield, the man who had caught the line-out ball of his life to present Andrew with that one opportunity. He was a key component in a drive reminiscent of the

San Francisco 49ers. Play was two minutes into overtime at 22–22 and destined for extra time when David Bishop, one of the referees of the tournament, blew for an England penalty. Mike Catt had enjoyed another fine game in his dream season, and by this stage he was trusted with the punting. He thought, 'If I slice it, my career is over. Luckily, I hit it well and the ball landed on their 10-metre line.'

Brian Moore took over. 'In the 1991 final we had a line-out on their line and I overthrew the ball at four [the middle jumper]. That was our one chance. I thought, we'll only get one chance this time. I called a forward ball to Bayf. If it's thrown well and he gets in front of Eales, he'll be barged and we'll get a penalty, or we'll get decent ball.' Moore hit the spot as the brilliant Bayfield took command. 'I thought we were too far out for the drop. I thought, get the ball and keep it alive. It was the right call. We had identified that Eales was weak coming forward at four. If you get a powerful drive, he can be exploited.' Big tick for the hated video screen and the coaches.

Eales was helpless, but still England were too far away, as Moore recalls. 'We decided to drive it. If they pulled the drive down, it would be a penalty. The drive almost stopped; someone shouted, "Give it back." We'd only made 5 metres so I shouted, "Keep it going!"' Exhausted, the pack found the requisite supply of energy, drawing it from 'the fear of failure, the knowledge that we'd let a lead go. That final drive showed our heart and commitment.' Bayfield had played his part to near-perfection.

The pack shoved towards their Holy Grail, revenge for 1991. As they ploughed on, Dewi Morris assumed the mantle of quarterback. 'We drove through the middle with Dean and then right into the midfield. I called players from left to right to keep the momentum going and get a penalty. When the ball hit the ground I knew what to do and I knew where Rob was standing. I just had to hit him. I threw it straight back and he hit it sweet as a nut.' Indeed he did. Andrew was mobbed as euphoria overwhelmed the side and supporters. Dennis Easby kissed Carling in the changing-room frenzy. Jack Rowell called a tense and limited affair one of the matches of all time and John Major, at a loss what else to do in Britain, made Rob Andrew an MBE. Given Major's ability to mess things up, Rob should have followed John Lennon's lead and politely declined it.

Later, the modest Andrew reckoned he could have slotted a 40-metre eighty-second-minute drop-kick to beat the world champions once in twenty attempts. One more than the rest of the world. Andrew's greatest virtue had always been the ability to focus inwardly. That was the secret behind his goal-kicking; practising for two hours a day also helped. With four minutes left he had already kicked a penalty to level the scores at 22–22. That was the extent of the knife-edge drama.

In the delirium of a Cape Town night few asked the pertinent questions. Why were the Australians overrun by the English pack for much of the game, yet still ahead four minutes from the end? Why did England's only try come about through a mistake by Lynagh? Tony and Rory Underwood looked incredibly sharp, but why did England ignore them, and, almost inevitably, Guscott? The answer was the one Rowell feared. The side had accepted that pressure games require pure safety tactics. England won the ball, kicked it back to Australia and waited for them to make a mistake. In victory the rest of the country accepted the method, but the reality was that this signalled the end for England. They would now believe that forward power and the Andrew boot would suffice. It was one of the most stirring and valiant of English victories, but it was also pyrrhic. Straight after the match, players like Campese and Horan insisted that England could not win the World Cup playing such limited rugby. Others also expressed the view that it would not be in the sport's interest, and they were right. As Bob Dwyer said, 'Had England won the tournament, I feared others might have copied their style, reasoning that it was a successful philosophy. I have been full of admiration for England. They beat us fair and square. But I would feel I had let everyone down – myself, the team, the game – if we hadn't at least tried to encompass all the things possible under the laws. There has got to be a more rewarding style of rugby than kicking the ball in the air nine times out of ten. If not, this is a pretty ordinary game.'

Dwyer was right, too, but his very ambition to create perfect, rather than winning rugby, combined with the demise of the greats, Lynagh and Campese, cost his side a champion's edge. I left the ground wistful. This was not the way to play the game. My mood lasted for all of eight seconds, until I remembered that there were Australian fans in town to be mocked. The raw heroism of the England team was sufficient reason to act the patriot. It was no act in most of the town. England would be back in a week for the semi, so the 15,000-strong Eng-er-lund hordes celebrated long, hard and affably. I travelled to Table Mountain the next morning. My head needed serious clearing. The sun shone as we neared the summit; a break from insanity, I thought. Then I heard it, 'Swing Low, Sweet Charriutt, cumin' for to . . .' Oh, please, fuck off. That was bad, but the humorous English rendition of the 'Marseillaise' that greeted Serge Blanco in a restaurant that evening was a treat. These supremely gifted England satirists then saw me with a mouthful of Kingklip and burst forth into 'There's only one Rob Andrew'. I was nearly sick with laughter. My chum Louis, a native of Cape Town, was not so pleased with this side effect of the English win.

So England would meet the tournament's most entertaining side, the All Blacks. They had terminated the great international career of Gavin Hastings an hour after England's triumph. Earlier in the week I had travelled to their team hotel in Pretoria to meet these men who were so reminiscent of the great 1970 Brazilian football team, yet another very weird element of this tournament with a twist. New Zealanders are dour, that is rugby folklore. Thankfully, the new breed were not so hot on their history. They were relaxed and smiling, in contrast to the majority of the England squad. They had learned a hard lesson in 1991, when siege mentality affected a side which had lost its characters. This team was loaded with characters. They were also supremely prepared. The negative judgement made in the light of the Super-10 tournament made fools of us all. While Queensland peaked, Mains ordered his squad to build slowly. They were on fire when they reached the tournament; the Aussie flames were dying down.

At their pre-quarter-final press conference, their management handled everything easily. Irrelevant questions were met with a smiling 'That's hypothetical,' from Laurie Mains. When asked about Scotland he said: 'We worry about our own game. We would be naïve not to consider Scotland, so we will not comment any further on their play as we see it.' The players had been away from rugby for two days and at the end of the conference Mains smiled. This was a confident team. Andrew Mehrtens, comfortably the most exciting fly-half of the tournament, summed up their refreshing attitude. 'Just playing is an enjoyment for me. Playing in a new place, playing in South Africa, is a thrill as well. I enjoy the thrill and excitement of it and the pressure on you can be good.' He was too young to know fear. It made him and his team a joy to behold.

Only Gavin Hastings sounded a warning note before the match. 'I have a feeling there's going to be one or two upsets, and the promise of this Scotland side is yet to be fulfilled. I don't think there has been an outstanding team in the tournament so far, and not too many teams in the last eight have shown their true form. From now on the games will be pretty competitive and may not be won by all that many points.'

Hastings had led Scotland quite gloriously. He had been the shining star of the northern hemisphere. But the All Blacks ended the outside chance of a fairytale end. Scotland played some fine, attacking rugby, scoring thirty points. Sadly for them, New Zealand scored forty-eight. Scotland glowered with intent and rocked the Kiwis as the Irish had in their group, but the New Zealanders' extra gear or three were always in reserve. Writing a feature on the England win, I looked up to see that beast Lomu doing some mean damage. The Kiwis looked good to me, but the English thought that if Scotland could score thirty points against them it made them beatable. The small matter of their forty-eight was ignored, as was the requirement to run with the ball to score tries. Carling's dream looked gloomy – no, black – but that was a view England were not taking, having overestimated and defeated the champs.

The previous day I had watched the quarter-final that mattered most to 43 million people: South Africa against Western Samoa, the bad boys of the sport. South Africa had beaten them by sixty points before the World Cup, but they were wary of another physical battering. Bryan Williams, their technical adviser, promised that they would be better prepared this time. It sounded ominous. James Small was missing with a hamstring strain, but the headlines concentrated on the return of God – whoops, I mean Chester Williams. The *Business Day* paper carried his picture on the front page and an inside advertisement read: 'Now the waiting's really over. Welcome aboard, Chester, it was well worth the wait.' Everyone – English, French and Japanese – was pleased to see him back. Or nearly everyone – I forgot the Samoans. Not all the ads were so cheerful. 'When you suffer from headache' – useful, I thought – 'feel good with Grand Pa, the fast way to fix a headache.' The photograph used to prove the product's therapeutic powers was one of James Dalton trudging off the pitch, presumably in the general direction of a phone to ask his father to fetch him. I had read a poignant interview with Dalton on the morning of match. He said he'd visit the players an hour before kick-off to wish them luck. 'Then I'll look at my No. 2 and think about what might have been.' Another man with bitter memories of the tournament.

His sadness was a rarity on a day when South Africans could be proud of their team and their nation. Western Samoa made Chester wait another fifteen minutes; it seemed inevitable that he would score with the first touch and start the paroxysms of adulation, and good ole Chester obliged. Three more tries followed and the headline writers went home, or to the bar, happy. Campese was on the verge of dethronement by the English and the time of Lomu was a week away. For today Chester was the king, and the South Africans won their expected berth in the semis.

But a moral darkness descended over Ellis Park, so long a home of racial injustice. This time it was the Springboks who nearly ran into the slaughter. The Samoans subjected them to a display of terror that probably convinced mothers throughout the land to stop their children from playing rugby. The combined fortunes of Rupert Murdoch and Kerry Packer would not convince me to come out of retirement if Western Samoa were the opponents. This was the violence many hoped for, until we realised that it was way beyond the pale. The Samoans might regard themselves as the popular islanders who burst on to the scene from nowhere, but in the interests of everyone playing the game, I propose they return in a hurry and stay away. They turned the body slam – apparently condonable, because they mention prayer meetings after playing – into an art form. It was a bit like athletes who test positive for drugs whose friends say, 'It can't be true. They are so religious.' God seems to approve of cheats and rugby psychos.

The only men with a right to thank God at full-time in Ellis Park were André Joubert and Joost van der Westhuizen. Both suffered intolerable punishment. Headlines were diverted by an unsubstantiated suggestion of a racist comment from Joost van der Westhuizen. The source of the story was a gregarious Kiwi journalist. Not more psychology. The broad evidence of the afternoon did not bear out the inherent racist theories that some of us liberals still espouse. I walked to my seat fifteen minutes before kick-off and the place was full of goodwill, just like the atmosphere at Newlands for the first match. The triumphalism of the older and more arrogant order seemed largely history. The new South Africa was epitomised by the diplomatic Springbok captain François Pienaar.

The policemen, a sure sign of tension, were missing. I saw just four, and they were smiling. Under the stands, the smell of Cornish pasties and pies wafted around the subterranean depths of the stand. It could have been Cardiff, except for the sun and the new South African flag painted on every member of 'Charlie Chow's' take-away staff. There were more cuddling couples than beer bellies, a remarkable sight at a rugby ground. When the 'World in Union' song proclaimed 'a new age has begun', it was difficult not to agree. Pop music is the one area of life that has suffered with the fall of apartheid. The bands, like American politicians with the end of communism, have nothing left to sing about.

The optimism surrounding the Springboks took some knocks during the game. André Joubert broke his hand. The common belief was that if Gavin Johnson replaced him, the chances of the side would be savagely diminished. Ruben Kruger departed, but not before he stamped his mark of rare quality on the game. Kobus Wiese and Mark Andrews also hobbled off wounded. Inspired by the four tries of Chester Williams, the hosts were through by 42–14, but comfortable it was not. In the wake of this battle few mourned the departure of the brutal islanders.

The Springboks would meet the winners of France and Ireland. Pierre Berbizier tempted fate before that quarter-final when he said: 'We are more concerned with the referee than with the Irish.' That referee was Ed Morrison, the gentle Bristolian who was to handle the final. There was nothing wrong with Morrison, but the match was another indictment of northern hemisphere rugby. Ireland were as bad as they had been against Wales, while the French half-backs, Hueber and Deylaud, were indescribably awful. Berbizier seemed blind in terms of his fly-half. Deylaud had produced a consistent run of poor performances, but still Berbizier waited for the miracle. It was Deylaud who created the space for the first French try two minutes from the end, but few understood why it had taken so long. Saint-André and Ntamack ran in a try apiece to give the score a realistic flavour at 36–12, but France, like England

and influenced by them, were intent on starving their stars of the ball.

In South Africa the locals remembered their poor provincial form before the Test series win over the Springboks. There was a fear that Berbizier had an undisclosed card which would be played in the semi-final the next Saturday in Durban.

The tournament was down to the last four. All the dreamers, like the Welsh and the Irish, were home; the nightmares of Japan and of life as an Argentinian forward were being endlessly re-lived on different continents. The debates about the merits of eighty-nine-point beatings and empty seats were over. The war was entering its final stages.

23

Full Steam Ahead,
Lomu Mania

E ven the importance of a World Cup cannot prevent moments of
depression. Twenty-six men are thrown together, often with little
in common bar the sport and a competitive drive. During the pool
rounds there had hardly been sufficient break between matches to worry
about tedium and tension. Combine playing, training and team meetings, and little time remained for anything but sleep. However, once
the knock-out stages arrived the players had too much time to fill and
in the quiet moments it can be hard to keep motivated. As the ultimate
tests loomed near, teams fought to maintain their adrenaline. These
battles can be as tough as the eighty-minute war itself. New Zealand had
taken two days off in the week preceding their quarter-final. England
followed suit after the drama of their Cape Town win and headed for
the hedonistic world of Sun City. That the place seemed the most popular venue for visiting teams convinced me of the wisdom of being an
ex-player. It is spectacular in its scope and its vulgarity. If you do not
like golf, gambling or wave machines, it is hell. If you like gambling
and you lose, you give it bad press. I had visited the casinos the previous
year.

New Zealand relaxed in the staggering role of the underdog as
England fever swept the country. Journalists who had dismissed
Carling's men after their first match were shouting the odds from hotel
bars throughout Jo'burg. If they could beat the champions playing static
rugby, the world could belong to the set-piece kings. Patriotism flooded
the pages of the British press. Considered pieces? Not a chance. In
the week leading up to the game, I had the distinct impression that a
cameraman was stunned to see me arrive for an interview on Sky in a
shirt and jacket, and not wrapped in the flag of St George. I feared he

216

had suffered apoplexy when I tipped the All Blacks. Many colleagues agreed, but to hell with admitting it. Being a patriot seems pretty mindless, but fun. I took refuge in Bob's Bar, near Ellis Park, where a combination of Namibian beer and pornographic Japanese lightshades created a suitably surreal and non-sporting atmosphere until the only sportsman to have visited the bar in a millennium spotted me. 'So, you think England can do it? What about James Dalton?' It was only cashflow that ruled out a day trip to Mauritius and a respite from all the rugby chat.

England were still in Sun City on the Wednesday morning before the match, but the All Blacks, having had an extra twenty-four hours to recover from their quarter-final with Scotland, were beginning to focus on the semi in the quiet capital of Pretoria. The only thing that shattered the calm of their preparation was the insistent ring of the telephone with requests for an interview with Jonah Lomu. Over a hundred approaches for interviews and 3,000 telephone calls had flooded into the New Zealand camp. Poor Ric Salazzo, the liaison manager, reverted to the role of Lomu's guardian. He spent entire nights telling irate tabloid journalists that he was not Lomu and that all the player's calls were being diverted. 'Try all you want, you will not get through.' But they did not quit, and Salazzo did not sleep.

He still found the energy to make a Lomu video. The idea was to give the media a chance to discover the man without fighting for exclusives. Just twenty and extremely raw, he needed the protection. An awesome force on the field, he was not about to win *Mastermind*. The video was memorable for one line: 'I could eat anyone under the table in fruit.' Jonah is a strange boy. He was also an immediate superstar, and a gossip story about him being in the back of a car with a female Free State student was a landmark as rugby entered the realms of trash journalism. The boyfriend did not ask Lomu for a man-to-man chat about the situation and the car must have been a stretch limo.

Such a car would have been in keeping with the style of a New Zealand team who had abandoned their unsmiling efficiency for flamboyance. It was as weird as watching Arsenal play total football. The paranoia of my earlier days had thankfully vanished, but I felt uneasy in the presence of free-spirited All Blacks. France, England and South Africa were all power and intensity; only New Zealand carried the flag for the purists. Unbelievable. To understand the transformation, it was necessary to watch these men outside the confines of the pitch. In their hotel it was left to the management to maintain the great tradition of solemnity. Brian Lochore and Colin Meads were born to wear blazers on tour. Fine men, but a little short on panache. Like genial parents, they looked fondly on the 'smiling happy people' who were overrunning their camp. The entire month seemed a fun occasion for this squad. What sort of heretics were they?

Hollywood's brat pack had its more engaging Kiwi equivalent in Jeff Wilson, Glen Osborne, Josh Kronfeld, the talkative Mehrtens and, of course, Marc Ellis, who constituted a gang of extras fit to grace the surfing movie *Point Break*. They appeared scared of nothing, including the All Black tradition of Calvinist rugby. Andrew Mehrtens said: 'If we screw up, we can blame it on inexperience.' The critics thought that the thirty points scored by Scotland cast doubt on their defensive attributes. Could they withstand the physical battering of the English task force? The world asked the questions and the All Blacks just smiled. If they were to move en masse to Earl's Court, London could be a fun place to hang out. For now, though, the one side to have altered the possibilities of international rugby travelled to Cape Town for England and their first match as underdogs in South African eyes. Australia's reputation had been bashed, but the performance of the England pack had been enough to convince the locals that the 'team who would be bad for the sport', according to Bob Dwyer, would squeeze the considerable life out of the All Blacks.

England, the great white dopes of Durban, were barely recognisable when they arrived in Jo'burg for their semi-final preparations. The clouds were replaced by gleaming smiles. God was an Englishman. Players were not taking the lift to their rooms, they were levitating on the euphoria of Rob Andrew's wonder-kick. Dreamy expressions replaced the scowls of Durban as the players patiently complied with whatever the television cameras asked of them. Foremost among them was Rob Andrew, the man with the incredible concentration skills, according to the team psychologist, Austin Swain. The spotlights barely left the new MBE, but Andrew maintained his legendary grace. I was asked to interview the national hero for the *Telegraph* and he agreed unconditionally. Considering our rivalry of a decade and my frequent outspoken comments on the subject, I would have respected his refusal. A number of his colleagues have found adverse publicity rather harder to accept.

We sat outside the England team hotel, barely three days away from the semi-final, and Andrew convinced me that England would lose. Reminiscing about the quarter-final, he said: 'We lacked the confidence to run. We have been quite conservative in our mental preparation.' Before the start of the tournament Les Cusworth had stated: 'You can't catch and drive a ball all tournament. We have plenty of pace and lots of moves to employ it, and we are still working on our flexibility.' England's win had been based purely on the conservative style. The flexibility was missing. Andrew continued. 'Jack has a vision of fifteen-man matches that suit the team. We put pressure on them with our kicking game, but the wider integration did not come.' Rowell's vision had been returned to its box leaving England to recall forward-based victories over all the remaining teams. The die was cast. Rowell had gambled on changing the attitude of the veterans when he took control. Three days before the semi-final, he and Cusworth ran out of time.

An England intent on static rugby was bad enough, but one that underestimated a side of New Zealand's calibre was a recipe for disaster. England made no special plans for Lomu. Andrew said that England had not been troubled by Tuigamala – what was the difference? Apart from about 10 metres over 100, 2½st, devastating acceleration and a brilliant sidestep, the answer was nothing. The victory over a poor New Zealand in 1993 and the limited win over a fading Australia had proved Dwyer right. England were susceptible to overconfidence.

The former Auckland coach, the highly respected John Hart, watched them train and declared later: 'Their own attitude cost them the semi-final. I saw them prepare before the game and it was obvious that they had overrated their ability to beat the All Blacks. They believed in themselves too much.'

The one man more apprehensive than anyone was Tony Underwood, the player who would be marking Lomu. The 'HOW DO YOU STOP LOMU?' headlines were gathering momentum. The media wanted answers from Underwood Junior. He consulted the team psychologist for advice on handling the press. If he could not handle them, how would he handle 19st plus on the hoof, with a set of inside backs happy to leave Lomu on a one-to-one?

I travelled down to Cape Town the Friday before the Sunday of the match. It was my bad luck to travel on a plane full of Kiwi supporters led by the former great Stu Wilson. He kindly informed his charges that a recent England player was aboard. It could have been an unpleasant flight. Then a saviour clambered on to the plane in the unlikely person of David Campese. 'Forget whatshisname, let's get stuck into Campo.' He took the abuse in good grace. He is a far better man than many people give him credit for. The Kiwi supporters were heavily out-numbered in town. My night finished in the Gecko Lounge at four in the morning. Swaying out to the tune of 'Walk on the Wild Side', I emerged into an unseasonal sultry night and a blast of the omnipresent 'Swing Low'. Bands of angels would be replaced by modern jets to carry the barmy army out of Cape Town after England's day of destiny in the shadow of Table Mountain.

Meanwhile, an entire nation crossed their fingers and legs and bit their collective nails to the quick. The nation was South Africa, and the barrier to the World Cup final was France. The next day the sunshine capital of Durban was a deluge, the drainage at the stadium almost non-existent and the game was delayed as people swept clear the lake on the surface of the pitch. In the western Cape it was a balmy winter day of 27 degrees as I joined the throngs from the Clifton district of

Cape Town in the idyllic La Med bar. Over 1,000 people were packed inside to watch one of the multitude of screens that made the bar look like David Bowie's viewing-room in the film *The Man Who Fell to Earth*.

According to Fred Rundle of the AWB party, every one of them was a traitor. When François Pienaar dedicated the side to Nelson Mandela, he declared his team betrayers of the white man's heritage. Rundle now urged his like-minded intellectual friends to watch the Springboks, once the bastion of the odious right, in the hope of defeat. Magnificent. As the sides sang the anthems, did Rundle ponder the likelihood that France's most gifted player was Emile Ntamack? The tournament was becoming an ideological nightmare for the racist minority in South Africa.

The Springboks ignored the dramatic conditions and dominated the opening quarter through the combined efforts of their pack, with Mark Andrews playing at No. 8 in place of Rudolf Straeuli – a brave and inspired selection by Kitch Christie – and the snappy incision of Van der Westhuizen. After twenty-five minutes Ruben Kruger was awarded a try. The conversion took the score to 10–0 and the celebrations began to bubble in La Med, where a fat hippy sought to exploit the refreshing display of national unity, a pretty coloured girl the target of his *joie de vivre*. The try was contentious. A week later Ruben Kruger quietly admitted that the ball had not been grounded and Louis Luyt was to present referee Derek Bevan with a watch in one of the least sensitive displays of generosity imaginable. Bevan's genuine error – nobody in the world of rugby would ever doubt his total integrity – did not kill the French; instead they fought back to 10–6 at half-time. The cameras focused on a lip-biting Pierre Berbizier. He could see the end of the road at Ellis Park, as he had said so poetically back in the northern winter. Here in the southern sun there was no French champagne, just brandy and cokes to settle the nerves. The celebrations were on ice.

In the second half, France, inspired by Laurent Cabannes, found the spirit that had eluded them all year as the game walked the tightrope. Fifteen minutes from time La Med became a morgue as Ntamack countered his way upfield. Memories of the score that beat New Zealand whizzed around the room. This time South Africa's granite defence stood firm. A Joel Stransky penalty goal ten minutes from time pushed the 'Boks seven points clear and the champagne was back on ice. Thierry Lacroix's penalty three minutes from time put France one try from the final. They were chipping away at the lead just as they had against Scotland. Seconds from the end, they almost repeated the finish, too, in the most gut-wrenching moment of the tournament. Abdel Benazzi grabbed a ball that bounced loose from a kick just 2 metres from the line. In the squelching conditions he was bound to slide over. The official credit went to the combination of Hennie le Roux and Ruben Kruger, but the presence of a *sangoma*, or even of Mandela, seemed to stop the French back-rower from crossing the line.

The bar erupted when the try was not allowed; seconds later pandemonium broke loose. Mandela's children raced into the sunlight, strangers kissed and hugged and the Tears for Fears song 'Everybody Wants to Rule the World' played on the stereo. Meanwhile, the savage director of the television coverage zoomed in on the tearful embrace of Olivier Roumat and Jean-Michel Gonzalez. It was a scene of utter desolation. A grave-faced Berbizier shrugged his shoulders and wished South Africa well. The decisions had fallen against him and Deylaud had failed to repay his faith when it most mattered, but defeat was taken with honour. The conditions might have diminished the spectacle, but not the occasion. I left the bar as the sun set on the mountains and on French aspirations.

And so the tournament moved on to its bloody Sunday, the day England's confident juggernaut of a side was reduced to a shambling disaster as New Zealand produced a succession of pre-emptive strikes which destroyed anything white. The strategy of Laurie Mains was perfect, the control of his field lieutenants admirable, but this battle will always be remembered as the day of the human bomb, Jonah Lomu. Tony Underwood was right to have been apprehensive; if his teammates had not been so inflated by the victory against Australia, perhaps his afternoon would not have been quite as spectacularly miserable.

'Jonah Lomu, just a name, a bit of hype, big deal,' was the feeling emanating from the England camp. Not long into the game – less than ninety seconds – it changed to a high-pitched 'Oh fuck, what do we do?' Nobody did anything until the deficit was too great. Lomu was the executioner after one minute. Bachop floated a pass to space, Lomu gathered and set off for the line. Tony Underwood failed to get his scent, Carling suddenly looked a schoolboy and Mike Catt's heady progress was steamrollered as Lomu ran him down. It was the most sensational solo try in memory. The crowd were stunned. A mixture of awe and confusion overwhelmed us all, from the press box to the England bench.

As the confusion subsided, admiration grasped the audience from the re-start. Calm down the game? Not a chance. The All Blacks ran hard from their own 22 and Walter Little fended off Jeremy Guscott and charged into the England half. A breathtaking passage of interpassing with Glen Osborne carried the attack to within yards of the line; England stopped them, but Josh Kronfeld arrived on the scene to score another hammer blow. This time Mehrtens kicked the conversion and it was 12–0 after three minutes.

England responded in the style they had adopted throughout the tournament. The pack drove into a fine attacking position and Andrew steadied for the drop. This time he missed. Then a penalty was missed, then a few more balls were kicked to the All Blacks. My match note showed six kicks and no running from England in the first twenty-two minutes. From one of these kicks Zinzan Brooke dropped an outrageous goal from 45 metres. England's noses were being rubbed deeply in the mire.

Jonah Lomu scored a second try, leaving Rob Andrew in his wake. Two tries for him and not even a touch for Rory Underwood yet. It said everything about the sterility of England. Carling and Rowell would later assert that Lomu was the difference. He was not. The difference was one of ambition and nerve. When England did increase the pace from a Dewi Morris quick tap, Rob Andrew dropped the ball with a clear overlap. The Midas touch had turned to rust since the vote-catching MBE from Major. The Conservative party were allied with the All Blacks. Heigh ho, who cared?

England were nearly helpless in the face of rugby as it should be played. Eventually they gained three points from a penalty given after a rolling maul. But 25–3 soon became 35–3 as Lomu scored another marvellous try, which was closely followed by an even better one from Graeme Bachop, the result of running from the revitalised Frank Bunce. The contest was over. England were out and they knew it. As the strains of 'Swing Low' finally disappeared into an African sunset, something strange occurred. England started to run the ball. True, New Zealand were off the pedal, but England were actually good. The tactical authority was grasped by Dewi Morris and Ben Clarke. England tapped penalties and surged through the heart of a defence that was supposedly weak, but woefully untested until too late.

Rory Underwood scored with his first pass after fifty-nine minutes. Will Carling got a try as Clarke continued to scatter opponents; another followed for the England captain and on full-time there was a second for Underwood. England had proved that they were as capable as any side, but they were incapable of conceiving the ambition to unleash their considerable array of talent. In contrast Lomu was the lucky guy. Oh, and he did score a fourth, in the second half.

Down and out, 45–29 and the glazed eyes of Carling told the tale. England could not believe what had happened. If Jack Rowell seriously believed that Lomu was the only difference, he too had lost the tactical plot. Ambition and vision were the words England had forgotten. The players admitted that a Lomu would not have been as effective in an England shirt; he would not have received the ball. The same old stories were trotted out. 'Not enough contact with the southern hemisphere', 'Poor leagues', 'Shitty weather' – try Invercargill in winter. Everything was the reason for the defeat except the truth. England were a side dominated by players ideally suited to winning Five Nations matches, in which the pack overwhelms. The same players lacked the vision and the ability to play the sort of game with which New Zealand were thrilling the world. Jack Rowell had sought to pick the old guard and change their style. It looked a masterstroke at Twickenham against the French, but ultimately they could not find the skill and determination until it was all over. This was one war that Rowell would not win. Carling praised his side for their comeback. Those in charge should have been castigated for refusing to expand until the pressure was off.

24

A Fairytale Ending

As a former player, I will doubtless be rebuked for voicing my opinion by some of the men involved in England's failed mission. They can think what they will, but all the talk of widening the experience of English players will never make England world champions until the side is stripped of the people who have done so much for the team, up to a certain point. The next World Cup is four years away. Some of the future players are probably still at school. Give them belief that enterprise is the path to the stars. Rowell must start to select players with the enthusiasm to run. Let them take risks and have fun and then pick them. The myth that England created about 'international rugby' and the 'pressure' that demanded negativity had been exploded by the New Zealanders.

Rowell's decision to persist with a side which had failed to play any constructive rugby for the third-fourth-place play-off against France was the low moment of his personal effort. His concept of development revolves around constant evolution rather than radical overhaul. If there is no one better, why change? At the start of his tenure, this philosophy dictated the gamble to change the style of the old guard as opposed to the players themselves. It had not worked in the real test, but gambles cannot always work. In the play-off little was at stake and he had a chance to state an intent for the future of the game in England. He should have played people like De Glanville, Bracken (although Morris had been one of England's doughtiest performers), Callard and even Catt at fly-half. These were the fresher men who actually ran the ball. Instead he stuck to the mentally jaded men who had won a Grand Slam but had failed when it mattered. The morale of those not selected was shattered, and for that Jack Rowell merits criticism. The magic of the autumn seemed to have deserted the side. I sensed an anti-climax brewing, but nobody dreamed just how poor the game would be. England kicked, kicked and kicked again. Even Ben Clarke kicked. Both sets of forwards looked tired, but with fifteen minutes left the England pack had found the energy to win 71 per cent, according to the television statistics.

France were little better until they realised that their lamentable run of eight defeats at the hands of England could be ended. Rowell's team were finished off by a sublime try from Emile Ntamack, one of the players of the tournament. The final score, 19–9 to France, was no worse than England deserved. When the excuses about 'long campaigns and tiredness' were trotted out, I wondered what the players who had shown such promise against Western Samoa thought. Perhaps they were being held back for the 1999 World Cup qualifiers that England must now contest.

New Zealand and South Africa were less concerned with the long term. The brief reign of Australia was over and the old powers were ready for 'the biggest New Zealand versus South Africa game of all time. There's no prizes for second and there's no second chance.' Brian Lochore is not a man given to exaggeration.

The final was a blow struck for the traditional order of rugby. But the headline news belonged to a new superstar, Jonah Lomu. No seedy sex sleaze, pop star or footballer was going to knock Lomu off the front page of every paper in England. Here was a man described by Grant Fox as the future of rugby. The brilliance of the Campese era, the vintage control of Lynagh, the athletic excellence of Michael Jones all belonged in the confined world of rugby proper. Lomu was pure headline. No technical appreciation was needed to groove to the sport the Lomu way. He had suddenly become the game's first real megastar, his name up in lights with Michael Jordan's, proof that great athletes play the sport. New Zealand are desperate to keep him in Union, and so the entire code should be. In the stunned England press conference after the semi-final, Carling suggested that the sooner Lomu left the game the better. In reality his loss would be a major blow. Rugby Union must keep its only world star if it is to be seriously perceived as a significant world sport.

Champagne was the order of the day for the demure New Zealand coaching staff, who dropped and recalled Lomu to the squad in the nick of time. The doubters and critics were muzzled by the dazzling style of their new-age team. It was entirely appropriate that the final hurdle between Mains and glory was the Springboks. Only one year previously, the man with the Mona Lisa smile had been seen as a false prophet in his own land. The nation wanted his head; defeat against the touring South Africans would surely have pushed him over the precipice after the series defeat against France. But the New Zealand Rugby Union stood firm in the face of angry public opinion. The backs coach, Earle

Kirton, grimaced at the memory of the recent past. Standing in the sunshine at training three days before the final, he recalled: 'I've never had so much shit thrown in my face. We were under tremendous pressure to change our style, but we stuck to our guns and our beliefs.'

New Zealand's young guns matured into the smoking machine-guns that blasted enough holes in the England defence to fill the Albert Hall. Mains' beliefs as a coach were forged in the province of Otago, dominated by students lacking the bulk to play a structured game. He created a pattern of frenetic pace and chaos. Playing for the 1993 Lions against them was the most bewildering experience of my rugby career. When they won ball in the second half, they ran us into the ground from all angles.

It was too much for every side New Zealand had met so far. Kirton described the first half against Japan as 'the nearest we have been to perfection'. It was a style which would not have graced the tournament had the series against the Springboks been lost, and even though it was won, the Bledisloe Cup defeat by Australia had still threatened to derail Mains' train. He argued that the side could win the World Cup if they could reproduce their second-half performance of that match. Most of the world scoffed at what they saw as the remarks of a desperate man. The critics included many of the great names of New Zealand rugby.

Even Brian Lochore, who was taking the media heat as campaign manager during the tournament, admitted to his confusion then. 'Like the rest of the world, I thought, what the hell is going on? There seemed no structure, no pattern.' The nation that had traditionally tamed the rugby world through efficiency was now as psychedelic in its rugby as Haight Ashbury. Weird.

Only the 1984 Wallaby coach, Alan Jones, saw through the mist of all-enveloping Kiwi misery. 'You've got some great players,' he said. 'You shouldn't be so desperate.' Mains knew that Jones was right, but having the courage to follow your instinct is a different matter. Where Jack Rowell accepted a reversion to the static style that he abhorred, Mains was true to his vision. Shane Howarth scored all his side's points and performed with distinction against Australia. Mains dropped him. Howarth had been faultless, but Mains wanted the free-running style of Glen Osborne. Untried youngsters such as Kronfeld entered the equation, travelling to an intensive training camp on the shore of Lake Taipo, where the management stripped back to the basics and 'sorted out the wheat from the chaff', according to Kirton.

Unfancied, the most exciting side of modern times arrived in South Africa. The players were bound to benefit from the profile their play had created, but for the management financial sacrifices had to be made. They received just their personal allowance, but, as Kirton said, 'You've got one chance in a lifetime to do something like this. Grab it.' No argument so far. They were grabbing their chance in large handfuls.

Training was relaxed. Nobody had informed the young charges that they were under pressure. Press conferences were held outdoors and players cracked jokes with the media. When Jeff Wilson said, 'We have prepared for six months. We knew it would be tough, hence the low key Super-10,' you knew just how focused the side were, but they had maintained their humour. As he recalled the Zinzan Brooke dropped goal, Wilson mused: 'I was happy at the time, then I realised it would be the worst thing ever.' Zinzan was keen to remind the backs that forwards could be 'playboys' too. Jonah Lomu was asked if there was anything or anyone who could stop him. 'My mother,' he retorted. May I never inadvertently offend Mrs Lomu.

Brian Lochore held his final press conference in one of the many Holiday Inn Hotels in Sandton with a picture of the 1905 All Blacks behind him. The weight of tradition did not seem to faze his team. 'I don't think the pressure has got to them at this stage. If they weren't going to handle it we'd know by now.' They were confident. On form New Zealand were favourites to beat the Springboks by ten to twelve points. The psychological games that had surrounded the first match were missing from the build-up to the final – everybody knew that the Blacks had the edge. Even the South African manager, Morné du Plessis, admitted that, man for man, it was a ten-point difference. Even the appointment of the referee seemed to go against them. The honour fell to one of the most decent referees in the game, the Englishman Ed Morrison. Unlike so many referees, Morrison does it for love, not ego. There are no tight shorts, no puffed-up chest and none of the 'You should hear what I said to so-and-so' type talk with which many of them entertain their friends in sad bars around the world. In South Africa, however, Morrison, was less popular. In 1993 he had sent off James Small against Australia. If you want to be popular in South Africa, you do not give an idol of the magnitude of James Small his marching orders.

The sending-off capped a traumatic period in the wild, wacky and gregarious career of the heart-throb Natal wing. That, and his axing for disciplinary reasons, were his career lows. But all this was history now as his name dominated South Africa's coverage. He was the man facing Lomu. Kitch Christie played his part in building the confidence of the wing. 'What is going to happen when Small runs at Lomu? He is not the type of player to get overawed and he is looking forward to the challenge. We cannot just focus on one guy. It is a World Cup final, a fifty-fifty game, and I am confident we can win it. You need to ask whether the devastation was done by the All Blacks or by England themselves.' A bit of both seems a good guess. Later in the week Christie added: 'The All Blacks are a great team. Lomu is only part of that, and we won't allow ourselves to forget that we have to be on our guard against all of them. James will not be scared of Lomu, because, frankly, I have never seen him afraid of anyone.' I remember thinking that being unafraid and able to stop him might be two different matters.

Logic demanded that New Zealand would win, but the nature of the Springbok self-belief that had expanded since the nervous phony favourite war at the start of the tournament was intimidating stuff for opponents. Balie Swart, the South African prop, captured its spirit with his recollection of the desperate final moments against the French as Berbizier's side strove for victory. 'This was our moment. No ways were they going to shove us back or cross our try-line. No ways.' Such conviction was not born out of rugby, but from a sense of well-being which literally seemed to crackle around the country. On the Wednesday before the final Du Plessis spoke of 'our destiny to win the tournament'. This was no religious freak or right-wing crackpot, but a fine man with deep, almost mystical, belief. This was imbued through-out the side. Under Du Plessis's guidance, the Springboks publicly embraced 'the spirit of *masakhane*. *Masakhane* is a Nguni word which 'captures the essence of nation-building; embodies the responsibility we all share to build each other'. Du Plessis's statement finished on a fervent note. 'We are rallying to the cause of the new country. One team, one country – *masakhane!*'

New Zealand were up against a nation, not a rugby team. Lochore knew this, but he hoped the pressure would tell against the South Africans. Those who had witnessed the opening game live thought it unlikely. He admitted that 'South Africa have more people with high expectations', calling them a 'nation clamouring for things to be seen good internationally'. He could also have added that they were a country with a legendary tenacity which had caused much good and much evil in the past. 'It is not in our nature to get blown away,' said Du Plessis. Iron in the soul. Confidence had matured as the management had 'seen everything develop almost to plan'. Christie had settled on a core of players at the end of the British tour, and by the Friday before the final he had decided on his XV, with Mark Andrews at No. 8. He had played the gambler's hand of sticking with three line-out forwards in an attempt to stop New Zealand obtaining ball for Mr Lomu and friends behind the scrum.

At the final Springbok press conference, André Joubert, with a broken hand which would need an operation the day after the final, told the world, 'You've got to be ready for everything.'

Saturday 24 June was the biggest day in the republic since the democratic elections that ended apartheid forever. There was a subtle difference this time: the entire nation was behind the same team. François Pienaar was nearly as popular as Chester Williams, and even in the football-mad townships black people spoke about 'national pride'. Only Fred Rundle and his moronic chums supported the opposition. The slogan 'One team, one nation' had pulled the people together. Sport had achieved something real.

So had our old friend, the *sangoma* from KwaZulu, the guy who told Keith Quinn that the Blacks would face the 'Boks in the final. Business was obviously brisk for such a power. On match day it was the turn of a female *sangoma* called Emily Zwane to make predictions. Now mock at your peril. In the Saturday *Star* we were informed that Springbok supporters 'can rest easy; the local boys will pull through, but only just'. The uncanny report forecast that the 'Boks and the Blacks were 'equally matched and both stand a fifty-fifty chance of winning. South Africa will win the match, but only by a very small margin. Maybe only three points.' The *sangoma* added that South Africa's win would be character-ised by mistakes on New Zealand's part, and that Lomu's luck would desert him.

By full-time, Mrs Zwane could command her own price among the world's media. This was a lady who really did know her stuff. The rest is history. South Africa exploded in a frenzy of wild emotion when Ed Morrison blew his whistle after 100 minutes of sheer will and desire saw South Africa defeat the infinitely more talented All Black side. South Africa defended as if the entire nation was helping, and in a way it was. After the match, François Pienaar was asked if the crowd of 62,000 had lifted the home side. He paused before replying: 'No, it was the 43 million people behind the side.' The temptation was to be cynical and admire his PR skills, but the atmosphere of the entire country demanded respect for the consummate captain.

The noise at Ellis Park was deafening throughout, from the moment that the spectacular low-flying aeroplane seemed on the verge of demo-lishing the main stand to the ecstasy when Joel Stransky became an immortal, albeit a minor one. The deity before whom all South Africa seemed to bow, with the exception of a few Zulus, was, of course, Mandela. He received a roar every bit as loud as that which greeted the final whistle just for waving to the crowd. When the band struck up the anthem, my dilemma over whether to support purely the rugby or the emotion of a nation was resolved. It was impossible not to share in the optimism of South Africa.

The match was only a classic in terms of South African defence and New Zealand's ambition. How strange that New Zealand, of all teams, should lose the game through idealistic attacking from deep. Jonah Lomu made breaks, but always from such a distance that Springbok cover was able to overwhelm him eventually. New Zealand started well. Glen Osborne made a scintillating break from deep and Mehrtens kicked a penalty. Only a typical surge by the remorseless Ruben Kruger lifted the siege. The first real sign of hope for the hosts was the form of Stransky. Calm and assured, he varied his game and disrupted the performance of Kronfeld, who suffered against the more powerful South African back row, as did Zinzan Brooke. This was a war of attrition designed for a side who believed the final was more than a game.

Slowly the South African pack asserted itself and Van der Westhuizen chipped them forward. Stransky kept his cool to kick a penalty and dropped a goal, and at half-time it was 9–6 to South Africa and the songs rolled around the ground. An appalling comic version of 'La Cucaracha' had even the most mild-mannered dancing. South Africa was going wild.

In the second half, Ian Jones suppressed the roars with a sublime display in the line-out. You felt a try must come from this monopoly, but the national wall held firm in defence as the nerve of the young Kiwis was finally found wanting. Lomu looked distressed, Mehrtens so vulnerable. Nevertheless, the fly-half levelled the scores fifteen minutes into the half as the favourites slowly dampened the local spirits by establishing belated territorial control. The clock ticked into the last two minutes and South Africa looked away as Mehrtens, one of the tournament's stars, steadied himself for the last rites, a drop at goal from 30 metres in front of the posts. Du Plessis admitted afterwards that he thought destiny had deserted him, even as the ball left Mehrtens' boot. His miss was greeted with a joy that South Africans will remember forever.

Du Plessis's faith would not be tested to such an extent in extra time. New Zealand took a 12–9 lead, but through their sheer will South Africa pulled it level to 12–12. Seven minutes remained when Joel Stransky struck a 30-metre dropped goal that rose above the desperate New Zealand arms and through the posts. I leaped from my seat, together with most erstwhile neutrals. I caught sight of my old chum Louis, suffering from a rare fit of delirium. Mass hysteria filled the ground as the realisation dawned that South Africa were on the verge of their greatest ever sporting moment. Brian Lochore left before the final whistle; Nelson Mandela, sporting his Springbok hat and Pienaar shirt, rose in real emotion and the Springboks collapsed in prayer – why did you spoil it, lads?

François Pienaar had been an inspiration on the pitch. In victory he remained inspired off it. 'When President Mandela gave me the trophy, he said, thanks for doing it for South Africa. I told him we could never do as much for the country as he had.' Nobody disagreed. The year of living dangerously had ended with a fairytale. Jonah Lomu left South Africa as the new superstar of the sport, but even he could not conquer the spirit of Nelson Mandela.

Epilogue

Extra Time – The Rugby Revolution

I n recent times we have learned of a new doctrine, the 'Frank Sinatra doctrine'. 'He had a song, "I Did It My Way". So every country decides, on its own, which way to take.'

Sound familiar? Nobody would be shocked to be told that Vernon Pugh, the outgoing chairman of the International Board, uttered these words after the historic meeting of his board in Paris during the last week-end in August, for that is effectively what the IB did: they authorised each rugby country to decide its individual destiny. Critics mumbled about a cop-out, but it was not the first time the world had seen those in power adopt such a strategy. Yet the Frank Sinatra doctrine was not voiced by Vernon Pugh, but was the philosophy of a man who had lost an empire. The words belonged to the Soviet foreign ministry spokesman, Gennady Gerasimov. He was explaining the end of communism and authoritarianism to an American television audience in October 1989.

If the great political revolution of the 1980s was the sudden collapse of communism, then the sporting equivalent in the 1990s is surely the dramatic demise of the amateur order in Rugby Union. Rugby's ruling ethos did not dominate the lives of so many, but its iron control outlasted communism by several decades. The implications of the two revolutions were obviously profoundly different, but the fall of both regimes follows a remarkably similar path. Both systems were based on an extreme defence of an unpopular order: in the Eastern Bloc it was communism; in rugby antiquated amateurism. While authority was implacably opposed to freedom and money, dissident voices were still. Communism fell when Gorbachev signalled a move away from the extreme position that the Soviet rulers had adopted. Likewise the rugby establishment sowed the seeds of their own downfall by tempting players with small perks such as off-field sponsorship deals. To those so long oppressed, suddenly the world becomes a wonderful oyster. In Eastern Europe it tasted of freedom; in Rugby Union, of money.

The events that formed a revolution in Europe came about when countries took matters into their own hands. They achieved it in different ways with varying degrees of elite and popular participation. One common factor was a total rejection of the previous system. Changes went further and faster than the leaders had either hoped or expected, just as the defenders of rugby's old order lost control in 1995.

There is one delicious ironic link between the two revolutions. On the day when East Germans walked through the Berlin Wall as free men, effectively ending the era of communism, Dudley Wood, the secretary of the RFU and defender of the faith, spoke out against the impending threat of professionalism in his sport. In response to a rumour that the IB would possibly allow fringe earnings, he painted a picture he described as 'alarming'. He said that the RFU would present implacable opposition to any relaxation of amateurism. 'Players would be represented by agents and they would be paid for all sorts of activities. Money would be asked for newspaper interviews and suchlike. There would be no end to it.' An English version of those South African *sangomas*.

Politically, the revolution in Eastern Europe careered out of control through the actions of a few different countries; in rugby the number was three – the mighty southern hemisphere axis of South Africa, New Zealand and Australia. Gorbachev and the other communist leaders were helpless against the cries of the people and the flood of emigration across the German border. In the southern hemisphere the authorities were powerless to heed the cries of the players and assuage the fear of emigration to Rugby League.

We all suspected that the sport was slowly marching towards reality, but few were prepared for the statement on 23 June, just one day before the World Cup final. Late on the Thursday night, long after the string quartet were safely in bed, I walked into the foyer of the Sanitary Sandton Sun, the safe house for the paranoid. Peter FitzSimons, that bulky Australian journalist, was leaving the bar as I approached; no surprise there, but he had the air of a man who knows about a conspiracy. He tipped me off about a press conference to be held the next morning at Ellis Park. Too late to file, I pondered the reason for his excitement over several beers.

As fresh as a used jockstrap, I arrived at Ellis Park early the following morning. Word was out, it was something big. Edward Griffith, the chief executive of the South African Rugby Union, passed by and told me I would enjoy the conference. Then I had a real inkling: the press were to be thanked for their objective coverage of the past month and granted a lifetime's supply of Hamilton Russell, my favourite South

African red wine. Er, not quite. Into the crowded room walked Leo Williams, Richie Guy and Mr Big himself, Louis Luyt, the representatives of the southern bloc. The television cameras in the room belonged primarily to Sky, rather than to ITV, the host broadcasters. I realised in a flash, albeit a belated one, what we were to be told. South Africa, New Zealand and Australia had formed a company, SANZA, which had reached a deal with Rupert Murdoch's Newscorp, Sky's owners (damnation, it was not a Bacchanalian eternity for me after all). The contract between Newscorp and the three unions was worth £340 million over ten years. Rugby had never dreamed of such riches. The three sides would play each other twice a year in an elite championship, while the Super-10 series would be enlarged to a Super-12. Newscorp had purchased exclusive broadcasting rights, along with the rights to all international tours in those countries from 1996, while the unions would keep control of their own destiny. That was the deal.

Louis Luyt informed a stunned media that it was 'the start of a southern hemisphere alliance, trying to get a better deal for every facet of rugby'. To Leo Williams it was simple: 'We have set up a competition and sold TV rights, just like the Five Nations.' Financial decisions had not been finalised, but the sums were clearly going to defend Union against the predatory League code that was chasing the likes of Lomu and Van der Westhuizen. Murdoch, the man whose injection of money had threatened to create that emigration of talent, was now the sport's white knight.

Louis Luyt was in rampant form. When asked why the deal had been struck so secretly if it concerned TV rights, he replied that there were 550 million reasons – the total in dollars for the deal for the decade. The media, even the generally more conservative northern element, were impressed. SANZA had initiated a lightning blow in defence of Union. They had finally taken the game into the realms of professionalism, although Luyt stressed that people would still not be paid for playing. The directors of SANZA believed that the deal was in the interest of the sport and its protagonists. Richie Guy informed us: 'The players will be happy with the deal we have struck,' while Leo Williams declared, 'We are representing the players.'

For once right, I wrote that rugby went professional at 9 a.m. that Friday morning, but, as a distant and dim historian, I should not have forgotten about the frustration of those people who had created the need for the violent swing towards professionalism: the players. Once again there was a lesson to be learned from 1989. Shortly before the Berlin Wall crumbled, East Germany's interior minister stated that all citizens would be entitled to a passport and that the crime of fleeing the Republic would be abolished. That was as radical as the Murdoch deal, but, like the citizens of Eastern Europe, many players were not prepared to wait. After all the years of frustration they wanted more, just as the impoverished Easterners dreamed of dollars, Deutschmarks and Levi's jeans.

The official IB line was that the future of the sport would be decided in Paris two months later. Between these dates the voices of the establishment suggested enough resistance to convince many players to drive the revolution even further. Ken Reid of Ireland could barely conceal his bile when he said: 'This deal is pushing rugby further down the professional road.' Dennis Easby predictably offered: 'I hope we don't have a system of match fees and contracts.' That was the official view of most British players; the only difference was that Easby was serious. Finally, Vernon Pugh, along with Luyt, refused to see the final barrier to full professionalism pushed aside. 'If it becomes pay for play, it may be impossible for the unions and the IB to retain control.'

Barely had the dust settled on the World Cup when the news broke that the players had been approached by Ross Turnbull, once a Wallaby and now perceived as an agent of Rupert Murdoch's old adversary, Kerry Packer. The rugby circus hit the headlines with a vengeance that knocked the cricket Test matches and Gazza's new hairdo off the back pages. The proposal was a three-year contract involving 900 of the world's finest players. It was to be the rebel tour to destroy the fabric and order of the old game. Instead of favouring the young talent over a ten-year period, this scheme was heavily weighted towards players with big names and a few years on the scoreboard. Internationals with a combined total of 2 million caps were to be the recruitment agents for one final pay day. I thought, 'Good luck to the lads' – until the official line of 'It's for the development of the sport' was bandied about. When Rob Andrew bemoaned the fact that 'the media are making out that it's all to do with money' a thought did cross my mind: were the players not asking to have their cake and eat it too? Peter Wheeler, the Leicester president, summed up my feelings when he said, 'These are ordinary blokes who have made a career decision.' Sport could become a lucrative business, and why not, but to claim the moral high ground of national interest was too disingenuous for belief. Nick Farr-Jones, too, was concerned. 'I hope the players don't see the money and lose sight of the essence and culture of rugby.'

Despite an excess of wildly inaccurate press stories, the plan was as flawed as John Jeavons-Fellows claimed. 'I have seen the document and the contract players are being asked to sign. You would have to be mad to sign. The whole thing has so many holes it is not true.' But who reads the small print? So the circus hype left town, but it had helped to accelerate the revolution. Where previously only the big three had acted, now the north had been forced to play a hand by the players' radically increased leverage. In the weeks leading up to the fateful weekend of 26 and 27 August, players sat down with their unions and discussed meaningful sums of money, and with it contractual obligations.

The stage was set for the death of the old order, but, like the fall of the Eastern Bloc, few expected it to come with such haste. Only days before the wall fell a foreign office spokesman said: 'There is a long way to go before the system in East Germany becomes genuinely democratic.' Likewise, the unions clung to the notion that while amateurism might have been 'in a state of rigor mortis', to quote incoming RFU secretary Tony Hallett, the final leap into the depths of true professionalism, pay to play, was still a distant concern. They should have remembered recent history. Helmut Kohl, the Chancellor of Germany, phoned Egan Krenz, Eric Honneker's successor in East Germany, and informed him of his hopes for a 'calm, sensible development'. But the external forces of revolution proved too much for Mr Krenz, as they did for Vernon Pugh and the International Board. On Sunday 27 August the rugby world was informed that the amateur regulations were to be repealed, rugby was to be open and that there would be no prohibition on payment or material benefit. After more than 100 years players were free to make their fortunes from the sport.

Vernon Pugh, in a funereal tone, according to my Sky colleague Jamie Salmon, spoke of the challenge to retain the special character which has helped make the sport so popular. That is a huge challenge. With every opportunity comes a threat. When the communist system crumbled, Western politicians toasted the golden dawn of democracy while impoverished Eastern Europeans nurtured visions of Western wealth. They may one day come to pass, but at the moment the communist parties of Eastern Europe are more popular than anyone would have imagined as free-market forces drive its countries deeper into crime, civil war and hardship while the dreams go unfulfilled.

Rugby is just a game, but it has the same problem. Tony Hallett, a bright light on the horizon of Twickenham, pondered at the RFU press conference days after the death knell of amateurism, 'How do you bail out the expectations that emerge?' In England, international players have seen the stadium of Twickenham arise like a phoenix on the back of their efforts. Now they want their slice of the pie, but who can bake it? I hope they receive their rewards; I hope even more fervently that they heed the reminders of the greatest of modern captains, Nick Farr-Jones. It would be a small tragedy to lose sight of the essence and culture of rugby, especially the legendary camaraderie. It is from a bar that I terminate my version of the year of living dangerously. One toast to the fond memories of the old amateur game, and another to the exciting potential of rugby's brave new world.

The 1994–5 Season: Results

National Leagues 1994–5

England: Courage Leagues Division 1

	P	W	D	L	F	A	Pts
Leicester	18	15	1	2	400	239	31
Bath	18	12	3	3	373	245	27
Wasps	18	13	0	5	470	313	26
Sale	18	7	2	9	327	343	16
Orrell	18	6	3	9	256	326	15
Bristol	18	7	0	11	301	353	14
Gloucester	18	6	1	11	269	336	13
Harlequins	18	6	1	11	275	348	13
W. Hartlepool	18	6	1	11	312	412	13
Northampton	18	6	0	12	267	335	12

Wales: Heineken Leagues Division 1

	P	W	D	L	F	A	Pts
Cardiff	22	18	0	4	672	269	36
Pontypridd	22	17	0	5	555	255	34
Treorchy	22	13	0	9	479	312	26
Neath	22	12	2	8	379	398	26
Bridgend	22	12	1	9	518	451	25
Swansea	22	12	0	10	475	400	20
Llanelli	22	10	0	12	459	409	20
Newport	22	9	0	13	366	433	18
Newbridge	22	8	0	14	302	452	16
Abertillery	22	8	0	14	349	604	16
Dunvant	22	7	1	14	333	542	15
Pontypool	22	4	0	18	293	655	8

236

THE FIVE NATIONS CHAMPIONSHIP 1995

	P	W	D	L	F	A	Pts
ENGLAND	4	4	0	0	98	39	8
SCOTLAND	4	3	0	1	87	71	6
FRANCE	4	2	0	2	77	70	4
IRELAND	4	1	0	3	44	83	2
WALES	4	0	0	4	43	86	0

21 January, Lansdowne Road

IRELAND 8
T: Foley
PG: Burke

ENGLAND 20
T: Carling, Clarke,
   T. Underwood
C: Andrew
PG: Andrew

21 January, Parc des Princes

FRANCE 21
T: Ntamack, Saint-André
C: Lacroix
PG: Lacroix (3)

WALES 9
PG: N. Jenkins (3)

4 February, Twickenham

ENGLAND 31
T: T. Underwood (2), Guscott
C: Andrew (2)
PG: Andrew (4)

FRANCE 10
T: Viars
C: Lacroix
PG: Lacroix

4 February, Murrayfield

SCOTLAND 26
T: Joiner, Cronin
C: G. Hastings (2)
PG: G. Hastings (4)

IRELAND 13
T: Mullin, Bell
PG: Burke

18 February, Cardiff Arms Park

WALES 9
PG: N. Jenkins (3)

ENGLAND 23
T: R. Underwood (2), Ubogu
C: Andrew
PG: Andrew (2)

18 February, Parc des Princes

FRANCE 21
T: Saint-André (2), Sadourny
PG: Lacroix
DG: Deylaud

SCOTLAND 23
T: Townsend, G. Hastings
C: G. Hastings (2)
PG: G. Hastings (3)

4 March, Murrayfield

SCOTLAND 26
T: Peters, Hilton
C: G. Hastings (2)
PG: G. Hastings (4)

WALES 13
T: R. Jones
C: N. Jenkins
PG: N. Jenkins (2)

4 March, Lansdowne Road

IRELAND 7
T: Geoghegan
C: Elwood

FRANCE 25
T: Delaigue, Cecillon, Ntamack,
  Saint-André
C: Ntamack
PG: Ntamack

18 March, Twickenham

ENGLAND 24
PG: Andrew (7)
DG: Andrew

SCOTLAND 12
PG: G. Hastings (2)
DG: Chalmers (2)

18 March, Cardiff Arms Park

WALES 12
PG: N. Jenkins (4)

IRELAND 16
T: Mullin
C: Burke
PG: Burke (2)
DG: Burke

THE WORLD CUP 1995

Pool A

	P	W	D	L	F	A	Pts
SOUTH AFRICA	3	3	0	0	68	26	9
AUSTRALIA	3	2	0	1	87	41	7
CANADA	3	1	0	2	45	50	5
ROMANIA	3	0	0	3	14	97	3

25 May, Cape Town

SOUTH AFRICA 27
T: Hendriks, Stransky
C: Stransky
PG: Stransky (4)
DG: Stransky

AUSTRALIA 18
T: Eales, Kearns
C: Lynagh
PG: Lynagh (2)

26 May, Port Elizabeth

CANADA 34
T: Snow, Charron, McKenzie
C: Rees (2)
PG: Rees (4)
DG: Rees

ROMANIA 3
PG: Nichitean

30 May, Cape Town

SOUTH AFRICA	ROMANIA 8

SOUTH AFRICA
T: Richter (2)
C: Johnson
PG: Johnson (3)

ROMANIA 8
T: Guranescu
C: Ivanciuc

31 May, Port Elizabeth

AUSTRALIA 27
T: Tabua, Roff, Lynagh
C: Lynagh (3)
PG: Lynagh (2)

CANADA 11
T: Charron
PG: Rees (2)

3 June, Stellenbosch

AUSTRALIA 42
T: Roff (2), Foley, Burke,
   Smith, Wilson
C: Burke (2), Eales (4)

ROMANIA 3
DG: Ivanciuc

3 June, Port Elizabeth

SOUTH AFRICA 20
T: Richter (2)
C: Stransky (2)
PG: Stransky (2)

CANADA 0

Pool B

	P	W	D	L	F	A	Pts
ENGLAND	3	3	0	0	95	60	9
WESTERN SAMOA	3	2	0	1	96	88	7
ITALY	3	1	0	2	69	94	5
ARGENTINA	3	0	0	3	69	87	3

27 May, East London

WESTERN SAMOA 42
T: Lima (2), Harder (2),
Tatupu, Kellett
C: Kellett (3)
PG: Kellett (2)

ITALY 18
T: Marcello Cuttitta,
   Vaccari
C: Dominguez
PG: Dominguez
DG: Dominguez

27 May, Durban

ENGLAND 24
PG: Andrew (6)
DG: Andrew (2)

ARGENTINA 18
T: Noriega, Arbizu
C: Arbizu
PG: Arbizu (2)

30 May, East London

WESTERN SAMOA 32
T: Harder, Leaupepe, Lam
C: Kellett
PG: Kellett (5)

ARGENTINA 26
T: Crexell, pen. try
C: Cilley (2)
PG: Cilley (4)

31 May, Durban

ENGLAND 27
T: R. Underwood, T. Underwood
C: Andrew
PG: Andrew (5)

ITALY 20
T: Vaccari, Massimo Cuttitta
C: Dominguez
PG: Dominguez (2)

4 June, East London

ITALY 31
T: Vaccari, Gerosa, Dominguez
C. Dominguez (2)
PG: Dominguez (4)

ARGENTINA 25
T: Martin, Corral, Cilley, pen. try
C: Cilley
PG: Cilley

4 June, Durban

ENGLAND 44
T: Back, R. Underwood (2),
  pen. try
C: Callard (3)
PG: Callard (5)
DG: Catt

WESTERN SAMOA 22
T: Sini (2), Umaga
C: Fa'amasino (2)
PG: Fa'amasino

Pool C

	P	W	D	L	F	A	Pts
NEW ZEALAND	3	3	0	0	222	45	9
IRELAND	3	2	0	1	93	94	7
WALES	3	1	0	2	89	68	5
JAPAN	3	0	0	3	55	252	3

27 May, Bloemfontein

WALES 57
T: I. Evans (2), G. Thomas (3),
  Taylor, Moore
C: N. Jenkins (5)
PG: N. Jenkins (4)

JAPAN 10
T: Oto (2)

27 May, Johannesburg

NEW ZEALAND 43
T: Lomu (2), Bunce, Kronfeld,
  Osborne
C: Mehrtens (3)
PG: Mehrtens (4)

IRELAND 19
T: Halpin, McBride,
  Corkery
C: Elwood (2)

31 May, Bloemfontein

IRELAND 50
T: Corkery, Francis, Geoghegan, Halvey, Hogan, pen. tries (2)
C: Burke (6)
PG: Burke

JAPAN 28
T: Sinali Latu, Izawa, Hirao, Takura
C: Y. Yoshida (4)

31 May, Johannesburg

NEW ZEALAND 34
T: Little, Ellis, Kronfeld
C: Mehrtens (2)
PG: Mehrtens (4)
DG: Mehrtens

WALES 9
PG: N. Jenkins (2)
DG: N. Jenkins

4 June, Bloemfontein

NEW ZEALAND 145
T: Ellis (6), Rush (3), Wilson (3), Osborne (2), R. Brooke (2), Loe, Ieremia, Culhane, Dowd, Henderson
C: Culhane (20)

JAPAN 17
T: Kajihara (2)
C. Hirose (2)
PG: Hirose

4 June, Johannesburg

IRELAND 24
T: Popplewell, McBride, Halvey
C: Elwood (3)
PG: Elwood

WALES 23
T: Humphreys, Taylor
C: N. Jenkins (2)
PG: N. Jenkins (2)
DG: A. Davies

Pool D

	P	W	D	L	F	A	Pts
FRANCE	3	3	0	0	114	47	9
SCOTLAND	3	2	0	1	149	27	7
TONGA	3	1	0	2	44	90	5
IVORY COAST	3	0	0	3	29	172	3

26 May, Rustenburg

SCOTLAND 89
T: G. Hastings (4), Walton (2), Logan (2), Chalmers, Stanger, Burnell, Wright, Shiel
C: G. Hastings (9)
PG: G. Hastings (2)

IVORY COAST 0

26 May, Pretoria

FRANCE 38
T: Lacroix (2), Hueber,
  Saint-André
C. Lacroix (3)
PG: Lacroix (3)
DG: Delaigue

TONGA 10
T: T. Va'enuku
C: Tu'ipulotu
PG: Tu'ipulotu

30 May, Rustenburg

FRANCE 54
T: Lacroix (2), Benazzi,
  Accoceberry, Viars, Costes,
  Techoueyres, Saint-André
C: Lacroix (2), Deylaud (2)
PG: Lacroix (2)

IVORY COAST 18
T: Camara, Soulama
C. Kouassi
PG: Kouassi (2)

30 May, Pretoria

SCOTLAND 41
T: Peters, G. Hastings, S. Hastings
C: G. Hastings
PG: G. Hastings (8)

TONGA 5
T: Fenukitau

3 June, Rustenburg

TONGA 29
T: Tu'ipulotu, Latukefu, 'Otai,
  pen. try
C: Tu'ipulotu (3)
PG: Tu'ipulotu

IVORY COAST 11
T: Okou
PG: Dali (2)

3 June, Pretoria

FRANCE 22
T: Ntamack
C: Lacroix
PG: Lacroix (5)

SCOTLAND 19
T: Wainwright
C: G. Hastings
PG: G. Hastings (4)

Quarter-Finals

10 June, Durban

FRANCE 36
T: Saint-André, Ntamack
C: Lacroix
PG: Lacroix (8)

IRELAND 12
PG: Elwood (4)

10 June, Johannesburg

SOUTH AFRICA 42
T: Williams (4), Rossouw,
  Andrews
C: Johnson (3)
PG: Johnson (2)

WESTERN SAMOA 14
T: Nu'uali'itia,
  Tatupu
C: Fa'amasino (2)

11 June, Cape Town

ENGLAND 25	AUSTRALIA 22
T: T. Underwood	T: Smith
C: Andrew	C: Lynagh
PG: Andrew (5)	PG: Lynagh (5)
DG: Andrew	

11 June, Pretoria

NEW ZEALAND 48	SCOTLAND 30
T: Little (2), Lomu, Mehrtens, Bunce, Fitzpatrick	T: Weir (2), S. Hastings
C: Mehrtens (6)	C: G. Hastings (3)
PG: Mehrtens (2)	PG: G. Hastings (3)

Semi-Finals

17 June, Durban

SOUTH AFRICA 19	FRANCE 15
T: Kruger	PG: Lacroix (5)
C: Stransky	
PG: Stransky (4)	

18 June, Cape Town

NEW ZEALAND 45	ENGLAND 29
T: Lomu (4), Kronfeld, Bachop	T: R. Underwood (2), Carling (2)
C: Mehrtens (3)	C: Andrew (3)
PG: Mehrtens	PG: Andrew
DG: Z. Brooke, Mehrtens	

Third-Fourth-Place Play-Off

22 June, Pretoria

FRANCE 19	ENGLAND 9
T: Roumat, Ntamack	PG: Andrew (3)
PG: Lacroix (3)	

Final

SOUTH AFRICA 15	NEW ZEALAND 12 (a.e.t.)
PG: Stransky (3)	PG: Mehrtens (3)
DG: Stransky (2)	DG: Mehrtens

SOUTH AFRICA: A. Joubert; J. Small (B. Venter), J. Mulder, H. le Roux, C. Williams; J. Stransky, J. van der Westhuizen; J. du Randt, C. Rossouw, I. Swart (G. Pagel), J. Wiese, J. Strydom, F. Pienaar (c), M. Andrews (R. Straeuli), R. Kruger

NEW ZEALAND: G. Osborne; J. Wilson (M. Ellis), F. Bunce, W. Little, J. Lomu; A. Mehrtens, G. Bachop (A. Strachan, temp.); C. Dowd (R. Loe), S. Fitzpatrick (c), O. Brown, I. Jones, R. Brooke, M. Brewer (J. Joseph), Z. Brooke, J. Kronfeld

Index